ELECTING A PRESIDENT

ELECTING A PRESIDENT

*

THE MARKLE COMMISSION RESEARCH ON CAMPAIGN '88

BRUCE BUCHANAN

Foreword by Lloyd N. Morrisett
Introduction by Robert M. O'Neil

UNIVERSITY OF TEXAS PRESS
AUSTIN

First edition, 1991

Requests for permission to reproduce material from this work
should be sent to Permissions, University of Texas Press,
Box 7819, Austin, TX 78713-7819.

♾ The paper used in this publication meets the minimum
requirements of American National Standard for Information
Sciences—Permanence of Paper for Printed Library Materials,
ANSI Z39.48-1984.

Library of Congress Cataloging-in-Publication Data

Buchanan, Bruce.
    Electing a president : the Markle Commission research on campaign
'88 / by Bruce Buchanan ; foreword by Lloyd N. Morrisett ;
introduction by Robert M. O'Neil.—1st ed.
        p.   cm.
    Includes bibliographical references (p.   ) and index.
    ISBN 0-292-72077-7 (alk. paper)
    1. Presidents—United States—Election—1988.   2. Press and
politics—United States.   I. Markle Commission on the Media and the
Electorate.   II. Title.
JK5261988h
324.973'0927—dc20   90-13079
                                                                   CIP

For my family

CONTENTS

Figures

Tables

FOREWORD

by Lloyd N. Morrisett

 The topic of political education is not often formally addressed in the United States. Civics, history, and social studies courses are thought to provide some orientation to political education. But it is assumed that an educated voter will result from a combination of family training, school experience, and participation in the political process. Although educators have paid comparatively little attention to the media, it is abundantly clear that the media have come to play an ever more important part in the political education of our citizenry and in our country's decision-making processes.

Network and local television, paid ads, newspaper and magazine coverage, and radio all go together to provide political education and information. Even though the goals of an individual media outlet may be a "show," news coverage, or editorial comment, the social objective of the aggregate coverage provided by the media is to enable the voter to be informed and to participate effectively in the political process. There is no coordination, no guiding hand, but we expect that an informed and educated voter will result from the "system."

From the point of view of society, it is not hard to outline the "curriculum" of political education that should be provided by the media. In a presidential year, the theme is how voters can best think about electing a president. What should they know? What does history have to teach? What are the issues? Who are the candidates? What are the requirements of the presidency and the qualifications of the candidates? Although these educational objectives may seldom be specifically addressed, the unstated assumption of the electorate is that the media will provide effective political education.

The experience of recent presidential elections has produced an increasing amount of criticism about the way candidates are chosen and elected. Several failed presidencies—the election of men whose experience or character led them to commit fatal errors during their presidencies—and a loss of certainty about America's mission in the world have all gone together to focus attention on the way our presidents are chosen. Much dissatisfaction has been expressed about the typical "horse-race" perspective provided by the media. Many observers have called for more and better coverage of the requirements for the presidency and the qualifications of candidates.

The 1988 election seemed to promise new opportunities. First, no incumbent president was seeking election, and the process was likely to be more fluid as a result. Second, new media outlets—particularly cable television—seemed to offer opportunities for new and/or extended presentations during a presidential election year. Third, many people were questioning the way candidates were chosen, and attention was again focused on the "apathy" of the typical American voter. This was the background that led to the formation of the Markle Commission on the Media and the Electorate. Its purpose was to examine objectively the information that was made available to the voters in the presidential campaign and how the voters used that information. Members of the commission were Robert O'Neil, former president of the University of Virginia and now director of the Thomas Jefferson Center for the Protection of Free Expression, who served as chairman; James David Barber, professor of political science at Duke University; John Culver, former senator from Iowa, now partner in Arent, Fox, Kintner, Plotkin & Kahn; Joan Konner, dean of the Columbia School of Journalism; Charles Mathias, former senator from Maryland and now partner in Jones, Day, Reavis & Pogue; Eugene Patterson, former publisher of the *St. Petersburg Times*; and Eddie Williams, president of the Joint Center for Political Studies. Bruce Buchanan, associate professor of political science at the University of Texas, was executive director of the project and planned and supervised the research that supported the commission's work. This book by Professor Buchanan reports the results of that research as well as the commission's recommendations, which have been previously issued.

Concentrating on the formal campaign period between Labor Day and election day, the commission believed it necessary to find out what voters knew at the beginning of the campaign, how much they learned, what information was provided by the media, and how the voters used that information provided by the media. Two national surveys, conducted by Louis Harris and Associates, allowed the commission to determine what the voters knew at the beginning of the campaign and how much they learned during the campaign. Content analysis of the campaign news presented by major newspapers, newsmagazines, and television networks allowed the commission to appraise the quality of information provided. Sixteen focus groups conducted throughout the country during the same period enabled the commission to examine how people were using the media and what their individual concerns were. In this book, Professor Buchanan discusses the theoretical framework in which this research was conducted, and the research results are reported and analyzed. The book concludes with the commission's recommendations, which were arrived at by considering both the research and American political experience. The overriding conclusion of this work is that the democratic faith in government by the people cannot be taken for granted. Voters must take renewed responsibility for educating themselves. The media must better inform voters and protect them from misrepresentation, and the candidates must shoulder the responsibilities to enlighten and inspire.

On behalf of the Markle Foundation, I want to thank all the members of the Markle Commission on the Media and the Electorate and especially its chairman, Robert O'Neil, and its executive director, Bruce Buchanan, for what they have accomplished. The extensive research conducted by the commission provides clear evidence of shortcomings in our electoral processes. The recommendations that follow begin to show ways in which voters, the media, and candidates can all work together to make government by the people even more of a reality.

LLOYD N. MORRISETT
AUGUST 1990

ACKNOWLEDGMENTS

This book, and the Markle Commission Report that preceded it, are products of the John and Mary R. Markle Foundation's multi-sided program in media and political participation. Markle Foundation President Lloyd N. Morrisett and Program Officer Edith C. Bjornson combined to provide extraordinarily gracious support and encouragement at every stage of this project's development, a fact I gratefully acknowledge here.

Others deserve thanks for their valuable contributions to the data collection stage of the project: Louis Harris, Ron Bass, and Ventura DiRocco of the Louis Harris and Associates organization, Bernie Richstatter and Wally Christofferson of the Luce Press Clipping Service, and Brooks Clapp and Mark Rovner, formerly of the Roosevelt Center for Public Policy Research.

Several scholars offered useful advice and/or helpfully criticized the early draft chapters. They include James David Barber of Duke University, Wayne Danielson and Roderick P. Hart of the University of Texas, Helmut Norpoth of the State University of New York at Stony Brook, and Doris Graber of the University of Illinois, Chicago Circle. Two political scientists reviewed the entire manuscript at the invitation of the University of Texas Press and made critical suggestions that improved the final manuscript. The staff at the Press helped make the experience of fashioning this large project into a book an enjoyable one. And Suzanne Colwell of the University of Texas Government Department skilfully produced the final manuscript.

None of the good people who helped me can be held responsible for the flaws and omissions that remain. Though much of any praise is deservedly theirs, the blame is mine alone.

BRUCE BUCHANAN
AUGUST 1990

INTRODUCTION
by Robert M. O'Neil

Electing a President offers a singular contribution to our understanding of what actually makes up a presidential campaign. The questions with which it begins are familiar ones to those who watch the electoral process. Yet the answers have been curiously elusive, despite the increasing sophistication of technology and political analysis, and the heightened media scrutiny which presidential elections evoke. Support of the John and Mary R. Markle Foundation, through the Commission on the Media and the Electorate, made possible a comprehensive research program to seek those answers.

The research described here proceeded along three parallel lines. Key to understanding voter perceptions and views were the two polls conducted at critical points during the campaign. In addition to the familiar questions that test voters' knowledge about the candidates, the issues, and the relationship between issues and candidates, these surveys also asked some unique questions about media coverage—what media the respondents read, watched, and heard, where they got their campaign information, how fairly they thought the media handled key issues. It was these findings, and the fascinating contrasts between the September and October polls, that charted the changing fortunes of Bush and Dukakis in the weeks before the election.

A second ingredient was the focus groups. Representative citizens in four communities were invited to talk about the election, the candidates, and the issues, and did so with remarkable enthusiasm and candor. They also provided valuable insight into the role of the media in covering the election—though more impressionistically than systematically. Apart from the immediate yield of the focus groups, this part of the research program suggests the utility of such sessions in future studies of elections and campaigns.

Content analysis of media coverage provided the third research component. A painstaking study of time and space actually allocated during the campaign confirmed a hunch that "the horse race" gets more attention than the personalities of the contenders, much less the issues on which they contend. But the content analysis revealed much more about sources of voter information and the extent and nature of presidential campaign coverage.

Since Professor Buchanan was the architect of the commission's research program, he is of course the ideal person to analyze and interpret the results. He brought to the study a rare understanding of presidential politics and campaign realities, along with a highly sophisticated sense of research design and methodology.

The contributions of this research program to the work of the Markle Commission on the Media and the Electorate have been legion. At the most basic level, the research findings helped to redirect our focus from media coverage to voter and citizen behavior. While we remained deeply concerned about the role of the media in reporting presidential campaigns, we came increasingly to appreciate the responsibility that citizens bear for their own participation in the political process. It was the research findings, quite as much as the experience of the campaign, that shifted our emphasis in this way.

The research program should also have significant bearing on analysis of future elections. Many of the questions that urgently needed to be answered in 1988 have been answered in ways that will make much easier and more rational studies of campaigning and voter response in 1992 and beyond. Any future research can and should built on the firm base that emerges from the data described in this study. To that extent, as in others, 1988 marks a watershed in presidential campaigns.

Appreciation is surely due to Lloyd Morrisett and Edith Bjornson of the Markle Foundation, not only for their support of the studies and the report, but for their deeply personal commitment of time, insights, and counsel throughout the process. Other members of the commission contributed either to the design or the interpretation of the research, or to both. But it is Bruce Buchanan who guided the commission through every stage of this complex process. It was an invaluable learning experience for us all—as it is certain to be for readers of this volume.

ROBERT M. O'NEILL
JULY 1990

ELECTING A PRESIDENT

1. WHAT WAS WRONG WITH THE 1988 ELECTION?

Campaign '88 had its defenders. A lead editorial in the *Wall Street Journal*, the daily newspaper with the largest circulation in America,[1] saw the discussion of the ills of liberalism, the American Civil Liberties Union, the Pledge of Allegiance, and prison furloughs for murderers as a needed opportunity to face fundamental differences over which values should inform America's civil and political life (The Moral Relativism Issue 1988).[2] *New York Times* columnist William Safire saw the campaign as the blooding of George Bush—a useful demonstration that a previously unassuming man had sufficient "fire in his belly" to be a leader (Safire 1988b). One professor, Michael J. Robinson of Georgetown University, suggested that 1988 was "a perfectly acceptable Presidential election campaign. We have a centrist political process, and the American people chose [between] two well-educated, decent, responsible men with long histories of public service" (Robinson 1988). And many veteran office-seekers from both political camps would argue that while the spectacle was neither inspiring or enlightening, the 1988 campaign was in keeping with life in the real political world. "Politics ain't beanbag," was a favorite refrain.

In fact, as many commentators would observe in the months following the election, 1988 did not represent an abrupt departure from previous American political practice. The avoidance by candidates of politically difficult, "no win" issues was certainly not unusual in presidential politics. Nor were aggressive attacks by one candidate against another. There had been more invective and innuendo in nineteenth-century presidential campaigns (Freund 1988). One historian finds a "mature flowering" of the "new politics" (scientific polling, media manipulation, negative advertising, etc.) in Lyndon Johnson's 1948 campaign for the U.S. Senate in Texas (Caro 1990:xxxiii). And as recently as 1952 there occurred what was described by one historian as "one of the bitterest campaigns of the twentieth century," one arguably as nasty in its way as was 1988's (Ambrose 1987).[3]

Nevertheless, 1988 did alter conventional political practice in at least two important respects. It saw the winning presidential candidate challenge the conventional political wisdom that voters will punish departures from strict truthfulness in one candidate's allegations against the other (Jamieson 1988). And it saw the emergence, for the first time at the presidential level, of a practice by then already common in state and local campaigns: the systematic and pervasive use of negative television advertising and candidate rhetoric to attack and discredit an opponent. "What is different," argued Curtis Gans, director of the Committee for the Study of the American Electorate, "is not the type but the volume. Where such ads were once limited to the occasional campaign and accompanied by howls of outrage, they are now the staple of all campaigns" (quoted by Oreskes 1989).

Too, the campaign's nastiness, shallowness, and evasiveness set the tone for the operation of the government in the election's immediate aftermath. For example, the failure of the 1988 candidates to discuss such urgent national priorities as the budget deficit, or the changing role of the United States in the world, plus the voters' demonstrated willingness to elect the most aggressive and least forthcoming candidate, encouraged elected officials to continue campaign-style posturing and the avoidance of difficult policy choices beyond November 8.

Thus, the 1989 debate between the Republican president and the Democratically controlled Congress centered around flag amendments, capital gains tax cuts, and other arguably peripheral matters.

It also became apparent that attack advertising was helping to erode political courage. "Fear among politicians . . . has become a pervasive and paralyzing force that keeps government from dealing with complex issues . . . A bill that includes anything that might possibly be taken out of context and used to attack its supporters is that much harder to pass" (Oreskes 1989).

Worst of all, a "sound-bite" campaign at the presidential level seemed to have hastened the deterioration of reasoned discourse about the means and ends of national policy. Principled stand-taking was increasingly replaced by overnight tracking polls aimed at discovering what positions were popular and how to manipulate public passions for political advantage. Disconnected images, bumper-sticker slogans, and ad hominem attacks supplanted serious efforts to understand and confront difficult problems in all their complexities. "The battle over the capital gains cut," for example, "had many of the trappings of a campaign, with competing sound bites and slogans, press releases and commercials" (Toner 1989). David E. Rosenbaum quotes Duke political scientist James David Barber: "The word 'plan' has gone out of style. What has happened in American politics is its drift to sentimentality and emotion, which substitutes for the facts that face you at the moment" (Rosenbaum 1989).

The Political Logic

Despite their role in intensifying these and other problems, Bush 1988 campaign tactics would be defended by Republican strategists like Ed Rollins, the 1984 Reagan-Bush campaign manager, as the only way for a candidate with Bush's vulnerabilities—the "wimp" factor, the "vision thing," and substantial poll deficits—to overcome his negatives (Runkel 1989).

The political logic was hard to fault. And the partisan skills of Bush advisors like Roger Ailes, Robert Teeter, Lee Atwater, and James Baker, were undeniably impressive. The media would celebrate the Bush campaign as a *tour de force* that, aided by what most observers saw as an inept Dukakis campaign that refused to fight back, managed to come from as far behind as sixteen points in early August (when a New York Times/CBS poll showed Dukakis leading Bush by 50 to 34 percent) to a 54 to 46 percent popular vote triumph on November 8.

The People's Choice

Whatever their reasons, those who voted preferred George Bush to Michael Dukakis by a margin of 54 to 46 percent. But the turnout of 50.16 percent was the lowest since Calvin Coolidge beat John W. Davis in 1924, some sixty-four years earlier. And the raw returns failed to reveal the great difficulty many Americans experienced in choosing between the two candidates. Some polls showed that as many as 25 percent of the voters did not decide until the last few days before the election (see Chapter 5, Table 5–1). Polls also showed that the public didn't much care for either candidate, wished that other choices were available, and flatly rejected the negative tone of the campaign (*World Almanac* 1989:35).

And the fact remained that, despite the arguments of defenders and the skills of the handlers, few observers were content with how the 1988 presidential campaign had been conducted. Voters, pundits, academics, and apparently even George Bush himself (Goldman and Mathews 1989) were all uncomfortable with the nature and tenor of the race. It felt wrong. The authors of numerous books, articles, and columns were moved to eloquence in expressing their disquiet: "A Moral Derailing" (Wills 1988); the "Year of the Handler," with a campaign waged "between high-tech button-pushers unburdened by contending visions or issues" (Goldman and Mathews 1989); a "trivial pursuit," in which "anything goes" (Germond and Whitcover 1989), and a year in which "civility took it on the chin" and "nastiness became a commodity" (McWilliams 1989).[4]

In 1989, gubernatorial elections in Virginia and New Jersey and the mayoral race in New York City tested the new conventional wisdom to emerge from the '88 campaign: that negative campaigning works. The candidates, Republicans all, who ran the nastiest attack ads—New Jersey's Jim Courter, New York's Rudolph W. Giuliani, and Virginia's Marshall Coleman—found themselves on the defensive, and lost (Schneider 1989:2862).

But whether or not issueless, mean-spirited campaigns would be the wave of the future (Bush media advisor Roger Ailes is alleged to have said, "If you didn't like 1988, you'll hate 1992"), it is clear from the widespread discomfort that a great many observers felt that some invisible line had been crossed during Campaign '88.

What Line Was Crossed?

What was wrong with the 1988 election? What implicit guideposts of campaign propriety were violated? By whom? In what specific ways? And with what consequences? Surprisingly, few of the many books and articles written about Campaign '88 attempted any thorough or systematic exploration of such questions.

That may be because they are daunting questions. They demand careful thought about the roles and responsibilities of the major actors in American presidential campaigns. And they require an orderly marshalling of evidence about the behavior of those actors.

They invite, in short, evaluation research. In this more systematic approach to assessment the moral and practical goals of American presidential elections are crisply defined for comparison with the record of what actually happened, as gauged by social scientific methods. The resulting map of the differences between ideal and reality clarifies the location of the "foul lines" and can point to those aspects of American political practice in need of rethinking or improvement.

Such a difficult and potentially controversial exercise is understandably avoided when things seem to be working more or less as they should or as well as can reasonably be expected. But when, as after the 1988 election, the widespread conviction emerges that something is wrong, it signals the need for a more fundamental stocktaking. If American political practice is not to drift too far from its ethical moorings, it behooves us to look periodically at how political practice squares with the ideals presumed to govern it.

Purpose

To illustrate how this can be done and to give evidence of the value of the effort are the reasons for this book. The work begins in Chapter 2, which offers definitions of democratic ideals as they apply to current presidential election practice.

There an exercise in values-clarification identifies the research information and the moral yardsticks needed to compare the reality of Campaign '88 with concrete standards of good democratic practice. The standards spelled out in the second chapter permeate the book.

Chapters 3 through 6 describe the research plan and give detailed results of an investigation that employed two national telephone surveys (Chapter 4), a content analysis of the election coverage of eighteen leading print and broadcast media (Chapter 5), and sixteen separate focus-group discussions with voters in each of four regions of the country (Chapter 6). The major findings, which shape the recommendations discussed in Chapter 7, show where and how the presidential campaign process has drifted off course.

The Major Finding: Voters Are the Problem

The findings are voluminous and deal at length with the performance of each corner of the modern "electoral triangle" (voters, candidates, and news media). But they all boil down, in one way or another, to a single, fundamental problem: American voters do not understand their rightful place in the operation of American representative democracy.

Our research (and other evidence) shows that the American people act as if they believe that presidential elections belong to somebody else; most notably, presidential candidates. They show no sign whatever of realizing the central democratic fact: that they actually "own" the electoral process. Nor do they seem aware of what a presidential campaign is supposed to accomplish (meeting their needs for relevant information and guidance, so that they can make an informed presidential selection). Perhaps most important, they do not grasp the fact that democracy grants them the power to demand candidate and media performance that is much more to their liking, and more responsive to their needs, than it was in 1988. Most felt the campaign was a charade, but few saw it as their problem or within their power to change.

That, in brief, is the explanation offered here for what our research disclosed, and for the fact that half of 1988's eligible voters simply ignored the presidential election altogether. That is also our explanation for why those who did bother to participate as voters expended so little effort trying to understand what was going on, as is clearly evident in our survey (Chapter 5) and focus group results (Chapter 6). Why invest significant personal effort in a process that is managed by and for the benefit of other people?

The Media

Our results show that there is very little encouragement offered by either candidates or the news media for the great mass of voters to adopt a more proprietary view of the election process. Consider, for example, this finding about media coverage: *the media devoted almost 60 percent of 1988 campaign coverage to the political horse race and to candidate conflicts, and only about 30 percent to issues and candidate qualifications.*

Table 4-1 (Chapter 4) reveals the distribution of coverage across these and additional categories that attracted the remaining coverage attention.[5]

What were the effects on voters of so much media attention to campaign strategy? It might have encouraged a public impression that strategic political effectiveness was the major qualification for service in the presidency and a sufficient test of suitability for office for the winning candidate to pass—as suggested in Chapter 6.

But, to their credit, participants in our focus group discussions showed no pronounced tendency to evaluate candidates in political horse-race terms. Instead, they focused mainly on the kinds of qualifications—competence and experience, issue positions, and character—most relevant to presidential performance in office (see Chapter 2). This evidence suggests that more informed media consumers like these focus group participants simply "tune out" the influence of any media coverage they deem irrelevant to their needs.

This is not to suggest that the media provided no quality coverage whatever of issues and candidate qualifications. In fact, we found that *what little voters did manage to learn about the issue agenda during the fall campaign was attributable mainly to the influence of the media.*

This conclusion is based on inferences drawn from Table 5-6, which summarizes responses to an open-ended question about the problems facing the next president that voters answered in their own words. There we see that only two issues—the budget deficit and drugs—showed enough change from our first survey to the second to indicate anything approximating "learning." And this was during the post–Labor Day campaign "prime time," when voters are traditionally thought to be paying closer than usual attention.

Other perceptions of important problems did not change significantly from the first survey to the second. This documents the absence in 1988 of anything approaching an influential national issues debate.

The budget deficit came to be perceived as the most important presidential problem by the largest single group of voters—23 percent in Table 5-6, just before election day. As with the drug issue, this also reflected a 5 percent increase above the post–Labor Day survey. But unlike the drug issue, this particular increase had to have been stimulated almost entirely by media coverage.[6]

The reason is that the candidates were avoiding discussion of the deficit, and the voters had no direct experience of budget deficit pain in their daily lives that could have increased the issue's importance to them. By a process of elimination, then, the media—which were covering the issue quite extensively and complaining of candidate inattention to it—can be identified as the source of the change. This is the clearest instance of media influence, and the best example of the media's contribution to an informed electorate, to emerge from the study.

Americans are traditionally most concerned with domestic and local rather than national and international problems.[7] In light of such localism, the media's ability to push the budget deficit to the top of the public agenda is all the more noteworthy.[8] Even a modest amount of media attention to issues during the 1988 campaign— Table 4-1 shows that television and newspapers devoted about 10 percent of their campaign coverage to issues—was able to have a significant impact on voter awareness. But some focus group participants noted that it took a good deal of targeted searching to locate such information amidst the saturation coverage of campaign hoopla.

The Candidates

As for the candidates, they offered voters little of substance concerning plans or agendas, concentrating instead on a barrage of misleading, largely negative television advertising, repeated so relentlessly as to be almost impossible to ignore. People reported finding the candidate contributions to their "learning" process depressing and insulting, even though *most of what they were able to recall about both 1988 presidential candidates came mainly from Bush campaign rhetoric and advertising.*

The major evidence is in Tables 5-8 and 5-9. There reported are the results of open-ended questions asking voters to identify, in their own words, what they had "learned about" each of the candidates.

The tables show that the biggest changes between Labor Day and election day in what was known of Democratic presidential nominee Michael Dukakis, for example, concerned his weakness on crime and prison furloughs, and his status as a liberal. The largest changes for Bush involved a decline in the percentage that saw him as a "wimp," a similar decline in the proportion of voters that interpreted his choice of Dan Quayle as "poor judgment," and increases in the percentages claiming to have learned that he was tough on crime and experienced in federal government leadership. In short, Dukakis's "negatives" went up as Bush's went down.

The Bush campaign originated most of these themes and repeated them endlessly in television advertising and candidate speeches. But television news programs and newspapers also covered them quite extensively in the "horse race" and "candidate conflicts" categories described in Chapter 4 (see Table 4-1), and thus surely helped to implant them in voters' minds.[9]

The Bush campaign thus succeeded in teaching the voters most of what they were able to recall about the 1988 presidential candidates. That raises important questions concerning the availability of credible and relevant information about the presidential qualifications of 1988's candidates.

But an equally important question, addressed in Chapter 6, is whether negative advertising actually determined the outcome of the election. This question is of special importance to assessing the health of democracy, as it pertains to the ability of ordinary citizens to resist unsavory influence as they attempt to make sense of their voting choices.

We uncovered some intriguing indications that the discussions people have with one another (whose contents in our groups tended to be far more enlightening about issues and qualifications) may have had as much influence as negative advertising, or more. We found, for example, that *voters had formed impressions favorable to Bush even before the advertising began in earnest.*[10] This suggests that the foundation for a Bush victory was already in place well before the major Bush advertising effort got under way in September, even though that advertising may have reinforced these pro-Bush impressions. The focus groups (Chapter 6) lend weight to the argument that citizen appraisals of candidate qualifications (e.g., Bush's status as a better-known quantity, his credible pledge to continue the policies that were linked in the public mind to peace and prosperity, plus the fear that the unknown Dukakis would turn out to be "another Jimmy Carter," well-meaning but ill-fated) may have had as much to do with the Bush victory as his hostile assault on Dukakis's "misguided liberalism."

And so, to paraphrase V. O. Key's trenchant observation, voters are not necessarily fools (1966).[11] Although they absorbed some distorted information from Bush advertising, they emphatically did not enjoy the experience. And many also learned important things about the issues and candidate issue positions from the media. But were they well-enough informed as an electorate to responsibly exercise the franchise? The evidence from our surveys is not encouraging. *Voters were poorly informed about candidates, issues, government operations, and their own responsibilities.*

Chapter 5 in particular contains abundant evidence of the electorate's ignorance in 1988. For example, 37 percent didn't yet know that Dan Quayle was Bush's running mate and 54 percent were unable to identify Lloyd Bentsen as Dukakis's running mate just after Labor Day (Table 5-1). This was despite extensive media coverage of both men, but particularly of Quayle following his controversial selection by George Bush as his running mate before the August Republican national convention. Clearly, saturation media coverage alone is not enough to guarantee "learning."

But that is not all. Even with a 50 percent chance of guessing correctly, over half of our survey respondents remained unsure or wrong about thirteen of twenty candidate issue positions as late as early November (Table 5-7). The uncertainty extended to the power situation then existing on Capitol Hill. Nearly half of eligible voters were unsure which party controlled Congress (see p. 78), a finding that argues against often-heard claims that voters are "deliberately" giving the White House to one party and Congress to the other.[12]

This kind of evidence is by no means unusual. Our results simply continue trends that first emerged with the initial national surveys of voter issue awareness and knowledge in the 1940's (Dalton 1988). The political ignorance of American voters is pervasive and longstanding.

This resurfaces and underscores our central interpretive point: voters have opted out of all but the most superficial involvement in the democratic game. Their ignorance is, for the most part, deliberate. It results more from a tacit belief that they are not really responsible for acquiring detailed political information than it does from any intellectual insufficiency. Focus group discussions summarized in Chapter 6 provide many convincing examples of the mental agility of ordinary Americans.

But the discussions also show that even very interested and attentive people simply do not see themselves in the way democratic theory regards citizens: as the owners and intended beneficiaries of campaigns for office (see Chapter 2). Instead, people view presidential campaigns as the special province of the candidates and the news media, and regard themselves as distant outsiders with little of personal consequence at stake.

Thus, instead of expressing their genuinely strong displeasure with the negative, issueless 1988 campaign in the manner of owners whose property had been misused, the focus group discussants responded with cynicism. And much of the larger electorate responded with avoidance (evinced by the disappointing 1988 turnout), in the manner of those whose real concerns were with other things. The result was candidate and media campaign performance undisciplined by a demanding political market test and tailored instead to goading a passive and mostly inattentive and indifferent audience.

There was, however, one type of campaign event that was able to pique real interest and attention throughout the electorate: the debates. *As many as 80 million people may have watched some or all of the presidential debates. Nearly half of our survey sample said they were influenced by the second presidential debate.*

This vast audience made the debates the single most important class of campaign events, and the most significant opportunities to learn about the candidates, of 1988. We have no direct evidence of their actual impact on voters beyond the testimony (Table 5-15) of respondents that they were influenced and some focus group testimony illustrating how such influence worked in individual cases. But inferential evidence from outside sources (e.g., post-debate media polls) suggests that the second presidential debate was a decisive factor in the eventual Bush victory.

The strong, widespread interest in the debates proves that the right kind of campaign presentations can engage even the otherwise indifferent mass electorate. Moreover, there is other evidence to suggest that most Americans are disposed to greater levels of political concern and involvement than their 1988 performance implies.

For *despite displeasure with the negativity and issueless content of the campaign, and despite the lack of an "ownership" attitude toward presidential campaigns, majorities of voters still claimed to regard voting as personally important and claimed to be interested in presidential politics.*

The evidence is in Table 5-2, "The Motivation to Vote." The internalized feeling of citizenship obligation is apparently alive and well. This is the most important source of hope for an improved electoral process.[13]

What seems to be lacking (as is argued at the close of Chapter 6) is a clear, strong sense of just what effective citizenship entails in an age of television campaigns and attack advertising.[14] This lack is accompanied by very low expectations of the news media and of presidential candidates. People weren't satisfied with the tone of the campaign. But they didn't think it was realistic to expect the candidates to change. And they did not regard the media as particularly responsible for checking on the truthfulness of candidates. The media's job in their view is simply to report the facts as objectively as possible.

These and other findings discussed later show why the problems that beset presidential campaigns begin and end with voters. It is ironic that just as a new striving toward democracy impels much of the rest of the world in the closing years of the twentieth century, a disconnection is widening between the American electorate and the very political process that has inspired others and kept Americans free for two hundred years.[15]

Evaluating Presidential Elections

Juxtaposing such research findings against reasonable concepts of "good democratic practice" for citizens, candidates, and the news media and reviewing what might be done to reduce the discrepancies between ideal and practice are the tasks that integrate the balance of this extended discussion of values, evidence, and reform.

The election analyzed below is 1988's.[16] But the work was done with 1992, 1996, and beyond in mind. The campaign of 1988 is but the starting point, the setting for an initial test of evaluative procedures and analytic concepts and definitions that can be refined and returned to use again and again. For if there is presently no tradition of systematic inquiry into the adequacy of evolving American political practice, the argument here is that there needs to be.

Evaluation research on the scale of an American presidential election is a large and expensive undertaking. But its potential for yielding significant returns, both in clearer values and in improved political practice, explains the willingness of the John and Mary R. Markle Foundation to fund this ambitious project. The Markle Foundation also established a national commission of distinguished Americans, identified in the Foreword, who reviewed the findings and made recommendations for improvements in the campaign–season practices of voters, candidates, and the media. The research described in this volume was prelude to their recommendations, which were released to the media in May 1990 (*Report* 1990; Oreskes 1990d). They are reproduced, with commentary, in the concluding chapter.

2. GOOD DEMOCRATIC PRACTICE: RESPONSIBILITIES IN PRESIDENTIAL ELECTIONS

There is something missing in evaluative discourse about American politics. It is an established tradition of discussing, clarifying, and updating the ethical moorings that define acceptable political practice. Every pundit, author, and voter has an opinion about the quality of the 1988 or any other campaign for the presidency. But the criteria that underlie and justify such opinions are usually left implicit and unstated, and therefore undebated and insufficiently clarified. There are fewer straightforward written definitions (or even unwritten understandings) of the responsibilities of the major protagonists in American presidential elections, less clarity regarding who is responsible for what, than might be expected.[1]

Evaluation, however, requires standards. Criteria for assessing the performance of the principal actors in American presidential campaigns are spelled out here. Use is made of published writings and discussions with experienced political thinkers and practitioners where appropriate as points of departure for developing the working definitions found below. The criteria will therefore be recognizable. But they are subject to modification. Indeed, their continuous refinement and updating for consistency with the widest possible consensus of informed opinion is a necessity, if improvement is to be possible.

The major actors in modern presidential campaigns are voters, candidates, and news organizations. What about political parties, political consultants, and other entities that play roles in the campaign process? Either they are not at present major forces in the electoral influence network, as is the case with political parties, or they can be subsumed within one of the three "estates" under discussion.

For example, political consultants act at the behest of candidates, who are responsible for the uses made of them.

Offered here is a model of "good democratic practice" focused exclusively on presidential campaigns and dealing with acceptable standards of performance for citizens, media, and candidates (see Figure 2-1). This concept of good democratic practice is intentionally positioned between the hopelessly unattainable ideals of democratic theory and the gritty realism of institutional and individual self-interest. This is intended to make its implementation "barely possible": not so idealistic as to be utterly unreachable in practice, yet substantially closer to democratic ideals than much recent political practice.[2]

What are ideals? Noble targets, standards of perfection and excellence, worth seeking but hard if not impossible to attain. Why are ideals needed? First, for their perceived intrinsic worth and inspirational power. Ideals give life meaning and make it worth living. Especially vivid examples were the spontaneous bursts of enthusiasm and sacrifice for democratic and humanitarian principles on display

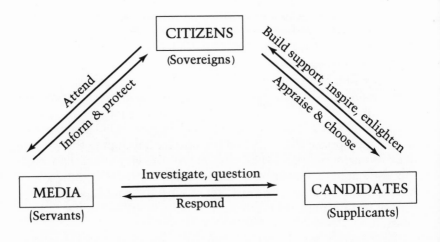

Figure 2-1. The Electoral Triangle (Ideal Model)

throughout the world in 1989. "No one can go to Eastern Europe in this season of its liberation, as I have just done, and come home uninspired by the power of democracy as a universal ideal," writes David Broder. "It would be grotesque, at such a moment, to watch without protest the strangulation or distortion of democracy in the United States—which symbolizes successful and sustained self-government to so much of the world" (1990a).[3]

But if ideals are inspiring, they are also useful: for specifying and motivating the behavior required to authenticate and sustain the identity and the health of specific political arrangements. "Good democratic practice" is defined here as political behavior by candidates, media, and citizens that has this effect. It is political behavior that is tempered and leavened with that measure of idealism needed to keep the political process meaningfully democratic. To identify such behavior is the aim of this chapter.[4]

If cynicism, selfishness, indifference, and other potentially corrosive and disintegrative forces are to be kept in check, the ethical implications of "routine" political behavior must be regular subjects of investigation and discussion. Explicit evaluative criteria of the sort offered here, themselves proper subjects of debate and refinement, are necessary for this task. Without ethical vigilance, each new departure from good practice is simply incorporated, after a brief flurry of complaints, into a benumbing sense of "normalcy" that masks a further erosion of the basic character of the American electoral system.

The Electoral Triangle

Figure 2-1 depicts the model relationships that, by the standards of good democratic practice defined here, should exist between the components of the electoral triangle.[5] The relationships depicted among the components represent hypotheses about the services these actors must exchange in the modern era if the triangle is to sustain itself as a democratic system of election, rather than slip into decline or evolve into some other kind of system.

Implicit in the figure is a concept of the citizen as proprietor and sovereign, and of the campaign as a process intended primarily for the benefit of citizens, in order to help prepare them to choose representative leaders responsibly. The roles of the media and the candidates are subordinate and pedagogical. Candidates are supplicants; they seek to attract votes and win a lease on power by demonstrating abilities to lead, inspire, and enlighten citizens. The news media are constitutionally protected servants of the electorate, as well as privately owned economic organizations. They are responsible for informing and protecting citizens by means of rigorous investigation of candidates and their proposed solutions (or inattention) to public problems. The figure captures these bare essentials. But it necessarily omits much of the detail to which we now turn.

The Meaning of Elections

The election, said H. G. Wells, is "democracy's ceremonial, its feast, its great function" (quoted in Sabato 1988:14). Elections are not only democracy's greatest ceremonies. They are its most definitive and character-defining events. This is because they represent "the last vestiges of democracy"; that is, the last remaining forum of consequence for the participation of individual citizens and for the expression of anything approaching the popular will.

Through a gradual process of downsizing, the most widely accepted understandings of democracy have evolved away from the conceptions of thinkers like Jean-Jacques Rousseau and John Stuart Mill, who placed great stress on citizen participation and involvement. In such views, democracy extended beyond elections to "a form of life marked by the promise of equality and the best conditions for human development in a rich context of participation" (Held 1987:165).

Following Joseph A. Schumpeter (1947:269), the most influential modern democratic theorists now regard democracy as simply an institutional arrangement for arriving at political decisions by vesting in certain individuals the power to decide on all matters as a consequence of their successful pursuit of the people's votes. The last vestige of democracy is the citizens' right, by their votes, periodically to choose and authorize governments to act on their behalf.[6]

As presently understood, then, democracy is primarily a method.[7] And "Elections are central to the democratic method because they provide the mechanism through which the control of the leaders by non-leaders can take place" (Pateman 1970:8). Citizens control leaders by electing them in the first place, and thereafter by virtue of the desire for re-election, which motivates leaders to act with the need to maintain voter approval in mind.[8] The requirement that leaders cultivate and maintain popular support in order to win election and re-election to positions of power is the most pervasive and forceful instrument available for democratic control of leaders.[9]

An American presidential election is thus an extraordinarily significant event. It is a tangible demonstration of real democratic power.[10] And it is the most visible symbolic expression of the reality of democracy within the United States. The stable and peaceful quadriennial recurrence of presidential elections since 1789 is perhaps the single most important reason that the United States remains the beacon of democratic inspiration throughout the world. Free and fair elections, regularly scheduled and peacefully conducted, represent the irreducible minimum requirement for a plausible national claim to the democratic label in the eyes of the world.

Beyond peaceful conduct, freedom, and fairness (things still of real concern in places like Nicaragua but long taken for granted in the United States), what constitutes good democratic practice in the conduct of presidential elections? Implicit in the critical writings of journalists, pundits, academics, and others are the following expectations.

First, each presidential election must give its own tangible evidence—in the form of majority voter turnout—that meaningful democracy endures.

The importance of this expectation is implicit in the large amount of attention paid to the question of turnout in academic and popular writings in all the Western democracies, but especially in the United States, where average turnout is far below the average of 80 percent of the eligible electorate that votes in other industrialized democracies (Powell 1986:17). There is no formal quorum requirement associated with voter turnout in presidential elections. But the majority-rule norm (imbedded in the amorphous web of psychosocial perceptions of political legitimacy in America) appears to underlie the discomfort often expressed as turnout figures threaten to drop below the magic 50 percent marker.

Much ink is spilled in the attempt to explain the low U.S. voter turnout, and in the search for remedies (e.g, Piven and Cloward 1989). Historically, U.S. voter turnout has fluctuated rather considerably. For example, it dropped from 79 percent in 1896 to a twentieth-century low of 49 percent in 1920 and 1924. In 1928 it climbed back to 57 percent, reaching 62 percent by 1940. It dropped again to 53 percent in 1948, but then rose to hover in the 60 percent range between 1952 and 1968. It began dropping again in 1972, reaching 57 percent, then 55 percent in 1980 (Burnham 1981). To the consternation of many, the recent downward trend continues. Turnout approached the record low again in 1988 by dropping to 50.16 percent.[11]

Second, the election results must be accepted as legitimately conferring the title and powers of the presidency.

The fact of peaceful transfer of the powers of the highest executive positon throughout American history is the envy of the world, and is among the reasons for the status of the United States as the oldest surviving government on earth and the most stable. Despite occasional grumbling by defeated partisans (e.g., 1824, 1960) the results of every presidential election, including 1988's, have been accepted as legitimate by the public as well as the defeated candidate and his supporters. If, as is often said, the American political system "works well" (Neuman 1986), this is an important reason why it is perceived to do so.

Third, a presidential campaign is expected to seek, and the election is expected to confer, informal public approval of a broad national policy direction.

Presidential elections have long been regarded as contests that crystallize the national sense of policy direction. The American expectation that elections represent choices between candidates who represent competing political philosophies and approaches to the solution of national policy problems can be traced at least as far back as the election of 1796 and the struggle between Adams the Federalist and the Democratic Republican Jefferson (Roseboom 1959:33). The more recent expectation is implicit in the fact that presidential candidates who do not discuss their plans or "the issues," or who fail to meaningfully distinguish themselves and their intentions from their opponents, are widely criticized and generally thought to be shirking a responsibility.[12]

In 1968, as one small example, third-party candidate George Wallace of Alabama would charge that there wasn't "a dime's worth of difference" between Republican candidate Richard M. Nixon and Democratic candidate Hubert H. Humphrey. The charge reflected a view that Wallace thought might touch a responsive public chord: that elections should offer genuine policy choices to the electorate. The failure of the 1988 candidates to seriously discuss such pressing national issues as the budget deficit and the U.S. role in a post–cold war world prompted a litany of journalistic criticism, rooted in the same expectation.[13]

The idea that elections reflect choices that confer broad policy mandates is linked to other beliefs. One is that there should be a relationship between campaigning and governing, such that campaigns help to prepare the ground for governing. This is accomplished by securing the electorate's prior approval for measures that would be much more contentious and difficult to achieve without such approval.[14] Another belief is that elections are in part intended as educational experiences for the electorate. There is no better time than a national election for the country as a whole to consider where it is, where it is headed, and where it wants to go. And with both candidates and news media attracting increased public attention as election day nears, there is no greater opportunity to update and upgrade the preparation of the citizenry, both to make intelligent choices between the candidates and policy options before them, and to oversee the performance of the eventual winner.

Fourth, presidential campaigns and elections should be designed to rekindle among citizens a positive sense of identification with and membership in the political order, in order to encourage voting.

This requirement follows from the circumstances of large representative democracies like the United States. For most Americans, voting is the sole act of official participation in politics. In preparing to vote, most citizens follow news accounts of the campaign and engage in discussions about the candidates and the issues, behaviors that constitute less formal modes of "participation." Except for the political socialization that takes place in families and schools, the repetition of such preparation and the act of voting every four years is the major means by which the connection of individual citizens to the national political order is periodically renewed and thereby sustained.

That is why, insofar as evolving national circumstances permit, and so long as voting remains voluntary, elections should be conducted with the ever-present need to attract and retain citizen participation in view. This means avoiding where possible those nonessential things known or plausibly suspected to discourage participation, such as cumbersome registration requirements, negative advertising, or hostile and aggressive campaign rhetoric. And this should also encourage more positive efforts, by schools, candidates, political parties, and journalists, to explain the importance of elections in the functioning of democracies, and to instill and evoke citizens' feelings of political obligation and concern for the polity.[15]

The Responsibilities of Citizens

Democracy places citizens in the sovereign position. It does so both because individual human beings are seen as intrinsically worthy and deserving, and because they are regarded as collectively the safest repository of ultimate power. "I know of no safe depository for the ultimate powers of society but the people themselves," wrote Thomas Jefferson. "And if we think them not enlightened enough to exercise their control with a wholesome discretion, the remedy is not to take it from them, but to inform their discretion" (letter to William Charles Jarvis, 1820).

What must citizens do in order to keep democracy viable? Early political thinkers demanded extensive citizen participation, as a safeguard against the abuse of power, but also because political participation was the vehicle by which citizens could develop the personal qualities needed to sustain democracy:

> ... the "classical" theory ... had an ambitious purpose, "the education of an entire people to the point where their intellectual, emotional, and moral capacities have reached their full potential and they are joined, freely and actively in a genuine community" and that the strategy for reaching this end is through the use of "political activity and government for the purpose of public education." (Pateman 1970:21, quoting from Davis 1964)

Theorists like Jean-Jacques Rousseau and John Stuart Mill set forth plans of action and specific prescriptions for citizen education capable of producing a "democratic character" that involved participation well beyond the mere act of voting.

In sharp contrast, such contemporary "empirical" democratic theorists as Schumpeter (1947), Robert A. Dahl (1956), and Giovanni Sartori (1987), taking the facts of political apathy and ignorance among ordinary citizens in Western democracies as evidence of the unworkability of such idealism, fashioned a different and much less ambitious concept of democratic participation as limited to the periodic choice between competing elites with election winners authorized to act on the people's behalf. Moreover, "Lack of political involvement can . . . be interpeted quite positively: it can be based upon trust in those who govern . . . Empirical democratic theorists held that pluralist (i.e., interest group) democracy was a major achievement irrespective of the actual extent of citizen participation. Indeed, 'democracy' does not seem to require a high level of active involvement from all citizens; it can work quite well without it" (Held 1987:192).

As a practical matter, the proposition must be granted that preparing for and casting a vote for president will remain the probable limit to the national political participation of most American citizens. But any argument that limited participation in the form of low voter turnout has positive implications must be rejected. As we have seen, a pattern of declining turnout adversely affects perceptions of democratic health and legitimacy. Too, citizen apathy and political ignorance invite destructive campaign practices on the part of candidates. It is likely, for example, that they encouraged the issue avoidance and negative emotional appeals critics found so deplorable in the 1988 presidential campaign (see Chapters 1 and 6).

What, then, must citizens do if use of their sovereign power is to motivate good democratic practice in the other parts of the electoral triangle? Four imperatives are clear.

First, they must regard presidential campaigns and elections as their "property" in two important senses: (a) as important, regularly scheduled ceremonial acknowledgments of their sovereign status, and (b) as their primary opportunity to acquire the insight and information needed to exercise their sovereignty responsibly.

The fact that elections anoint leaders has focused disproportionate citizen and media attention on the candidates. This fixation tends to overshadow the equally important fact, implicit in the logic of democracy, that campaigns and elections exist primarily for the benefit of citizens. Only citizens have the power to confer the presidency. And by any reasonable construction of democracy, they have an obligation to do so with care.

The campaigns preceding presidential elections exist so that citizens can prepare themselves to exercise the power of leader choice. A proprietary attitude toward campaigns and elections must be nurtured so that citizens will recognize their right to demand the kind of media and candidate campaign presentations needed for responsible citizen preparation. Treating campaigns and elections as celebrations of citizen sovereignty is a way of rekindling and reinforcing the needed proprietary attitude.

Second, citizens must insist upon candidate and media behavior that respects their sovereignty and responds to their need for relevant information and guidance.

As the ultimate wielders of the political (votes) and economic (consumer) power to which candidates and news organizations respond, citizens get the kind of presidential campaigns and news media campaign coverage they are willing to tolerate or demand. But before candidates and media can respond to citizen demands, those demands must be clearly specified and explicitly communicated by citizens themselves. Coherent, widespread demand for responsive presentations and relevant information from candidates and media are unlikely unless citizens fully understand the responsibilities of candidates and media (described below), as well as their own proprietary status. Citizen ignorance of the ground rules—who is responsible for what—invites candidates to define the rules to suit themselves. Thus emerged the idea, for example, that campaigns are only about winning, and not about national stocktaking. If they are to serve as a corrective force in American politics, voters must claim and use their political and economic power to decide what constitutes acceptable practice by the other elements of the triangle.

Third, citizens must be sufficiently well informed to recognize mis-information and sufficiently inner-directed to resist demagoguery.

One clear implication of vesting followers with the power to choose leaders is that the former must acquire sufficient information about matters under public discussion to avoid being easily duped about the facts by self-interested candidate misinformation or distortion.[16] If citizens do not know enough to distinguish truth from falsity on matters of public record, there can be no meaningful control of or check against leaders who distort, deny, or conceal the truth, and democracy is defeated.[17] Ignorance also invites evasive and (from the standpoint of the national agenda) irrelevant campaigns. Uninformed voters are ill equipped to prevent the substance of issues and candidates' qualifications from being supplanted by candidate emphasis on self-serving "wedge" issues.

Democracy additionally assumes and requires a significant degree of self-possession and maturity on the part of citizens sufficient to protect them from self-interested candidate appeals to coarser emotions such as fear, anger, or prejudice in pursuit of votes. But if, as Schumpeter (1947) argued, ordinary citizens are "generally weak, prone to strong emotional impulses . . . [and lacking in] the sense of responsibility that comes from immediate involvement"; and if "ir-rational prejudice and impulse" make citizens "highly vulnerable" to emotional appeals (Held 1987 : 167), then democracy is again de-feated.[18] If an electorate is to be in fact capable of responsibly assess-ing alternative leaders (as representative democracy by definition requires), then it must not only be motivated to acquire the infor-mation needed to do so, but also able to resist appeals that it suspend critical thinking in favor of unreasoning passion.

Fourth, citizens must regard the act of voting as the ultimate civic responsibility, neglect of which undermines the prospects for viable representative democracy.

Such attitudes, and the accompanying tendency of an electorate to actually vote in large numbers, are the definitional bedrocks of democratic legitimacy and of de facto democratic control of leaders by followers. In a system where voting is the primary expression of citizenship, the widespread refusal to vote signals a dangerous ab-negation of civic responsibility.

The Responsibilities of Candidates

The literature of democratic theory does not give extensive atten-tion to the responsibilities of candidates for high public office in democratic polities. But the very existence of that literature is an unflattering reflection on the tendencies of leaders, and by implication on the candidates who seek to become leaders. For democratic thought was born of the desire to protect citizens against their excesses. Political and other leadership skills are recognized as essential to effective representative government (Schumpeter 1947). But the tendency of power to corrupt—with results like tyranny and demagoguery—are the reasons why such democratic forms as separation of powers were invented in the first place (see Madison, *The Federalist* 47 and 48).

We should of course ask presidential candidates—prospective leaders—to voluntarily embrace democratic norms of propriety in mounting campaigns for office. But as with government itself, enforceable citizen expectations must supplement the good intentions of candidates to insure respect for such norms in practice.

In an age of television, presidential campaigns are "candidate centered" in ways not seen in the earlier eras of party labels and political bosses (Abramson, Arterton, and Orren 1988:16). As already noted, this candidate-centeredness deflects attention away from the sovereign status, as from the needs, of the electorate. Of special importance here, however, is the fact that it also invests contemporary presidential candidates with much greater powers to help or hinder the operation and the democratic character of the electoral system. This fact makes it essential that the consequences of presidential candidates' campaign practices be closely monitored.

As prospective leaders of the nation, whose declarations of candidacy imply willingness to swear to "preserve, protect, and defend" the nation's Constitution and values, candidates for the presidency have responsibilities to the political process that go well beyond simply trying to win election, and that constrain what may be done in the effort to win. For in addition to seeking victory, candidates must at least avoid depleting, and arguably should also act to replenish, democracy's "capital," defined as the accumulated store of psychological and social assets (citizen feelings of obligation, goodwill, loyalty, etc.) that undergird the system's durability.

What specific campaign practices are likely to contribute to the health and durability of the political order?

First, candidates should seek to educate voters about the state of the nation and the priorities facing the next president.

To be effective, democratic leaders must be teachers. And in demonstrating such capacities during a campaign, presidential candidates should try to upgrade the understanding of the electorate by explaining the situation to be faced by the next president. The "situation" includes the domestic, economic, and international policy problems and priorities of the United States that exist at the time of the election and that are likely to continue into the presidential term to follow.

The contents of such explanations should reflect good-faith efforts to increase public understanding, not covert attempts to exploit public anxieties or to otherwise cast favorable partisan light on the national circumstances. By this test, candidates gain competitive advantage from cogent and effective explanation, and from demonstrating the ability to increase public understanding, not from guileful manipulation of public emotions and perceptions. To the extent that voters become more aware of the state of the nation and its problems because of candidate presentations, the democracy benefits.

Second, candidates must strive to prepare the ground for governing; that is, they must seek to create positive public support for themselves as leaders and as representatives of a clear sense of national policy direction.

Having created, by their explanations of the situation, a context for proposing and advocating solutions to national problems, candidates then must put reasonably specific proposals before the electorate. The proposals, and the candidate's presentation of them, should convey a clear and realistic sense of direction to the electorate, so that voters may make reasonable predictions concerning the policy consequences of supporting either candidate. If the ground is to be adequately prepared for the work of government after the election, candidates must discuss the realistic possibilities for any necessary public sacrifice, such as increased taxation, as well as politically more palatable intentions.

The shortcomings of opponents may sometimes be legitimate subjects for mention or discussion by one or both candidates. But the importance of avoiding the election of the opponent should never become the major selling point of any presidential candidacy. The preparatory function of campaigns is defeated if the majority of each candidate's pronouncements do not deal with his or her own qualifications, explanations, and policy intentions.

Third, candidates must expose themselves and their policy proposals to sustained critical scrutiny, discussion, and debate.

Candidates have a responsibility to defend their plans and outlooks in debate with one another and in response to the questioning and commentary of ordinary citizens and of nonpartisan policy experts and analysts.[19] The major televised events of any presidential campaign—candidate debates, interviews, talk shows—should be devoted to the fullest possible airing of the comparative merits of candidate proposals relating to priority national problems. This airing constitutes the major educational experience of the campaign for the electorate. To the extent that candidates make themselves available and participate vigorously in this comparative assessment of policy alternatives, they help to sustain the democracy.

Finally, candidates must use their influence on citizens in ways that facilitate their citizenship. This implies striving to maintain citizens' respect for the political process and actively helping to sustain those positive citizen dispositions—feelings of political obligation, clear-headedness, civic enthusiasm—upon which viable representative democracy depends.

At a minimum, this responsibility entails avoiding calculated appeals to negative emotion, or the systematic use of misrepresentation or deceit. For by most available evidence, citizens are repelled from politicians and politics (and possibly from voting) by such tactics, even though their candidate preferences may be influenced by them (see Chapter 6).[20] Moreover, people in the sway of feelings of estrangement or negativity do not appraise evidence as fairly or as objectively as is desirable in a democracy. Nor can they function competently if the evidence they are given is inaccurate or misleading.

More positively, this requirement demands campaign conduct that inspires respect by displaying respect for, and by giving evidence of genuine commitment to, communitarian values that transcend the candidate's electoral self-interest.[21]

Election Coverage Responsibilities of Print and Broadcast News Media

The First Amendment makes the press (i.e., the print and broadcast news media) the only private business in America that is expressly protected by the Constitution.[22] The Communications Act of 1934 requires those who are permitted to use the public airwaves for commercial purposes to devote a significant portion of their programming to the public interest. The corporations that control newspapers and the airwaves collectively hold dominion over a crucial resource: the communications link between the government and its citizens, without which a modern political system cannot function.

These things justify substantial expectations for public service from the media in all the circumstances where such service is needed to promote the public interest. And indeed, many journalists regard their industry as "the fourth branch of government, surveying the political scene for the public" (Graber 1988:123). The Constitution "gave journalists a special immunity from government·regulation and placed us outside the system of checks and balances, not because of our charm, our virtue or our brilliance, but because the Founders believed that a free press, even if fallible, would be a healthy check on government" (Broder 1989b:4). Checking government includes checking those—notably presidential candidates—who would assume its mantle.

Significant disagreement exists among leading representatives of the print and broadcast media concerning the obligations their industry should assume during a presidential campaign.[23] Nevertheless, three services can be identified that a democratic society can reasonably expect of private-sector news organizations in return for constitutional protections and near-monopoly control of the public information space. At a minimum, the leading print and broadcast news media should:

1. *Make available to the public information and analyses of the problems facing the nation and the qualifications of those who would be president.*

This straightforward expectation implies certain media practices intended to maximize the chances that the public can genuinely benefit from media coverage of national problems and candidate qualifications. For example, such coverage should reach its peak on the airwaves and in newsprint publications at the time—usually after Labor Day of a presidential election year—when the largest audience is attentive to the campaign.

The coverage should also, in accordance with well-established principles of learning, be somewhat repetitive, so that nonpartisan accounts of national problems and priorities and candidate qualifications have the opportunity to become as familiar to audiences as do the contents of candidate-sponsored political advertising, which is repeated continuously during the campaign season.[24]

The substance of the coverage of national problems and candidate qualifications is of special importance and should reflect the current state of the evolving needs of the electorate for information and guidance. There is evidence to suggest, for example, that in 1988, voters lacked a coherent sense of the national agenda (see Chapters 5 and 6). Thus they could have profited from an emphasis, during that particular year, on news stories that summarized debates among policy analysts and experts concerning the relative urgencies and priorities among the many problems that would clamor for government's attention in the election's aftermath. Such an educational service would have helped to create an integrative context for additional stories that examined individual public policy problems in greater detail.

As for candidate qualifications, there is need for media presentations on the general importance of particular qualifications for the presidency, as well as for detailed and repetitive coverage of the credentials of particular candidates. For example, three distinguishable kinds of qualifications for office are usually given some attention by citizens and media: character, competence, and issue positions. Voters want to know whether a candidate is personally stable and trustworthy, whether she or he is talented and experienced enough to meet the demands of a difficult job, and they want to know something about the candidate's solutions to the problems facing the country (see Chapter 5, Table 5-3).

Within these broad, familar categories, the media should seek to enhance voter sophistication. That is done with stories that address questions like the following. What dimensions of character are most relevant to the presidency and why? (J. D. Barber 1985). How can a citizen "read" the character of a presidential candidate from a distance? (Buchanan 1987b). What specific kinds of skills and talents are most useful in the presidency, and how can they be spotted in would-be presidents? (Buchanan 1987a). How well did the campaign promises of past presidential candidates predict what they actually tried to do in office? (Fishel 1985). In a campaign season that begins as much as two years before election day, shouldn't candidates with character and competence problems be screened out first, so that issues can take priority when voters compare the finalists after the nominations? (Buchanan 1988). Having written and read stories that probed the status of each qualification and its best use, journalists would be better positioned to examine, and citizens to comprehend, the strengths and weaknesses in the qualifications of particular candidates.

2. *Seek to protect the public from misinformation and self-interested distortions purveyed by candidates.*

If "surveying the political scene for the public" has any meaningful application to presidential campaigns, it is that news organizations must routinely and vigorously call public attention to distortions and inaccuracies in candidate speech or advertising. But a peculiar circumstance of Campaign '88 illustrates how this seemingly straightforward expectation for public service may thrust the media into unexpected and uncomfortable situations.

Traditionally, if a presidential candidate levied an unfair or inaccurate charge at his opponent, the opponent would assume the major responsibility for calling public attention to the impropriety of the charge. That gave the news media a "peg" on which to hang stories of its own about the inaccuracies. In 1988, however, Democratic candidate Michael Dukakis largely ignored misleading Bush campaign charges.[25] That left the media without its customary justification, and faced with a dilemma: whether or not to step in as surrogate for a candidate who did not vigorously defend himself.

Making more of the opponent's distortions than the wronged candidate himself does risks a public perception that the press is choosing sides and invites the lying candidate to allege media unfairness. Still, when ABC News reporter Richard Threlkeld finally did a televised segment comparing advertising fiction with fact on October 19, 1988, it was regarded as a media breakthrough. It came two-thirds of the way through the fall campaign, however; much too late to have had a significant corrective impact on the ad distortions.

The late appearance of "truthsquadding" in 1988 reflects the ambivalence about the practice within the journalism community. Some regard it as inappropriate for the media to compensate for the failure of the candidates to police each other. Others may be reluctant to be too critical of ads for fear of alienating important news sources inside campaigns.[26] But increasingly, journalists like David Broder are coming to feel that greater activism is in order: "The public is sick and tired of being assaulted for weeks before Election Day with horrifying recitals of the opposing candidate's supposed record on some issue—which magically disappears when votes have been counted . . . That means that we must be far more assertive than in the past on the public's right to hear its concerns discussed by the candidates—in ads, debates and speeches—and far more conscientious in reporting those discussions when they take place" (1990a). If such assertiveness is to influence the quality of campaign practice, it must include an aggressive policy of media attention to candidate distortions.

Finally, the media's credibility as a check on the candidates is enhanced to the extent that journalists and editors show themselves willing to turn a critical lens on the campaign coverage practices of television and print news media as well.

3. *Continually rethink and refine political coverage practices in response to the evolving methods of candidates and the changing needs of the electorate.*

If they are to adequately serve the public, news media organizations must develop and maintain the ability to counter any candidate technologies or practices that undermine the public's right to distortion-free information. But the increasing technological and psychological sophistication of campaign influence attempts makes this a difficult task.

The problem is illustrated by 1988 Bush campaign misrepresentations, most apparent in television advertising. The infamous prison-furlough ad, for example, showed a group of prisoners coming and going through revolving prison doors. It also contained factually accurate audio commentary about the Massachusetts prisoner furlough program. But as Kathleen Hall Jamieson suggests, the misleading visual conveyed a more powerful message than the narrowly truthful audio.[27] Watching the prisoners moving in and out of the barred prison doors on the video encouraged viewers to amalgamate the voice and video messages; that is, to infer inaccurately that a large number of Willie Horton-like killers were routinely being freed from Massachusetts prisons because of Dukakis policies, and that they were bent on committing the same crimes that Horton had committed.

What does it take to counter this kind of subtle misrepresentation? Apparently something more than simply replaying the ad on national television, accompanied by a voice pointing out its inaccuracies. For according to Jamieson, efforts to do just that, like the Threlkeld piece mentioned above, actually made the situation worse. Since video messages routinely override audio messages in determining what sticks in the minds of viewers, the effect was to reinforce rather than correct the distortion. Apparently, then, keeping up with candidate innovations in persuasion involves attention to such subtleties as "visual grammar" and its impact.[28]

In the past, the effort to stay abreast of the changing needs of the electorate has led news media to enter, with mixed success, gaps opened by the collapse of other institutions. For example, when political parties stopped pre-screening the qualifications of presidential candidates, leaving the task to voters in primaries, media organizations sought to fill the vacuum with increased attention to the qualifications of primary candidates. Their performance of the screening function has been criticized as inadequate (e.g., Patterson 1989). But even if the criticism has merit, the willingness to try to fill an unmet need should be credited.

In the 1920's Walter Lippmann warned that the press is not equipped for, and cannot be expected to bear alone, the burden of insuring the health of democratic institutions. Nevertheless, democracy benefits greatly from the existence of privately owned organizations staffed with those who have the political expertise and information-gathering skills of journalists to monitor the health of its political institutions on behalf of the public.

Finally, meeting the ever-changing needs of the public requires constant surveillance of the state of the voters as well as of institutions and candidates. For example, an informed electorate must be equipped with a grasp of its own responsibilities as well as with information about national problems and the qualifications of candidates. And if, as in 1988, there is evidence to suggest that public awareness of such matters as the place and importance of elections in a representative democracy has seriously diminished, who is better positioned than print and broadcast news organizations to join in an effort to mount a remedial civics education initiative? Other actors, including the candidates and voters themselves, share responsibility for deploying an educated and an informed electorate. But no other actors can muster the communications reach needed to project a sufficiently timely and comprehensive message.

Conclusion

The foregoing performance expectations for citizens, candidates, and media supply the criteria for assessing the performance of each corner of the electoral triangle, as well as for the system as a whole. They are implicit in the evaluation of the 1988 campaign by the Markle Commission in the concluding chapter. They guided the design of the research program to be described next. And their influence is apparent in the discussion of the results of survey, content-analysis, and focus-group studies sandwiched in between.

The standards are ideals from which practice can be expected to depart. But they force a confrontation with the question "How good is 'good enough'?" in each corner of the electoral triangle. And that, it is to be hoped, is enough to stimulate a public conversation that can pinpoint where, and by how much, political practice has gotten beyond acceptable bounds.

To suggest that the relation between ideals and practice warrants periodic and systematic checking is not to imply incipient crisis or impending doom. A president was, after all, duly elected in 1988. And he went on to enjoy record-breaking public approval after a year in office. In this sense, the machinery of American democracy worked as usual. The pervasive sense that something was wrong with Campaign '88, discussed in Chapter 1, was never a signal of imminent system breakdown. Rather, the spirit during and immediately after the 1988 election was one of inchoate discomfort. It was rooted in the fact that the campaign was too blatantly at odds with American ideals, and in addition did not meet the practical, informational needs of the electorate. The response suggested here is one of prudence, not alarm. Just as people undergo routine physical examinations in order to spot and correct health problems that could otherwise gradually and imperceptibly worsen, so should their political arrangements.

Explicit attention to definitions of good democratic practice serves other purposes as well. It can deny self-interested practitioners a luxury they now enjoy by default: the uncontested privilege of deciding for themselves, without the inconvenience of sustained critical input, what constitutes acceptable political practice in their spheres of operation. Left unchallenged, they naturally gravitate toward definitions that do the least harm to their interests. That way, however, if recent experience is any guide, lies subtle debasement of principles needed to sustain the integrity and vitality of our political arrangements.

It is important to recognize that the moral status of those arrangements has always had international as well as merely domestic implications. The United States has served as the global democratic model through much of its history. But with the sea change in the Communist world, and the move toward democracy in Eastern Europe and elsewhere, the American example looms even larger. Insuring that America's status as international exemplar is deserved is yet another incentive, with both pragmatic and idealistic overtones, for habitual ethical stocktaking. It serves neither U.S. interests nor pride when a pundit can write: "The tacky, morally cheap and financially extravagant U.S. campaigns of late provide a shameful example to those who are switching to democracy" (F. Lewis 1990).

But the most important reason for a revival of explicit attention to the allocation of campaign season responsibilities stems from the pressing need to reconstitute the grammar of citizenship, as it is taught in families and schools, and as it is understood by voters, candidates, and news organizations. The meaning of citizenship requires updating and clarification. Its present ambiguity, as we shall see, underlies many of the political practices—nonvoting, simplistic advertising, negative, issueless campaigning—now widely deplored. New, more relevant language must be invented to teach citizens— the sovereigns in representative democracies—what they owe, and what they must expect, from the other components of the electoral triangle.

3. THE RESEARCH STRATEGY

What is the best way to determine how closely campaign practice in 1988 approximated the ideals just reviewed? The answer begins with a measurement model (Figure 3-1) that identifies the necessary information and implies its utility.

In keeping with the previous chapter's view of an election as a learning opportunity for citizens, the model casts the electorate in the role of "dependent variable," that is, the intended target of an election-season influence network that is expected to change (increase) what citizens know about candidates and issues, to sustain various positive attitudes toward the political process, and to encourage voting.

The "independent variables," presumed causal forces, are the candidates and the news media, who share responsibility for helping citizens to prepare themselves. Social interactions (i.e., citizen exchanges with one another) are expected both to mediate the influence of candidates and media and to have independent impacts of their own on what citizens learn and believe.

Measuring Performance: Multiple Methods, Data Sources

The implications for measurement are straightforward. To discover if the electorate has treated a particular election as a learning opportunity and actually acquired information about national problems and candidate qualifications, it is necessary to measure what voters learned. If attributions of learning are to be credibly made, the extent to which learning took place during the campaign, and did so

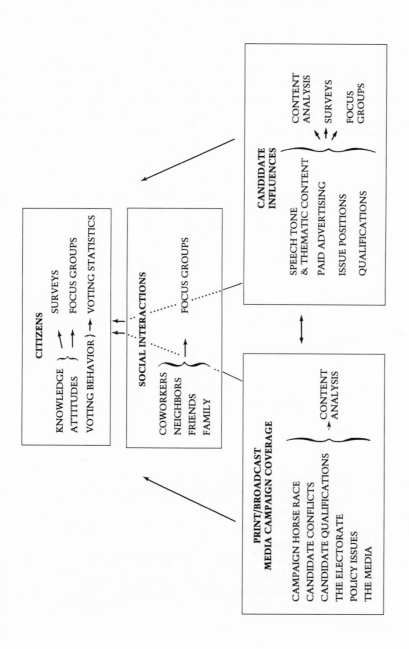

CITIZENS

KNOWLEDGE ⎫
ATTITUDES ⎬ → SURVEYS
          ⎭ → FOCUS GROUPS
VOTING BEHAVIOR } → VOTING STATISTICS

SOCIAL INTERACTIONS

COWORKERS ⎫
NEIGHBORS ⎬ → FOCUS GROUPS
FRIENDS   ⎪
FAMILY   ⎭

CANDIDATE INFLUENCES

SPEECH TONE
& THEMATIC CONTENT ⎫
PAID ADVERTISING   ⎬ → CONTENT ANALYSIS
ISSUE POSITIONS   ⎪ → SURVEYS
QUALIFICATIONS   ⎭ → FOCUS GROUPS

PRINT/BROADCAST
MEDIA CAMPAIGN COVERAGE

CAMPAIGN HORSE RACE   ⎫
CANDIDATE CONFLICTS   ⎪
CANDIDATE QUALIFICATIONS ⎬ → CONTENT ANALYSIS
THE ELECTORATE   ⎪
POLICY ISSUES   ⎪
THE MEDIA   ⎭

Figure 3-1. Measurement Model

as a consequence of influence exerted by candidates, media, and social interactions, must also be estimated. Data for these purposes were generated with survey research and focus groups, as described below and detailed in Chapters 5 and 6.

In order to learn the extent to which the media offered sufficient relevant information, sought to protect the public from misinformation, and tried to stay abreast of other campaign-season needs of the voters, it was necessary to examine what news organizations actually published and broadcast about the election. This was done by content analysis of their election coverage, as discussed below and in Chapter 4.

Information about the candidates, including how they influenced citizens' learning, beliefs, and morale, was implicit in the nature of many of our survey and focus-group results. The details of candidate messages, their television advertising, information about their qualifications and about their day-to-day performance on the hustings, were all obtained from newsprint accounts of their travels and pronouncements and political backgrounds. Candidates are not given a chapter of their own below, however, as their actions and influences are sufficiently described in later reviews of the survey, content-analysis, and focus-group data.[1]

Obtaining insight into how 1988 citizen-voters understood their own role in presidential campaigns, how they responded to competing influence attempts, and how they screened and processed political information called for an approach less formally preconceived and structured than survey questionnaires and content-analysis protocols. Accordingly, we used the more subtle, flexible, and qualitative group depth-interview methodology, more popularly known as focus groups, to pursue these questions (Goldman and McDonald 1987; Krueger 1988).

In ways spelled out in Chapter 6, the group discussions revealed something of the comparative contributions of media, candidates, and social interactions to group participants' attitudes and knowledge of the candidates and issues. They were also quite revealing of the general state of people's civic orientations.

Finally, frequent use is also made in chapters below of the many additional sources of valuable information and insight developed by others, including polls and focus groups sponsored by other organizations and the published reflections of journalists, scholars, and other analysts.

Monitoring Change: A Longtitudinal Design

The aim of assessing and explaining changes in voters' knowledge and attitudes dictated a multi-method (survey research, content analysis, focus groups), longtitudinal (Labor Day to election day) design. Figure 3-2 juxtaposes the data collection schedules for each method.

We see that the surveys proceeded in two waves, one immediately following the Labor Day weekend, the other in the weeks prior to the November 8 election. The sixteen focus groups were conducted in four waves of four groups each, every two weeks between Labor Day and election day, in each of four regions of the country (Elmsford, N.Y., Chicago, Ill., Houston, Tex., and Sacramento, Calif.). The election coverage of eighteen leading print and broadcast news organizations was clipped and video-recorded for each of the sixty-two days from September 8 through November 8, 1988.

For both practical and theoretical reasons, data collection was limited to the traditional Labor-Day-to-election-day fall campaign season. Theoretically, this is the time when citizens are assumed to be most attentive to election information. A practical constraint was that the research planning started too late to begin data collection any earlier.[2]

		SEPTEMBER		OCTOBER		NOVEMBER	
		(5 LABOR DAY)				(8 ELECTION DAY)	
SURVEY WAVES		1 (9/6 – 19/88)			2 (10/18 – 11/4/88)		
		1 (9/19 – 22/88)	2 (10/3 – 6/88)	3 (10/17 – 20/88)		4 (10/31 – 11/3/88)	
FOCUS GROUP WAVES	NY	X	X	X		X	
	IL	X	X	X		X	
	TX	X	X	X		X	
	CA	X	X	X		X	
PRINT/ BROADCAST MEDIA— CONTINUOUS RECORDING		9/8/88				11/8/88	

Figure 3-2. Data Collection Schedules

Measuring Citizen Preparation

Telephone Surveys. The telephone survey instrument was assembled by a Markle Commission planning group in July 1988.[3] The completed instrument was administered under contract with the Markle Commission by Louis Harris and Associates to random national samples of the eligible electorate as indicated above.

The survey was designed to elicit four bodies of information: citizen attitudes toward voting and understandings of the presidency, appraisals of the issue agenda, knowledge and beliefs about the candidates, and attitudes toward the media. Two unique features of the surveys, discussed in greater detail in Chapter 5, were the use of several open-ended survey questions to assess candidate and issue learning and the fact that the survey was administered twice, in nearly identical form, in order to capture any changes in attitudes and information.[4] The changes represent the study's operational definition of "learning."

Focus Groups. The focus-group protocol was designed by the author and refined in consultation with the Roosevelt Center for American Public Policy Studies, which coordinated and moderated the groups by arrangement with the Markle Commission.[5] Discussion topics included presidential qualifications, the issue agenda, the candidates, and the media. Implicit research questions involved the general state of civic preparation and concern evinced by participants.

The group discussions permitted investigation of these subjects at two levels. The first, the "intentional" level, yielded volitional answers to straightforward questions. This kind of information is similar to what is obtained through telephone surveys, although it can be more readily amplified and elaborated by moderator prompting in the group setting.

The second, "unintentional" level, concerns information revealed as a byproduct of discussions about other topics. Information obtained in this "unobtrusive" manner is often richer and more revealing than that obtained through direct "obtrusive" questioning, which often motivates the respondent to edit responses out of concern for the opinion or approval of the questioner.

To illustrate, group discussions of unrelated topics were particularly valuable sources of insight into questions like this: Do citizens regard themselves in any meaningful sense as "owners" of the campaign process? This kind of question is arguably best answered without ever being asked directly. In this instance, we simply watched the groups engaged in discussions of other facets of the unfolding campaign. The emotional shading, belief patterns, and the substance of their commentary on other matters portrayed quite vividly how people conceived of their own relationships to the political process, as can be seen in Chapter 6.

Such discussion also clearly revealed, both directly and indirectly, what the participants expected of candidates and media, and whether (to recall another criterion discussed in the previous chapter) the candidates were thought to have encouraged citizens to respect the political process.

Measuring Media Coverage

Content Analysis. Recording, transcribing, and coding of print and broadcast news election stories were done under contract with the Markle Commission by Luce Press Clipping Service. Coders were trained for the task by the principal investigator, who also developed the coding scheme.[6] Of the eighteen news organizations whose election coverage was coded, five were television networks (ABC, CBS, NBC, CNN, and PBS) and thirteen were print media (the *New York Times, Washington Post, Wall Street Journal, Christian Science Monitor, Los Angeles Times, New York Daily News, Chicago Tribune, Sacramento Bee, Houston Chronicle, Newsweek, Time, U.S. News and World Report,* and the *National Journal*).

Stories were coded into six categories and numerous subcategories. The six major categories, as shown in Figure 3-1, were campaign horse race, candidate conflicts, candidate qualifications, the electorate, policy issues, and the media. The definitions of these categories and subcategories, explanations of their relevance to appraising media performance, and a review of what the coding disclosed, concern us next.

4. THE NEWS MEDIA IN CAMPAIGN '88: WHAT THEY COVERED AND HOW THEY COVERED IT

Media watching has become an industry. Increasing numbers of both partisan and public interest research organizations now routinely monitor the content and tone of television and newspapers from a great variety of perspectives (Bonafede 1989a:856). These relative newcomers join an enterprise—content analysis of news media output—once dominated by nonpartisan university researchers (e.g., Graber 1988: 206; Krippendorff 1980:13–20).

The content analysis results reported in this chapter are in the nonpartisan tradition. They were obtained according to strict canons of social science research.[1] Three coders independently analyzed over seven thousand campaign stories, representing the Labor-Day-to-election-day campaign coverage of eighteen print and broadcast news organizations. These organizations included many of the leading national and regional news media in the United States. Research has shown that regional media closely reflect the coverage patterns of these leaders, which makes them good representatives of the U.S. media as a whole (Graber 1989:66). The coding scheme is implicit in the discussion to follow.[2] Table 4-1 summarizes the findings, identifies the organizations whose news products were coded, and reports inter-coder reliability estimates for each of six major coding categories.

These findings were assembled in order to confront the value questions that emerged in Chapter 2 on democratic practice. There it was suggested that in return for unique First Amendment protections and in light of their privileged and profitable dominion over the public airwaves and other information space, it is reasonable for

Table 4-1. *1988 Presidential Campaign Media Content-Analysis Summary*[a]

Coded Categories	Number in Category	Coder Agreement(%)	Percentage in Category
Total campaign stories coded			7,574
News stories	5,078		
Editorials	2,442[b]		
Photographs	54		
Total story allocations to coded categories[c]			10,373
Campaign horse race	3,744	83.9	36.1
Candidate conflicts	2,162	85.6	20.8
Candidate qualifications	1,995	78.7	19.2
The electorate	1,009	82.6	9.7
Policy issues	1,003	79.5	9.7
The media	460	76.2	4.4

[a] The September 8–November 8, 1988, campaign coverage of the following eighteen news organizations was content-analyzed: *New York Times, Washington Post, Christian Science Monitor, Wall Street Journal, Los Angeles Times, Newsweek, Time, U.S. News and World Report, National Journal, New York Daily News, Chicago Tribune, Houston Chronicle, Sacramento Bee,* NBC, ABC, CBS, CNN, and PBS.

[b] Includes both official editorials and signed op ed pieces.

[c] Some stories fit multiple categories.

[d] Three coders analyzed each story. Percentages refer to the extent of agreement—by two of three or three of three coders—that stories put in category actually fit category.

this democracy to expect leading private-sector news organizations to inform its citizens about presidential candidates and national issues, to provide a counterweight against misinformation and self-interested distortions by candidates, and to continually refine their coverage practices in response to changes in candidate practices and voter needs. Do the coverage patterns summarized in Table 4-1 and elaborated in other tables throughout this chapter constitute an acceptable measure of collective media effort and success at meeting these expectations? That is the pivotal question about media coverage posed in this book. Although the principal business here is to present findings rather than pass judgment, note will be taken of the relevance of various findings to the appraisal offered in Chapter 7.

Results

If we are to ask how well the media served the electorate's need for information and explanation during the 1988 presidential campaign, we must first examine what the media covered and how they covered it.

The six coding categories in Table 4-1 reflect a mixture of the kinds of stories known to have dominated past election news coverage practice (e.g., "horse-race" stories) and categories of coverage our normative model suggests ought to be well represented in responsible election coverage (e.g., stories about candidate qualifications). We begin our review of the findings with the perennial media favorite: stories about the strategic political contest between the candidates and their campaign organizations.

Campaign Horse-Race Stories

"Political journalism," writes George F. Will, "has become more preoccupied with mechanisms and cosmetics . . . As the machinery of politics—polling, direct mail, and all the rest—has become more elaborate, there have been more nuts and bolts for political journalists to know about . . . Television, especially, has encouraged the notion that a vivid gesture or memorable 'sound bite' seen by millions of people at a dramatic juncture of a campaign must be as consequential as it is conspicuous" (Swerdlow, ed. 1989:218).

Stories classified in Table 4-1's "campaign horse-race" category emphasize the ebbs and flows of the campaign (e.g., stories about momentum, who seems to be winning and losing, whether the candidates are comfortable and impressive on the stump, etc.); evaluations and comparisons of campaign strategy (e.g., Dukakis's "middle-class squeeze" theme is not playing as well as Bush's anti-crime message); and the contributions and quality of the campaign staff and organization (e.g., John Sasso rejoining the inept Dukakis campaign never provided the hoped-for "shot in the arm"; James Baker's smooth orchestration of the Bush campaign gives Bush an edge).

This category dominated media campaign-season coverage during the 1968, 1972, 1976, and 1980 presidential elections (Graber 1989: 415; Patterson 1980). It contained the greatest number of stories during the 1988 primary season (Lichter 1988:45). It comes as no surprise, therefore, to discover that it also got the most media attention between Labor Day and election day, 1988.[3]

Table 4-2. *1988 Campaign Horse-Race Coverage:*
18 Print and Broadcast News Organizations (9/8–11/8/1988)

	Total Stories	Horse-Race Stories	Per-centage
Broadcast News			
CNN	249	165	66
CBS	184	111	60
NBC	139	83	60
ABC	165	97	59
PBS	185	73	39
Publications			
National Journal	76	45	59
New York Daily News	738	419	57
Chicago Tribune	426	234	55
Washington Post	939	483	51
Newsweek	113	56	50
New York Times	825	396	48
Los Angeles Times	1,022	491	48
Time	96	45	47
Sacramento Bee	761	348	46
Christian Science Monitor	246	108	44
Houston Chronicle	1,057	446	42
Wall Street Journal	249	101	41
U.S. News and World Report	104	43	41

Table 4-1 indicates that this was the case for all eighteen news organizations included in this study. Did some news organizations play up the horse race more than others? Table 4-2 shows the answer to be yes. While 49 percent of the 7,574 total stories from all eighteen news outlets coded had some horse-race content,[4] the table shows considerable variation from one news organization to another. The percentage of stories containing coverage of the horse race ranged from a low of 39 percent for PBS to a high of 66 percent for CNN. Despite having the lowest (PBS) as well as the highest (CNN) entry, television news gave the horse race significantly more coverage (an average of nearly 57 percent of their campaign-related stories had horse-race content) than newspapers (average, 48 percent).

Did pace-setting newspapers like the *New York Times* or the *Washington Post* allocate less coverage to this dimension of the campaign than others? Not significantly. Several publications in the sample did have higher percentages. But the *Times* was right on the average of the thirteen print outlets, with the *Post* slightly higher. Interestingly, the highest percentage among print outlets was the *National Journal*, an influential, elite-circulation weekly news magazine that emphasizes in-depth issue and policy analysis.[5] The print news outlets with the lowest percentages of coverage devoted to the political horse race were the business-oriented *Wall Street Journal* and *U.S. News and World Report*.

As noted, the majority of horse-race stories involved comparisons of various features of the two campaigns and the appeal of the two candidates. Although both candidates experienced a good deal of criticism,[6] the story balance tilted increasingly against Dukakis as it became apparent that the Bush campaign was more effectively managed. Whatever impact this coverage may have had on voters, it undoubtedly worked to the advantage of the Republican candidate.[7]

This advantage is clearly the unintended result of journalistic norms and not a partisan effort to help any particular candidate (Robinson and Sheehan 1983:302). Candidates are helped or hurt in unplanned ways depending on how news values interact with campaign developments (Patterson 1989). One scholar aptly terms this unintended effect "random partisanship" (Seymour-Ure 1974).

An aspect of the 1988 horse-race coverage that clearly favored one candidate and that got substantial critical attention in pre- and post-election stocktaking among journalists was the tendency to treat the election of George Bush as inevitable. Among the first such stories to appear was one entitled, "Top Democrats See Dukakis in Deep Trouble." It ran on September 21 in the *Los Angeles Times* and asserted that "Democratic Party power brokers" were beginning to say privately that Dukakis's "goose was cooked" (Nelson 1988:1). The volume of such stories swelled after ABC News, on the night before the second (October 13) debate between George Bush and Michael Dukakis, featured its own fifty-state electoral college poll that showed Dukakis to be much worse off in the electoral college race than in the popular vote. In a piece about the post-debate "landslide" talk, E. J. Dionne, then of the *New York Times*, noted that "many journalists [are] troubled about the seeming rush to be the first to declare Mr. Bush the victor . . . " Dionne quotes *Chicago Tribune* national political correspondent Jon Margolis: "It's a difficult situation. You have to do your job and say things are looking pretty good for Bush. But when you say that, it influences the process" (Dionne 1988e:1). On October 17 CNN media analyst Martin Schram opined on the air that the media were portraying the

Dukakis campaign as "apocalypse now," and admonished his colleagues to "tell the story, don't be the story."[8]

Why do the news organizations in our sample, which include many of the most highly respected national and regional news operations in the United States, devote so much coverage to the political horse race? Is it because horse-race coverage attracts more viewers and sells more papers? It may do so, though it would be difficult to document this directly. In any event, news executives believe it does, or they wouldn't allocate the resources to the horse race that they do. Locked in ratings and sales competitions, they apparently find the pressure, for example, to make news by commissioning another poll, or to be the first to declare the probable winner, too intense to resist.

Does such coverage serve journalism's institutional values and imperatives better than would the sort of coverage the critics want? Here the answer is a clearcut yes. The political contest is highly newsworthy. It serves "here and now" news values like originality and immediacy. Unlike the budget deficit or the qualifications of candidates, the campaign story unfolds anew each day, providing something fresh to put in the paper or on television. Plus, it can be made to seem dramatic, colorful, exciting, and even tension-filled, all qualities which help attract and hold audience attention.

Entertainment aside, is it possible that such coverage actually helps voters in ways not sufficiently credited by the critics? This view has an influential supporter. In his book *Behind the Front Page*, David Broder offers a spirited defense of the practice, suggesting that the news audience has a right to know who is likely to win the election: " ... it is ... a genuine and legitimate response to the curiosity about 'who's going to win this thing?'" (1987a:242). Too, horse-race coverage tells something of the candidates' ability to interact with the public. And most horse-race stories also contain at least some information about issues and candidate qualities. Broder also argues that horse-race journalism takes nothing away from other important categories of coverage: " ... I am not convinced that horse-race journalism blinds us—or the voters—to the importance of issues in the election ..." (1987a:259–260).[9]

Broder cautions that while horse-race coverage may be legitimate, the challenge is to provide it without losing sight of other aspects of the coverage—especially the issues. We will have the opportunity to examine the issue coverage patterns of our sample of news organizations later in the chapter.

Why have social scientists and others been so critical of the media's emphasis on the horse race during presidential campaigns? In part because, as recent research on "priming" and "agenda setting" has shown, what people watch on television affects not only their beliefs about which national problems deserve priority attention, but also their beliefs about how candidates ought to be judged (Iyengar and Kinder 1987). In ways too subtle to be easily reflected on or guarded against by the mass audience, media coverage emphases can instill concepts of what sort of information about presidential candidates is most relevant to the voters' choice. By devoting the largest proportion of their coverage to the campaign horse race, news organizations may convey a repetitious subliminal message that the horse race generates information that bears on who ought to be president. Viewers and readers are implicitly invited to assume that the strategic political contest is a worthy and possibly a sufficient test of suitability for office, and that the shrewdest candidate with the most effective campaign both wins and deserves the presidency for that reason alone.[10] Critics believe that the media should convey a more accurate sense than this of what candidate qualifications are relevant to the presidency. They particularly want more attention to policy issues and programs. Media defenders retort that anyone willing to put forth some effort can acquire abundant information about candidate qualifications from media sources. We will see in Chapter 5 that people who said they paid close attention to media coverage of the campaign did significantly better than others on a test of knowledge about the candidates' issue positions. Still, for the more typical voter who "follows" the news rather than studying it, the 1988 presidential campaign was mostly a story of horse race and strategy (Patterson 1989:98). Critics believe that unless casual viewers encounter at least as much coverage of issue positions and other qualifications as they do of the horse race, they will end up ill equipped to select the president.[11]

Candidate Conflicts

The second most heavily populated coding category, with some 2,162 story allocations (Table 4-1) is labeled "candidate conflicts." In previous coding studies, this kind of story has usually been included in the "campaign horse-race" category. If the two categories were combined here into one omnibus category, it would encompass 57 percent of the story allocations.

Stories coded as candidate conflicts dealt with what the presidential and vice presidential candidates (or their surrogates) said to or about each other. Use of the word "conflicts" in the label stems from the fact that candidate exchanges about issues or each other—whether in formal debates, media exchanges, or stump speeches—are more often critical than neutral or favorable, and are often confrontational. Candidate A levies a charge at Candidate B, who usually responds and often counterattacks. Or Candidate A makes an assertion about a policy or a problem that Candidate B disputes.

The category was included in order to bring some data to bear on whether the 1988 campaign was unusually negative, and particularly on whether media coverage emphasized the conflict between Michael Dukakis and George Bush. The campaign has, of course, been widely described as one of the most negative in history (e.g., Jaroslovsky 1988; Dionne 1988f:11), evoking cynicism among voters and helping to reduce voter turnout (Broder 1989d:4; Berke 1988a:1). But what of the media's coverage of the campaign? Did allocating over 20 percent of its coverage to conflict (Table 4-1) constitute undue attention to the confrontational side of the campaign, and thus accentuate the perception of negativity? Consider the following.

Available evidence suggests that past presidential candidates spent most of their time talking not about their opponents, but about goals, problems, and past performance. One researcher analyzed the contents of a random sample of Kennedy's and Nixon's campaign rhetoric in 1960 and found that both candidates devoted most of their rhetorical time (49 and 43 percent respectively) to goals and problems. Only 9 percent of Kennedy's comments dealt with himself or his opponent, while 26 percent of Nixon's comments fit this category (Page 1978:156). We do not have comparable data for 1988, but that year's presidential candidates probably did devote a larger proportion of their rhetoric to one another's shortcomings, particularly since the thrust of the Bush campaign strategy was to highlight Dukakis's weaknesses and to attack his "liberal" performance record.

But it is still quite possible that the category received media attention out of proportion to the rhetorical space the candidates actually devoted to the conflict. The fact that "candidate conflicts" was the second-largest media coverage category invites suspicion that this was indeed the case.

At least one of the candidates thought so. At the second 1988 debate between the presidential candidates, for example, George Bush complained that journalists following his campaign ignored his policy statements and position papers and focused instead on the critical things he and Michael Dukakis had been saying about one another.[12] Candidates often assert that media coverage does not faithfully reflect what they actually say. Scholars often note the media's particular attraction to controversy and divisiveness (e.g., Seymour-Ure 1974; Patterson 1989). And, in an often-quoted appraisal, Bush media strategist Roger Ailes identified "attacks" as one of only four things he believed the media were interested in (the others were polls, pictures, and mistakes) (McCarthy 1988:70).

Even if conflicts are overplayed, however, not all conflict coverage can be dismissed as mere sensationalism. Certain features of the conflict between candidates yield information that can be relevant to the voters' choice. The formal debates are one obvious example. Though sanitized even more than usual in 1988 by format restrictions imposed by cautious candidates, debates are face-to-face confrontations that may offer crucial insight into various aspects of the candidates' suitability for office. The value to the citizen may come more from watching the debate itself than from absorbing the post-debate print and broadcast accounts. Debates are the only opportunities voters usually have to observe the candidates thinking "on their feet," in the least controlled and least-scripted settings of the campaign season. Direct observation of such relatively informal performance supplies invaluable sensory data about the candidates as people that is simply not available from other sources. Still, post-debate coverage can help viewers think through their own reactions.

Another aspect of the conflict between candidates of at least potential relevance to the voters' decision is commentary by one candidate or the candidate's surrogates about the qualifications of the other candidate. (e.g., Bush's claim that Dukakis would be "weak" on national defense, and that he lacked foreign policy experience, implying that he, Bush, would be stronger by comparison). Such commentary is, of course, highly susceptible to self-interested distortion. And it might well get more media attention than needed for strictly informational purposes. But it does pertain to the fitness of candidates for the presidency. Such coverage can therefore credibly claim to serve the voters' interests.

What sort of candidate-conflict coverage, then, is not relevant to the voters' task, and can thus be considered newsworthy only for its ability to attract an audience? One type of candidate exchange in particular seems to qualify: direct attacks by one against another that target some real or imagined shortcoming which, even if true, is of dubious relevance to gauging fitness for office. Bush's relentless attacks on Dukakis for the Massachusetts prison furlough program that released convicted murderer Willie Horton are an example.

Such criticisms have an ad hominem flavor. The connection between the criticism and suitability for office is murky at best—and in any case is not the real intent of the allegation. Ad hominem attacks contribute little or nothing to the voters' store of relevant information. Extensive coverage of this sort of candidate exchange would give credence to complaints about undue media emphasis on conflict and might afford grounds for the charge that responsibility for a negative campaign was shared by media as well as candidates. Reduced media attention to such attacks would likely discourage them, as candidates noticed that they had lost their publicity value.

An effort was made to capture these distinctions between types of conflict stories, and the results appear in Table 4-3. The percentages include stories in each category for both presidential and vice-presidential candidates. We see that both print and broadcast media devoted more than half of their coverage of candidate conflicts to the subcategory just identified as least relevant to serious candidate appraisal: attacks made by the candidates against one another. The remaining conflict coverage gave slightly more attention to debate stories than to partisan comparisons.

Additional information not reported in tables sheds better light on the nature of the coverage within the subcategories in Table 4-3. Within the debate-stories subcategory, for example, it was found that only 22 percent of more than 800 debate stories dealing with all three 1988 candidate debates identified winners or losers. This is at least partly because many of these stories appeared before the debates they dealt with took place. But it shows that debate coverage was not solely about winning and losing.

In fact, each debate seemed to generate a particular issue or question of its own that attracted a great deal of media attention. In

Table 4-3. *Media Coverage of Candidate Conflicts: Subcategories[a] (9/8–11/8/1988)*

	Debate Stories (%)	Partisan Comparisons (%)	Attack Stories (%)
Aggregate sample	27	19	54
Broadcast news	21	21	58
Print news	28	19	53

[a] Conflict subcategory coding project is the work of a single coder.

stories just before and just after the first presidential debate on September 25, for example, a frequently addressed question was whether the lesser-known Dukakis could (or did) establish himself as credible presidential material in a verbal exchange with the more experienced George Bush (e.g., Drogin 1988). The October 5 vice-presidential debate was widely portrayed as Dan Quayle's big opportunity to redeem himself as a serious and deserving national candidate (e.g., Rogers 1988). And the final (October 13) presidential debate was often written and spoken of as the aloof Dukakis's last chance to establish himself as a warmer and more likeable person (Toner 1988c). Such stories were clearly relevant to the various concerns voters had expressed about the candidates.

As for the partisan-comparisons subcategory, partisan commentary about candidate competence edged out issue position to receive the larger share of media attention (34 to 33 percent, not shown in tables), while 23 percent of the stories dealt with opponents' appraisals of the other candidate's personal attributes. The distribution of these partisan-commentary percentages probably reflects what the 1988 candidates themselves emphasized in discussing one another's qualifications. Both Bush and Dukakis partisans did devote a good deal of their appeals to unfavorable comparisons of their candidate's to his opponent's competence. The Bush indictment of Dukakis's competence featured his lack of foreign-policy background, while the latter's criticism of Bush featured his implication in such policy failures as Iran-Contra and the war on drugs.

Coverage of the candidates' attacks on one another defy easy summary, except to say that the majority of such stories featured mention by the attacker of several of the target's alleged shortcomings. Summarizing such a Bush speech, a *New York Times* editorial says: "He portrays the Massachusetts Governor as a closet liberal who favors unilateral disarmament and furloughs for felons and hates the Pledge of Allegiance" ("The Pledge vs. the Good Old U.S.A." 1988). And in a story titled "Dukakis and Bush Trade Fire in Heavy Barrages," a *Times* staff writer notes about the same charges: "In Mr. Bush's telling, all these issues came together as representing the lowest form of liberal reasoning" (Toner 1988b).

Bush started sooner and persisted longer and more successfully in the attack mode than Dukakis, and the stories reflect it. As one story noted, "Mr. Dukakis is struggling for some low concept ways of making his high concept fly. The best he's done so far [as of September 5, 1988] is to turn his speeches into the 'Where Was George?' show. The question is aimed at showing that Mr. Bush failed to do this or that in the Reagan Administration. The crowds, primed by the repetition of the question at the Democratic Convention, love to yell 'Where was George?' whenever they get a chance" (Dionne 1988c).

Candidate Qualifications

Table 4-1 shows candidate qualifications to be the third-largest category, with nearly 20 percent of the story allocations. Stories classified here deal not with partisan attacks by one candidate on the qualifications of the other, as described above, but with nonpartisan, primarily journalistic efforts to explain the qualifications of the candidates.

An ideal often expressed in assessments of media campaign coverage is that it ought to convey information about presidency-relevant qualifications. This coding category was included to measure the extent to which the 1988 coverage implemented that ideal.

The major presidential qualifications can be conceived in three categories: character, competence, and issue position.[13] By "character" is meant "the kind of person" the candidate is, particularly in moral and temperamental terms. Stories will often mention such attributes as trustworthiness, or whether the candidate is a forceful or inspiring person, whether he or she seems compassionate, and the like. The following excerpt from from a primary season story about Democratic presidential candidate Michael Dukakis is an example:

> . . . it's no mystery why Dukakis is touchy about [being called a technocrat]. It is code for the qualities, real and perceived, that give people their deepest misgivings about him: the rap of blood-lessness, of a managerial mentality, of dread Jimmy Carterism. It is code, too, for the fact that voters still don't know quite what to make of him . . . Exasperated by all the psychologizing, one of his campaign aides says, "He's just a guy, you know. He's just a guy!" (Trueheart 1988:8)

By "competence" is meant the skills, abilities, or capacities that television or news stories mention as relevant to the candidate's ability to lead, work with Congress, devise foreign policy, and meet other presidential job demands. For example, stories about whether Dukakis has enough foreign-policy experience would fit here, as would discussions of Republican vice-presidential nominee Dan Quayle's youth and inexperience. Previous experience in government posts is taken by reporters and citizens alike as significant evidence of probable presidential competence in a candidate. Most

Campaign '88 competence stories focused on experience. In a column about George Bush, James Reston provides an illustration:

> The Vice President has benefited greatly by his record as co-pilot in the White House, former head of the Central Intelligence Agency, member of Congress, businessman and ambassador to the United Nations and China. He claims fairly that this is what sets him apart. (Reston 1988a:19)

Issue positions, of course, concern where the candidates want to take the country in terms of policy direction if they are elected. The 1988 presidential candidates were criticized for their failure to address such pressing matters as the budget deficit and the savings-and-loan crisis in any detail. But each man took numerous stands on other matters, and the press both reported and evaluated those positions, as the following example shows:

> Governor Michael S. Dukakis, whose views on foreign policy are unfamiliar to many foreigners, sought today to assure Western allies and those involved in American foreign policy about his commitment to the North Atlantic Treaty Organization . . . The Massachusetts Governor repeated his call for a strengthening of non-nuclear military forces. He also denounced the Reagan Administration's plan for a space-based defense against missiles and affirmed his opposition to the Midgetman and the mobile MX missiles, a position that concerns some leaders of his own party . . . Representative Dave McCurdy, Democrat of Oklahoma and one of the party's defense specialists, said later that he and others continued to be concerned about Mr. Dukakis's opposition to the mobile MX and the Midgetman systems. (Toner 1988a:13)

Previous research shows that there has been substantial coverage of the various candidate qualifications in past presidential campaigns, but less than many regard as desirable (Graber 1988). Reasonable people may differ as to whether 20 percent represents a sufficient share of 1988 media attention for this important category (see Table 4-1). But at least as important a question as "how much" coverage is "what kind" of coverage. Table 4-4 breaks the candidate-qualifications coverage down by candidate and story type. To avoid cluttering, the table does not report percentages along with the

Table 4-4. *Candidate-Qualifications Stories*[a]

	Bush	Dukakis	Both	Quayle	Bentsen	Both
Character	143	67	36	142	26	4
Competence	121	70	59	177	18	8
Issue positions						
Economic policy	87	44	106	5	1	2
Domestic policy	123	99	158	19	7	5
Foreign/national-						
security policy	67	49	95	25	6	2
Candidate						
summaries						
Total stories	541	329	454	368	58	21
Percentages[b]	31	19	26	21	3	1

[a] 1,771 stories were classified in these categories. The sum is less than the 1,995 figure in Table 4-1 because stories were included here only if two or three of three coders agreed on each classification.

[b] Percentages do not sum to 100 because of rounding.

number of stories in each category. Percentages are reported in the text below where appropriate.

First worth inspecting is the distribution of stories across qualification categories. Calculation shows that candidate issue positions received the lion's share of attention, 51 percent when economic, domestic, and foreign-policy/national-security stories are combined. The remaining 49 percent divided almost evenly between character (24 percent) and competence (25 percent). Such results will not displease those who argue that issue stands deserve priority attention. Within the candidate-qualifications category in 1988, they got it.

What of the distribution of stories about the candidates? It is interesting that George Bush's qualifications received more press and TV attention (31 percent) than those of the less well known Michael Dukakis (19 percent), although a substantial body of stories dealt simultaneously with the attributes of both presidential candidates (26 percent).

Why were there more stories about Bush? One possibility is that reporters simply knew more about him and covered him more extensively because of it. The greater likelihood, however, is that the belief—widespread among reporters as early as mid-September—that Bush would win the election led to closer and more extensive scrutiny of his credentials (Nelson 1988:1).

It is easier to account for the large share of attention given the qualifications of Republican vice-presidential candidate Dan Quayle. Once the furor over his alleged use of family influence to gain entry into the Indiana National Guard had subsided, Quayle's relative inexperience and perceived lack of stature would keep him alive as a media focus. Note that 48 percent of the Quayle stories deal with competence, compared to only 31 percent for Texas Senator Lloyd Bentsen.

Bentsen, the Democratic vice-presidential nominee, was the principal subject of only 3 percent of the candidate-qualifications stories, an astonishingly low figure. This despite the fact that he was perceived—in poll after poll—as better presidential material than Quayle. Some polls showed him to be the most credible of the four 1988 candidates in the eyes of the public. For better or worse, most of the attention goes to front-runners, particularly when they are controversial.

How was media attention allocated among the various qualifications of the presidential candidates? The category totals in Table 4-4 show that 26 percent of Bush qualification stories dealt with character as against 20 percent of the Dukakis stories. Twenty-two percent dealt with Bush's competence (compared to 21 percent for Dukakis). And 51 percent concerned Bush policy positions, with Dukakis positions accounting for 58 percent of the stories. The slightly greater concentration on Bush's character and Dukakis's policy positions may reflect nothing more than chance. Or it might reflect special interest in Bush's emergence as a forceful campaigner, for example, or the fact of Dukakis's advocacy of a greater number of domestic programs.

Later, the tone of the media coverage for all coded television and newspaper stories about the two major presidential candidates will be discussed (Table 4-8). But we extracted tone information specifically for candidate-qualifications stories as well, and the results (not reproduced in any table) are worth discussing for what they imply about the media's evaluative stance toward candidate qualifications.

It is clear, for example, that the tone of coverage for both candidates is preponderantly critical. Most (55 percent) of the Bush stories were negative in tone, with 32 percent mixing positive and negative assessments. Only 13 percent of the stories were positive. Dukakis's largest category was mixed (43 percent), with 38 percent negative and 19 percent positive. Clearly, news organizations appraise candidates skeptically. If there is any imbalance, it is toward sterner scrutiny of the front-runner.

Another media pattern is to concentrate attention on particular candidate strengths and weaknesses. The largest cluster of positive Bush stories, for example, dealt with competence and experience (37 percent of the positive category), and the biggest group of negative Bush stories dealt with the vice president's character (32 percent). Bush's record of experience—Congressman, U.N. ambassador, Republican National Party chair, CIA director, China envoy, and vice president—was regarded favorably. His abidance of a negative, aggressive campaign, his record of policy flip-flops on matters like abortion and economics, his choice of Dan Quayle as vice president, his exaggerated loyalty to President Reagan, and his verbal gaffes were among the things cited in stories questioning Bush's personal fitness for the presidency.

Praise for Dukakis in news stories was allocated more evenly to his character (22 percent of positive stories), competence (27 percent), and domestic policy proposals (25 percent). These stories acknowledged his unimpeachable integrity, the achievements that led his fellow governors in 1986 to rate him in a *Newsweek* poll as the most effective governor in the nation (Osborne 1988), and the creativity of his domestic campaign proposals for such programs as national health insurance and welfare. Negative coverage emphasized his wooden, uninspiring demeanor (character, 33 percent of negative qualifications stories) and his lack of foreign-policy experience (competence, 30 percent).

Press scrutiny of Republican vice-presidential candidate Dan Quayle was preponderantly mixed (45 percent) and negative (43 percent), with only 11 percent of his stories classifiable as "positive." Fully 51 percent of the negative stories dealt with competence, with character criticism preoccupying some 40 percent. Negative stories about Lloyd Bentsen accounted for 40 percent of his total, and concentrated mostly on the character category. The fifteen positive stories (26 percent of the stories devoted to his qualifications) were evenly divided between character and competence.

In summary, candidate-qualifications coverage gave more attention to the Republican ticket, more attention to issue positions than character or competence, and was decidedly critical in tone. An interesting question is whether these coverage patterns had any discernible impact on the news audience. The links cannot be specified with precision, but responses to the Harris surveys (Chapter 5) and our focus-group discussions of the two presidential candidates (Chapter 6) suggested that voters knew more about Bush and Quayle than they did about Dukakis and Bentsen. Our respondents also tended to focus on the candidate traits—Bush's experience, Dukakis's cold-bloodedness—that were emphasized in the media.

Issue positions, however, were not well known, despite the attention given them in stories fitting the candidate-qualifications category.

The Electorate

The media pay considerable attention of varying kinds to the voters themselves during a presidential campaign. There are, for example, stories about polling results that detail public sentiment (who's ahead and who's behind in the race for the White House; what people believe are the most important problems facing the nation). There are stories about the mood of the voters (e.g., people are anxious about the economy, or don't know either presidential candidate very well, or are not paying close attention to the campaign, or are unhappy with their choices for president). There is usually coverage of this or that voting block (e.g., big labor has used its influence more effectively in 1988 than it did in 1984; the Reagan Democrats are the main target of the Dukakis campaign, the Black vote is not as predictably Democratic as it used to be). And there are stories about nonvoters (e.g., why does 50 percent of the electorate not bother to show up at the polls?).

The reasons news organizations cover the electorate as extensively as indicated in Table 4-1 involve economics as well as journalism. Economic imperatives are said to dominate news organizations as never before (Cose 1989; Boyer 1988). That spawns intense network competition for ratings, such as the race to be the first television network to identify the voters' choice on election day. The practice has attracted wide criticism because projections are broadcast before polls close in the West and may dissuade otherwise likely voters in western states from showing up at the polls.[14]

As for news values, in a democratic political contest the voting public and its component parts are key players, legitimately deserving coverage. Shifts in candidate preference or in sentiments toward national priorities are crucial parts of the campaign story. In the effort to stay abreast of the election prospects of the candidates and of the public expectations the winner must face, serious journalists can hardly afford to ignore the voters. One of the biggest stories of the 1988 election was of this type: the dramatic late summer–early fall shift in voter sentiment away from Michael Dukakis and toward George Bush. Dukakis went from poll leads of 17 to 25 points in late July to the underdog position—behind and fading—by mid-to-late September. Many of the the explanations focused on Dukakis's own shortcomings. But the thing that most needed explaining was why

the public underwent such a striking change in its collective perception of the candidates. Many competing explanations were advanced
by different journalists. These explanatory efforts were needed to
increase their audiences' understanding of the state of the electorate.[15]

Such coverage can yield both hard news and useful analysis. But
the competitive dimension has spawned other less clearly valuable
practices, most notably a rise in media-commissioned polls. Such
stories often deal with polling results assessed from the standpoint
of the political contest and the question of who is winning or losing.
The value of this brand of journalism seems worthy of reasoned debate. As little more than an extension of the campaign horse-race
category, such coverage adds more column inches and air time to an
already overreported phenomenon. Further, such polls may have an
undesirable impact on the race itself. The now-famous ABC News
Electoral College poll, released the day before the second presidential debate, is a case in point. As noted elsewhere in this book,
many believe that poll unfairly raised the debate stakes for Michael
Dukakis and also contributed to a premature journalistic conclusion
that a Bush victory was inevitable.

Still another journalistic motive, with roots in both professional
norms and federal statute, is to serve the public interest.[16] Stories
about citizens afford a particularly good opportunity to do so. Examples of coverage with a public-service impact might include a
story about nonvoters that encourages someone to vote,[17] an op-ed
piece about the obligations of citizenship that sparks a reader's sense
of civic identity and duty,[18] or a heartening expression of democratic
pride like this 1987 encomium to the citizens of Iowa by David
Broder:

> . . . in the park outside Cedar Rapids as the Linn County Demo-
> crats had their picnic . . . It was quiet and peaceful and friendly
> and—most of all—thoughtful, a place where good and gentle
> people in a sylvan setting could perform one of democracy's most
> important but unheralded acts: listening carefully . . . [to the six
> Democratic presidential candidates in attendance] . . . This night,
> the Iowans were determined no one would lose, and no one did.
> If there was a winner, democracy was its name (1987b: A10).[19]

How, then, did the leading news organizations apportion story
space among these and other subcategories during the final stage of
Campaign '88? Table 4–5 shows the patterns. We see that polling
results were by far the most heavily covered electorate subcategory.

Table 4-5. *Electorate Coverage Subcategories (%)*

Polling results	49
Citizenship and miscellaneous	18
Voters' mood	17
Voting blocs	10
Interest groups	6

Second largest was the residual category that included citizenship stories and others not classifiable elsewhere. Coders did not explicitly differentiate stories that seemed to reinforce pro-citizenship attitudes. But it is reasonable to assume that they comprised only a small fraction of the 18 percent residual category. The mood of the voters also accounted for only about a third as many stories as the polling results.

Voting blocs and interest groups attracted relatively little media attention in an election year that saw more attention paid to the choice between continuity and change, and to the negative tone of the campaign itself, than to demographics or special-interests politics. One heavily promoted, nonpartisan study classified the electorate into some eleven voting groups (Enterprisers, Moralists, Upbeats, Disaffecteds, Bystanders, Followers, Seculars, '60's Democrats, New Dealers, Passive Poor, and Partisan Poor) on the basis of responses to questions about political, personal, and moral issues. The study was conducted by the Gallup organization for the Times Mirror Company (Dionne 1987 : 14). Though these groups became familiar largely because of paid Times Mirror advertising, they may have attracted enough "free media" attention to have contributed to the 10 percent voting-blocs figure in Table 4-5.

Perhaps in part because of Democratic candidate Michael Dukakis's deliberate avoidance of the interest-group alliances he believed had helped to undermine the prospects of the party's 1984 nominee, Walter Mondale, there was less available material for such stories than in previous election years. Speculations about Jesse Jackson's ability to deliver Black votes for the Democratic ticket probably accounted for a significant proportion of the 6 percent interest-groups figure. But another potential contributor was what *New York Times* columnist Tom Wicker called the Hispanic factor (1988 : 21). The Hispanic population had experienced a 34 percent population increase since the 1980 census, and it was concentrated in California, New York, and Texas, the three most populous states. Hispanics thus figured prominently in the electoral calculus of both campaigns, and became newsworthy as a result.

Policy Issues

We turn next to a coverage category—policy issues—that represents the most accessible source of nonpartisan information about national problems that is available to ordinary citizens. This category excludes candidate issue positions, which were classifed under candidate qualifications. Policy-issues stories might mention the candidates or their positions in passing. But coders were instructed to include only those stories whose principal emphasis was on the substance of the issues themselves rather than on what the candidates had to say about them.

Independent media coverage of policy substance represents just about the only way that voters can learn about national problems and priorities independently of candidates and election politics. Ideally, these stories provide the means for citizens to develop a sense of the problems, decisions, and demands the next president will face that can inoculate them against the distortions and misrepresentations that are typical of presidential campaigns.[20]

The 1988 presidential campaign discourse between George Bush and Michael Dukakis, for example, focused on "hot-button" issues like capital punishment, the American Civil Liberties Union, the polluted status of Boston Harbor, and whether Michael Dukakis was too "liberal" to be trusted. It featured virtually no systematic discussion by the candidates of the specific problems—what to do about the savings-and-loan crisis, how to respond to the stunning overtures of Soviet President Mikhail Gorbachev, how to contend with the massive budget and trade deficits—that President Bush would be forced to confront in the days and months immediately following his inauguration.

Some problems, like the spring 1989 Exxon tanker oil spill in Alaskan waters, are unpredictable and thus can't be subjects for campaign discussion. Such unpredictabilities are often cited as evidence that it is pointless for voters to emphasize issues in assessing candidates. But each of the other problems just mentioned was known by Washington elites and the candidates themselves to await the early attention of the next president. They were simply unwilling, for reasons of political expediency, to discuss them. Speaking of his candidate's tacit understanding with the opposition that a serious discussion of deficit-reduction alternatives would not be part of the fall campaign, an anonymous Dukakis staffer said: "I'm not sure you can prepare the country for what you would have to do and still be elected" (Taylor 1988:16).

Fortunately, there were in-depth news accounts of these problems available at least to attentive citizens willing to search for and read them. But without television and newspaper stories about major, presidential-level problems the candidates wouldn't discuss, voters would have had no way to construct a realistic sense of the agenda they were about to elect someone to confront.

This is why one of the most important contributions the media can make to the preparation of the electorate during a presidential campaign season is simply to make available nonpartisan information and analysis of issue substance and national-policy priorities. And to be of maximum value, such coverage must be independent of and additional to coverage of candidates' policy speeches or how the campaign is going.

Evidence strongly suggests that voters need this kind of help. Markle focus-group discussions (Chapter 6) showed that even people who claim to follow newspaper and campaign coverage lack a coherent sense of the policy agenda that the new president will be forced to confront. Survey research (Chapter 5) shows little concrete knowledge of issue substance or candidate issue positions.

These findings show a need, but they also reflect the fact that much of the information the media makes available is ignored (Graber 1988:224). The political apathy and striking political ignorance of average Americans is well established (Kinder and Sears 1985; Kagay 1989:15). Still, other research shows that even though random samples of voters usually retain much less information than was available in the news products to which they were exposed, the knowledge they did possess paralleled that offered by news outlets (Graber 1988:223). Before information can be absorbed, or increases in public attention to issues contemplated, news organizations must make the information available.

How much attention, then, do the media pay to issues? Previous content-analysis research shows that there is some campaign-season attention to policy problems, but that it lags behind coverage of the horse race and candidates' personal characteristics (Graber 1988:215). That is a fair characterization of the 9.7 percent figure in Table 4-1, which represents the 1988 fall campaign's story allocations to this important category. Compared to other Campaign '88 coverage categories like the horse race and candidate conflicts, media attention to policy issues was quite modest.

Table 4-6. *Policy-Issues Stories (%)*

Domestic policy	46
Economic policy	30
Foreign and national-security policy	24

Table 4-6 shows the distribution of stories across policy categories. We see that domestic-policy stories were the most frequent. Interestingly, this was also the case in the last months of the 1968, 1972, 1976, and 1980 elections, at least for the twenty-newspaper sample coded by Doris Graber (1988:217).

Why should domestic policy get more coverage despite the usually equal or superior urgency of economic and national-security problems? Graber offers an explanation:

> These stories, which are available from regular beats, are usually tied to familiar names and widely salient domestic events. Therefore they require little background information, and pictorial coverage is easily arranged. All of these considerations make it very tempting to report domestic politics stories. (1988:216)

Economic policy, which in Graber's study varied widely from one election year to another (1968, 22 percent; 1972, 10 percent; 1976, 11 percent; 1980, 7 percent) in 1988 received much more extensive coverage (30 percent, Table 4-6). This is not surprising, in light of the fact that policymakers and the reporters who interviewed them for their stories came to regard the budget deficit as the most urgent problem, linked to trade deficits and U.S. international economic competitiveness, as the priority agenda for the end of the century.

Many stories fitting this category chastised the candidates for their failure to speak forthrightly about their economic plans and priorities (e.g., Kilborn 1988a:1; Broder 1988:A12).

The *Wall Street Journal*, for example, featured an issue series on what it termed the "absent agenda," running stories with headlines like "Bush and Dukakis Duck $50 Billion S&Ls Problem That One of Them Will Have to Face as President" (Seib and Tayler 1988:A26).

Table 4-6's 24 percent for foreign and national-security policy reflects an increase over the three recent presidential campaigns for which comparable figures were available. Graber's findings show that foreign-policy issues coverage declined from a high of 30 percent in 1968 to 18, 14, and 5 in the three subsequent campaigns of

1972, 1976, and 1980.[21] Intensified 1988 media attention, prompted in part, no doubt, by recent arms-reduction accords and the sea change in the world order originating in the Soviet Union, was not matched by the candidates. This was particularly true with respect to the changes in the Soviet Union. Each candidate staked out various defense and foreign-policy positions more thoroughly than he had done in economic policy. But neither Bush nor Dukakis used the campaign as an opportunity to articulate or debate America's new role in a more economically interdependent, post–cold war world: ". . . the immense foreign policy challenges that will face the next administration have scarcely been discussed in the long and tortured campaign of 1988," wrote two critics, "and it's likely that voters will go to the polls Nov. 8 without the benefit of even a primitive national debate on some of the global shifts that lie ahead in the 1990's" (Ignatius and Getler 1988). Were it not for the press, then, Americans would have had no way of knowing the extent to which foreign-policy rethinking and global repositioning would be required of the next president.

During the period leading up to the fall campaign, analyses and op-ed pieces in the elite press dealt with such questions as how the United States might avoid the kind of "imperial decline" described by Paul Kennedy in his *Rise and Fall of the Great Powers* (Blumenthal 1988:6), the need for NATO allies and Japan to assume a larger portion of the defense burden in Europe and the Pacific Rim (Nunn 1988:31), and whether the space-based anti-missile shield known as Star Wars would survive the Reagan administration as a viable defense initiative (Roberts 1988:1). Thoughtful newspaper essays on these and other matters provided the kind of orientation to the future that the campaign did not.

Finally, we sought information about two additional characteristics of the policy-issues stories content-analyzed for this project. Coders were instructed to evaluate each story's complexity and to take note of whether each issue story included any discussion of the issue's importance or priority to the nation.

Complexity. An effort to assess the usefulness of the policy-issues category of print and broadcast journalism to its citizen-consumers should, it seemed to us, try to take account of the extent to which such stories as a class presented often complicated policy questions and problems at a level appropriate both to their intrinsic complexity and to the comprehension of "average" readers. Accessibility and appropriateness in these terms could be assumed for technically undemanding coverage categories like horse-race stories or candidate conflicts. Too, the public's comprehension is less of a concern in these areas than in policy matters.

Previous research had shown that people's comprehension of television news was surprisingly low, largely, the researchers contended, because of program producers' lack of sensitivity to viewers' information-processing needs (Robinson and Levy 1986). A coding project like this was not equipped to check reader or viewer comprehension directly. That would require giving people stories to read or watch and then asking them to submit to a test of their comprehension.[22] But coders could subjectively assess how well policy stories struck a balance between the needs of the readers and the demands of sometimes technical policy topics.

The experience of reading more than eight hundred policy stories (plus thousands of other kinds of stories) put the coders into as good a position as anybody, we felt, to judge whether any particular story met these standards. Stories were classified as either complicated, simplistic, or average. Calling a story "average" meant that it achieved an acceptable balance between accessibility to the reader and appropriateness of issue treatment, in the judgment of at least two of three coders. The expectation was that the great majority of stories would be average in this sense, and the results generally showed this to be the case. Seventy-two percent of the economic-policy stories, 74 percent of domestic-policy stories and 69 percent of the foreign-policy stories met the standard. The percentages fitting into the complicated and simplistic categories were miniscule across the board. There was no coder agreement, however, on a rather high 20 percent of total policy stories, suggesting room for improvement.

Policy Priorities. Though the policy-issues stories were comprehensible by coders' standards, as a rule these stories did not make explicit efforts to situate their subjects within a hierarchy of national priorities. Only implicit clues to importance were provided, such as the story's place in the order of presentation, the amount of air time or column inches it got, or simply the legitimizing fact of being on television or in the newspaper. Apart from such subliminal cues to importance, which offer no explicit rationale or justification for the priorities they may communicate, readers and viewers are left to decide without guidance which of the great many policy problems discussed in news stories is deserving of priority presidential attention.

The budget deficit was an occasional exception in 1988. And stories about the drug issue sometimes mentioned the fact that 1988 polls often showed a plurality of Americans to regard drugs as the most pressing national problem.

This suggests that when a consensus does exist that a particular policy problem is the single most urgent confronting the nation at a particular time—Vietnam in the '60's for example, or inflation in the late '70's—some stories about the problem will mention that consensus. But any regular news reader or viewer knows that journalistic discussions of the order among national policy priorities are not common, in 1988 or any other year. It is just as rare to encounter a story about an isolated issue—the homeless, for example, or acid rain—in which the featured policy problem is assigned a place in a ranking of national priorities. To learn, therefore, that our coders found the issue's priority to be "unclear" in all but 2 percent of the relevant stories is not surprising. In 1988 as in other election years, the audience was generally left to make sense of the issue agenda by itself.

The need for a public discussion of national priorities is always high on any list of campaign-season desirables. Why, then, in the relatively small amount of time and space devoted to issues, don't journalists pay more attention to the larger national policy agenda that is likely to command the attention of the president-to-be, as well as to the relative position of particular issues among the nation's priorities? Reasons are not hard to find. For one thing, producing "big-picture" feature-story analyses of national priorities is demanding work, requiring considerable expertise, time, and effort. The budgets and deadline-driven political-coverage priorities of most news organizations rarely encourage such efforts. The dramatic and the recent—two classic news values—usually enjoy priority over abstract considerations of the long-term national interest.

For another thing, such stories can smack of subjectivity or advocacy, things news-section editors want to avoid. Briefer editorials or op-ed pieces can sidestep these problems and also can convey a sense of the agenda at less cost. But even these opinion pieces are relatively rare. Producers and editorial-page editors seem reluctant to consistently devote limited editorial space to sustained projects of any sort.

Most important, however, is the fact that the business of educating the electorate about national priorities during presidential elections has been regarded by media leaders as essentially someone else's responsibility. Some media leaders, as we saw in Chapter 2, do believe they serve an inchoate educational purpose during presidential campaigns. But most do not regard themselves as ultimately accountable for devising and purveying a conception of the national agenda, nonpartisan or otherwise. Developing a list of national policy priorities has traditionally been a partisan political task that is the special province of political parties. Communicating policy priorities to the voting public and building support for them has heretofore been, and despite recent contrary evidence is still thought to be, the job of presidential candidates and the special focus of presidential campaigns.

But as parties have declined in significance, and as candidates increasingly shy away from substantively specific issue campaigns, responsibility for making sense of issues and clarifying the priorities among them increasingly falls by default on citizens themselves. And since Americans get the vast majority of their political information from the media, they also (unavoidably) take many of their cues about national priorities from the same source (Iyengar and Kinder 1987; Graber 1988). Although news organizations have not sought this responsibility and many news leaders resist accepting it, they increasingly help to shape the agenda that takes root in the public mind.

Respected analysts such as Walter Lippmann have argued since the 1920's that the media are poorly equipped for this or other major responsibilities for organizing public opinion (Lippmann 1965). Contemporary analysts maintain that the media lack the incentive, the legitimacy, and the capability to undertake these large responsibilities on behalf of the political system (Patterson 1989). Whether the media can adequately serve—or even should serve—as the principal intermediaries between candidates and voters remains a controversial matter. But controversial or not, the media continue to assume additional intermediary roles.

Since the decline of party kingmakers and the proliferation of primary elections began in 1968, for example, the media's participation in helping to winnow the pack of presidential candidates during primary season has increased to the point of near-dominance. More recently, at least one major network has announced plans to use its control over the airwaves to influence how presidential candidates conduct their campaigns. Disturbed at the manipulation of their campaign coverage by the 1988 presidential candidates, ABC News announced that henceforth candidate "photo opportunities," such as George Bush's infamous visit to a New Jersey flag factory or Michael Dukakis's ride in an Army tank, will not appear on the television evening news unless the candidate is willing to submit to reporters' questions (Apple 1989:12).

Each of these moves represents a major increase in the media's intermediary role between candidates and voters. In each case, one or more media organizations stepped in to fill a public need no longer being met by traditional political institutions or means. As presidential candidates have moved away from policy-oriented campaigns, the education of the public about national priorities is emerging as another vital but increasingly unmet need, no longer fulfilled in traditional ways. Should the media be asked to explicitly accept another intermediary responsibility, an educational function they now fill implicitly and somewhat haphazardly?[23] We will return to this question in Chapter 7.

Media Stories

The final category of coverage involved stories about the media. Two kinds of media stories are included in the 460 stories noted in Table 4-1: news reports on the use of paid advertising by the candidates and stories about the nature and quality of the media's own coverage of the campaign. Lumped together, stories about both "paid" and "free" media accounted for only 4.4 percent of total story allocations, the smallest of the six categories in Table 4-1. Table 4-7 shows how the eighteen leading news organizations whose stories and editorials we coded covered each of the media subcategories between Labor Day and the election.

We see that political advertising commanded more attention than news stories about the media (62 to 38 percent), that most of the ad stories (45 percent) featured both candidates' campaign ads, and that the remaining such stories were nearly equally divided between the two campaigns. Not shown in Table 4-7 is the fact that story tone was coded as well, to provide a measure of how critical the stories were of the advertising practices of the candidates. In fact, fewer

Table 4-7. *Media Stories (%)*

Campaign-advertising stories		62
Republican advertising	27	
Democratic advertising	28	
Both	45	
Campaign news-coverage stories		38
Print	26	
Electronic	58	
Both	16	

than 2 percent of the stories were critical in tone. The vast majority had no clearly negative or positive tone.

As for attention to the media's own performance in covering the campaign, the bulk was devoted to electronic journalism (58 percent), with print getting just 26 percent of the stories. Relatively few stories (16 percent) dealt simultaneously with print and broadcast-media campaign coverage. The story tone, important here for reasons explained below, was again pervasively neutral. Slightly more than 2 percent of the stories could be called negative in tone, while just under 7 percent were positive. Stories in the neutral category either had no evaluative content at all or balanced critical and and complimentary coverage evenly enough to avoid setting a clear tone.

Information about these two kinds of media stories serves quite different purposes. The first, which is to shed light on the media's credibility as a source of reliable, valid, and relevant information, is served by stories about how the major news organizations covered the presidential campaign.

Media Self-scrutiny. Few would dispute that news organizations, which enjoy the special protections of the First Amendment, and which constitute the primary source of political information available to the mass public, should engage in some form of ongoing self-scrutiny and criticism. Such coverage is regarded as a mark of professionalism. It keeps journalists sensitive to the ideals and standards governing their craft. And if it is perceived as thorough and rigorous, it reinforces the credibility of journalistic products in the public mind.

Critical self-scrutiny also serves the public interest. By alerting viewers and readers to shortcomings, such coverage may help to make citizens more intelligent and sophisticated consumers of the news.

These worthy purposes are served both by straight news reports (i.e., reporters investigating and reporting on the work of other reporters, just as they routinely do for government officials and candidates for government offices) and by publishing or broadcasting op-ed commentary by critics outside the media.

An example of the first is a story worth quoting at length about the media's treatment of Republican vice-presidential nominee Dan Quayle's alleged misuse of family influence to get into the Indiana National Guard during the Vietnam War. The story, titled "'Quayle Hunt' Turns News Media into Target for Angry Public," was written by Eleanor Randolph and appeared on page A10 in the *Washington Post* on August 25, 1988. The publication date was a week too early for the story to have been included in the coding figures in Tables 4-1 or 4-7. But it would have been classified as "neutral" in tone because of its even-handed attempt to weigh the case for and against press treatment of Mr. Quayle. The story has several qualities that make it a good example of effective journalistic self-scrutiny.

Randolph begins by making it clear that the criticism deserves to be taken seriously, noting that both Republican partisans and members of the journalism community found things to criticize in reporters' treatment of the little-known Republican vice-presidential nominee. Bush media adviser Roger Ailes is quoted as saying, "This is guilt by press . . . We might as well have hanging by press." Randolph then has *Chicago Tribune* political correspondent Jon Margolis describe some unlovely press characteristics displayed at Quayle's mid-August hometown press conference: "We did look kind of rude . . . when we are all together, we can be rude and we are collectively often simple-minded."

In response to the concern expressed by "some journalists" that "the media had begun piling on Quayle unfairly," *Post* staff writer Randolph next examines some of the evidence least flattering to journalistic practice. She compares the handling by several leading print and broadcast organizations of one sensational aspect of the Quayle story—allegations by former Washington lobbyist Paula Parkinson, who was soon to pose nude for *Playboy Magazine*, that Quayle had once propositioned her.

Randolph notes that all three major networks used the unsubstantiated Parkinson charges, and that the CBS and ABC nightly newscasts made them the opening story. Most leading newspapers also ran the story, though giving it less prominence: "The New York Times, for example, used the story . . . on Page 7 of its second section; The Washington Post used a story on Page 1 but did not specify the charges in its headlines. The Wall Street Journal steered clear of the Parkinson charges and used only one front-page paragraph on the ongoing question about Quayle's National Guard service."

Journalists' defense of their Quayle coverage appears late in the story. *Chicago Tribune* editor James Squires is the spokesman: "George Bush wanted the press to have no story at the convention except his announcement of vice president, and that's exactly what he got." By picking an unknown in New Orleans, he virtually guaranteed that thirteen thousand nervous reporters in search of a story would examine Quayle's background minutely, seizing upon any evidence of character or behavior that could be construed as relevant to his fitness for high office.

Only in Randolph's two closing paragraphs, which react to criticism of reporters using interviews with the same people to reach different conclusions about Quayle's use of family influence, does a hint of defensiveness appear. "A public that criticizes the press for drawing different inferences from the same interviews at the same time it lambastes the press for acting like a mindless herd of sheep is nothing new to veteran reporters, who do not expect to be loved for their efforts."

Randolph's story about Quayle's media treatment supplied readers with enough relevant information and rival opinion to support reasoned conclusions of their own about media shortcomings. It may have been more thorough and more balanced than the typical such story.[24] But, as noted earlier, research shows that elite media coverage patterns tend toward remarkable similarity, and also that regional media take their cues from elite news organizations like the *Post* (Graber 1989:66). The tone data mentioned earlier showed that the great majority—over 90 percent—of these stories was objective and/or balanced rather than positive or negative in tone—more evidence of the similarity of the approach taken by different news organizations.

Op-ed and editorial commentary about the adequacy of the media's campaign-coverage practice is more difficult to summarize, as it was much more diverse. But it is fair to say that most of the serious misgivings thoughtful critics had about various aspects of the media's coverage of the 1988 campaign got hearings on the airwaves and leading editorial pages. This is evinced in the numerous citations to op-ed columns critical of the media throughout this book. Among the many specific charges levied were allegations that television treated the presidential debates too much like prime-time sporting events (Zurawik 1988:E3), that television has an antiliberal bias (Miller 1988:25), that the media care more about "red meat" than policy speeches or position papers (Carter 1988:19), that the press trumpeted Bush victory predictions too much (A. M. Rosenthal 1988:27), that the media portrayal of the Dukakis campaign as "apocalypse now" put them at risk of replacing the candidates as the season's major story,[25] that television news made no sustained effort to elicit issue discussions from candidates (Kalb 1988:19), and that the nature of television coverage may help explain why voter turnout in the the United States continues to decline (C. B. Gans 1988b:sec. 2, p. 1). Whatever the merits of specific charges, such a highly visible drumbeat of media criticism can hardly fail to alert the attentive public to the existence of skepticism about the fourth estate's performance.

Taken together, then, the weakness of news and op-ed media self-scrutiny is not that it lacks bite, but that, as Tables 4-1 and 4-7 show, there was comparatively so little of it. Given the potential contribution to journalistic excellence, news credibility, and public sophistication, there is room for more than 4.4 percent.

Campaign-Advertising Coverage. The public needs met by news coverage of campaign advertising are of a different order than those met by media self-criticism. The latter highlights the limitations of the media. The former is a check on the abuses of the candidates.[26]

As noted in earlier chapters, the content of the political advertising used in the 1988 presidential campaign represented a sharp downturn in respect for factual accuracy and norms of civility. American political discourse has, of course, descended to nasty levels before (Freund 1988). Notable recent examples are found in the criticism of President Roosevelt in the 1930's and in the character assassination common during the McCarthy era. But modern presidential campaigns have not usually featured the kind of distorted advertising and personal attacks seen in 1988 (Jamieson 1984; Oreskes 1988d : 1).[27]

In its unofficial role as democratic watchdog, vigilant against the abuses and distortions of the powerful, the fourth estate would be expected to complain editorially about the negative tone of the campaign and in news space to beard any misleading ads. Both did happen. Commentators bemoaned the adverse consequences for the political system, and the networks eventually began calling attention to candidate misrepresentations and inconsistencies. But a review of the contents of the advertising coverage depicted in Table 4-7 shows that while the negativity and distortions were reported, other issues got more attention.[28]

Perhaps the largest number of stories emphasized strategic guile. Coverage of the Democrats, for example, dealt mainly with the political ineffectiveness of their advertising. "A disorganized Dukakis advertising team allowed . . . ads attacking Mr. Dukakis's handling of crime and of pollution in Boston Harbor, to go unanswered for a substantial period, a cardinal sin of political advertising" (Oreskes 1988c). The Democratic television spots that featured a group of cynical political advisers discussing how to manipulate public opinion, intended to expose the tawdriness of the Bush campaign style, became particular media targets, roundly dismissed as confusing and therefore politically impotent.

Stories about Republicans advertising, on the other hand, took special note of the manipulative skills of such GOP media masterminds as Stuart Spencer and Roger Ailes, while simultaneously noting the cynicism of the Republican approach to campaigning. Several fall 1988 news accounts illustrated it with an anecdote from the 1984 presidential campaign. Reagan campaign operative Stuart Spencer, in a tape-recorded 1984 strategy session, was heard saying that the Reagan administration had run out of ideas and programs and that there was "nothing in the pipeline." "But not to worry," he continued, promising that a series of carefully staged photo opportunities dutifully covered by television cameras would be more than enough to restore the luster of vitality and leadership (Scheer 1988:1).

By mid-October, as the polls showed increasing public displeasure with the aggressive tenor of the campaign, news stories finally began to take note of the inaccuracies in candidate advertising. But it took a particularly misleading ad to provoke a concerted media response. "Only when the Bush 'tank' ad rumbled into the World Series did its obvious distortion of Dukakis's defense posture prompt ABC, and then the other networks, The Washington Post and the other major papers to set the record straight" (Jamieson 1988).[29]

Most of the complaining about the unusually negative tone of the campaign appeared in editorials and op-ed columns, although some found its way into straight news accounts via quotation of the critics. Unsurprisingly, liberal columnists who blamed the campaign's negative tone on Bush were the most disturbed. John B. Oakes, former editorial-page editor of the New York Times, exemplifies their outrage: "Have you no sense of decency, sir? . . . [Joseph N. Welch's famous question to Joseph R. McCarthy] spotlight[s] the level of indecency that has marked the Bush campaign, for which Mr. Bush and his mentor, James Baker, are basically responsible" (Oakes 1988). And bemoaning the fact that "George Bush's handlers have made this a low, ugly, evasive campaign because that kind of campaign wins American elections," New York Times columnist Anthony Lewis also criticizes his press colleagues for "accepting the corrupt techniques of the political packagers as legitimate" (A. Lewis 1988).

More admiring of what they regarded as welcome evidence of Mr. Bush's toughness, conservative columnists like William Safire still acknowledged Bush's authorship of the campaign's tone: "Bush now poses as the great foe of crime and liberalism, embracing the death penalty, and blazing away at gun control, prison furloughs, and unpopular defenses of civil liberty. Does this application of his knee to the opposition's political groin trouble him? [He is said to find it distasteful,] but experience taught him that Mr. Nice Guy wins no ballgames" (Safire 1988b).

Following the election (and thus not included in our content analysis), more allegations that the media had not properly handled its coverage of the campaign's negative tone appeared in print. Among them were charges that the media had conveyed the inaccurate impression that both campaigns were equally engaged in mudslinging, when in fact the Bush campaign was both the initiator and the principal purveyor (Boot 1989), that reporters are generally reluctant to police campaign commercials for fear of estranging valuable news sources among the campaign consultants who produce the spots (Broder 1989c), and that the media too easily permitted candidates to set a negative, issueless tone by granting uncritical access to the airwaves for candidate media events (Holloway 1989).

Because it engages so many fundamental issues of electoral propriety and responsibility, the debate over campaign advertising and the press's role in policing it can only intensify in subsequent election years. It is a safe prediction that the volume of media coverage of negative advertising in 1990, 1992, and thereafter will considerably surpass the percentage figures in Tables 4-1 and 4-7.

The Question of Fairness

A longstanding criticism of the media that remains to be considered here is that they are politically biased. Most frequent of late have been allegations of liberal bias (e.g., Rusher 1988), but it has also been contended that the media operate to mobilize support for "the special interests that dominate the Government and the private sector" (Herman and Chomsky 1988). Academic researchers, however, generally find little evidence of systematic bias of any kind in content analyses of media products. Reviewers of their research discover instead that "cautious and overwhelming objectivity show[s] up in study after study" (Iyengar and Kinder 1987:131).

Still, suspicion of unfairness of one sort or another is so persistent that it is necessary to continuously monitor the objectivity of media coverage of important events like presidential elections. Accordingly, we devised a simple measure of the treatment given the two major presidential candidates in the news products we analyzed. Coders assessed the tone—positive, neutral, or negative—of each mention of either presidential candidate in every story included in the study.

Table 4-8 shows the tone breakdowns for the 6,271 print and broadcast stories that could be classified as preponderantly about one presidential candidate or the other.[30] Classifying stories by the positive, neutral, or negative "tone" of "candidate mentions" is too

Table 4-8. *Tone of Media Candidate Coverage*

	Television Stories		Print Stories	
	Number	(%)	Number	(%)
Bush stories	369	(52)	2,930	(53)
Positive	1	(0.3)	77	(3)
Neutral	324	(88)	2,051	(70)
Negative	4	(1)	440	(15)
No dominant tone	40	(11)	362	(12)
Dukakis stories	336	(48)	2,636	(47)
Positive	0	(0)	24	(0.9)
Neutral	236	(70)	1,625	(62)
Negative	8	(2)	96	(4)
No dominant tone	92	(27)	891	(34)
Subtotals	705		5,566	
Grand total			6,271	

insensitive a measure to capture the substantive ideological slant (if any) of the stories. But it does disclose whether media treatment of the two candidates was similar, which is an index of a certain kind of fairness. And it reveals the extent to which the media's general approach to candidate coverage was critical, supportive, or nonjudgmental.

As is clear from the table, there is little basis for a charge that one candidate got strikingly better press than the other. George Bush did receive slightly more coverage than did Michael Dukakis (4 percent more television coverage and 6 percent more print coverage). But the great majority of the stories about both candidates fell into the "neutral" category. Clearly, then, the trend toward nonpartisan, nonjudgmental media coverage remained undisturbed during the 1988 election (Abramson, Arterton, and Orren 1988: 85).

Newspapers were somewhat more critical of George Bush (15 percent) than of Michael Dukakis (4 percent). But almost as large a portion of newspaper stories about Bush, 12 percent, had no dominant evaluative tone (that is, the mix of positive and negative mentions was precisely in balance). For Bush's television coverage and for television and print Dukakis coverage, "no dominant tone" was the second-largest category after "neutral."

Television in particular was extraordinarily reluctant to broadcast a story about either candidate that outsiders could perceive as clearly positive or negative in overall tone. The networks did, however, pass judgments of both kinds somewhat more often on Dukakis than on Bush. This is indicated by Dukakis's 27 percent to 11 percent "no dominant tone" lead over Bush in the television category, indicating both more positive and more negative judgments about the Democratic candidate. The same was true of newspaper coverage. Dukakis got fewer negative mentions than Bush, but more evaluative attention (34 to 12 percent "no dominant tone").

Conclusion

We conclude by returning to the questions that oriented this content analysis of news products. Did media coverage of the 1988 presidential campaign provide citizens with adequate information and guidance about the presidential candidates and national policy problems? Was there sufficient media vigilance against campaign distortions and misinformation to make available an accessible source of corrective information? What impact, if any, did coverage patterns have upon cynicism, feelings of political obligation, morale, and other public sentiments relevant to effective participatory democracy?

Such questions measure the extent of the media's contributions to the public interest during any campaign season. Results from this content analysis of 1988 election coverage provide relevant evidence.

The six coding categories in Table 4-1, which reflect the normative and measurement models set forth in earlier chapters, organize the findings. Campaign horse-race stories, at 36 percent, constituted the largest category of Labor-Day-to-election-day coverage. Horse-race story dominance is deplored by critics because of the repetitious subliminal message—strategic political skill is a sufficient test of presidential mettle—it may send to voters.

Candidate conflicts, the subject of 21 percent of the coverage, was a category that featured partisan attacks by the candidates against one another. Such emphasis may have contributed to the widespread perception that 1988's was an extraordinarily negative campaign, as well as to increased cynicism among voters. Candidate qualifications, the third-largest category with 19 percent of the story allocations, devoted over half of its story content to the candidates' issue positions, with the balance divided equally between assessments of character and general leaderly competence. The stance toward the candidates in these appraisal stories was decidedly critical.

Stories about the electorate, which mainly described media-commissioned polling results, accounted for just under 10 percent of the coding allocations. Though largely an extension of horse-race coverage into the ranks of voters, this category also contained a few stories about the state of the electorate and the health of the democracy. Coverage of policy issues, though scant in comparison with the largest categories, provided a comprehensible review of important issues generally slighted by the 1988 candidates. Like the candidates themselves, however, these stories offered few explicit cues about the priorities the next president would face.

Finally, stories about the media comprised a scant 4.4 percent of the total, and were divided between scrutiny of media campaign coverage habits and the uses of paid media by the candidates. Both kinds of coverage serve important public purposes. But the small number of stories, plus the late appearance of stories calling attention to advertising distortions, raise questions about the extent to which these purposes were served in 1988.

5. WHAT THE ELECTORATE LEARNED

The 1988 campaign saw the commissioning of the largest number of polls in presidential election history: by some estimates as many as 135, said to be three times the number done in 1984. Most were short, completed in little more than forty-eight hours, and focused on the campaign horse race. A few, such as the Times Mirror-Gallup series and the surveys discussed in this chapter, were more ambitious.

The Markle Commission telephone interviews, conducted by Louis Harris and Associates, had a number of unusual features. They probed fundamental orientations toward the presidency, presidential candidates, and issues rather than topical "horse-race" concerns. They took nearly a half-hour per interview to complete, because they included several open-ended (i.e., non-structured) questions. These required the persons being interviewed to come up with their own words and concepts in response to questions, instead of simply choosing one of the options spelled out by the interviewer.

By the standards of current polling practice, such questions are unusual. There were other unusual features as well, such as an effort to probe the extent of respondent knowledge about candidate issue positions. One recent study of polling question patterns showed that questions probing the extent of respondents' knowledge about various topics have all but disappeared from current surveys (Smith 1987).

Perhaps most unusual, however, was the fact that the Markle survey was repeated. The same questions were asked on different occasions of two different random national samples of Americans eligible to vote in the forthcoming election. This was done so that changes in public sentiment could be documented and the factors producing change investigated. Our two telephone surveys of the American electorate each took several days to complete. They were conducted September 6–19 and October 18–November 4, 1988. The surveys drew samples of 1,876 and 1,875 people, respectively. The demographic characteristics of each of these samples are statistically representative of the American electorate as a whole.

Purpose

The purpose of the Markle Commission survey research was to measure the readiness of the electorate to vote in the 1988 presidential election. The readiness of the electorate—defined as what voters know and believe about candidates and issues—is a good indicator of the campaign performance of the print and broadcast news media. It is also a worthy indicator of the influence of the candidates and the campaign. For the electorate and the media are part of an influence network that also includes the candidates. All three components interact dynamically during a campaign season. Because each is inevitably influenced by both of the others, meaningful evaluation requires taking them all into account.

Standards

To evaluate something requires standards. The standards that influence the organization and discussion of the survey and other findings are rooted in American democratic ideals (see Chapter 2).

Among the ideals of democratic citizenship is the expectation that voters become reasonably well informed about the qualifications of the candidates and the problems confronting the nation. Only the informed will be equipped with a workable picture of what they are choosing a leader to face, and with grounds for appraising the suitability of candidates.

The basic responsibility for acquiring information and insight about national problems rests with individual citizens. But it is recognized that citizens need help. The help is to come in part from campaigns for office in which candidates educate the electorate about national problems as well as about their plans for solving them.

Help is also expected from the news media. In return for constitutional and statutory protections and privileges, the press has traditionally sought not only to inform the public, but also to protect it against misinformation and self-interested distortions by candidates.

These ideals point to the central evaluative questions that the surveys and other research can help to answer. How well informed did the voters become about national problems and priorities? Did the candidates use their platforms to clarify problem priorities and suggest solutions? And did the media work to inform the voters and to shield them from campaign flimflammery? We will see that the survey results shed both direct and inferential light on each of these questions.

Setting the Stage

Before delving into complexities, we first set out some general findings that convey the broad outlines of what the electorate knew and how much remained to be learned about the candidates and the issues in the weeks between Labor Day and election day.

Table 5-1 shows that at the time of the Labor Day survey, some basic information had yet to be absorbed and that the most important decision—whom to support for president—had not yet been made by a large segment of our first survey sample. Clearly the initial survey did not take place too late to demonstrate that a sizable proportion of the electorate was still open to influence. Much remained to be learned and much would change, as the second survey results in Table 5-1 demonstrate. Forty-seven percent of those surveyed were undecided or unsure about which candidate to support as late as September 19, and as many as 31 percent were still not committed four days before the election.

As for basic information, among the most basic is the identities of the men who were the running mates of George Bush and Michael Dukakis.

It is astonishing that 54 percent—a majority—did not know that Lloyd Bentsen was the Democratic nominee for vice president at the time of the initial survey. That suggests a widespread, glacial indifference, given the near-saturation media coverage of the Democratic convention, extensive commentary about Dukakis's strategic gamble in going for the electoral votes of Bentsen's home state of Texas, and the lead-story, front-page attention that both presidential candidates were receiving on a daily basis at the time. Clearly, media coverage alone is no guarantee of audience awareness.[1]

It is only slightly less surprising that a smaller 37 percent couldn't

Table 5-1. *Changes in Voter Knowledge and Candidate Preference between Labor Day and Election Day, 1988*

Survey	1 (%)	2 (%)
Have decided who to vote for:		
Yes	53	69
No	42	25
Not sure	5	6
Preferred candidate of decided voters[a]		
George Bush	48	54
Michael Dukakis	50	45
Undecided but leaning toward		
George Bush	40	48
Michael Dukakis	39	32
Not sure	21	20
Who is Bush's running mate?		
Dan Quayle	63	76
Not sure	34	22
Other	3	2
Who is Dukakis's running mate?		
Lloyd Bentsen	46	65
Not sure	49	30
Other	5	5

Harris Survey 1; N=1,876; conducted 9/6–19/1988.

Harris Survey 2; N=1,875; conducted 10/18–11/4/1988.

[a]The Markle surveys differ from some that were conducted in September, such as the *New York Times*/CBS poll conducted between September 8 and 11, which showed Bush leading Dukakis 47 to 39 percent. The Markle Harris surveys offer a more stable picture of electoral sentiment at that time because they were spread over many more days than most other polls (eleven and seventeen, respectively) permitting short-term events to "wash out" with the passage of time, whereas polls taken in three or four days were more susceptible to the short-run impacts of events. For example, the *NYT*/CBS poll began just two days after the Bush campaign opened its TV push in vote-rich California, stressing Dukakis's responsibility for the Massachusetts prison-furlough system. Those ads may have contributed to a temporary inflation of the gap between the candidates.

identify Dan Quayle as George Bush's running mate. For Quayle, it will be recalled, had been the subject of the most extensive and sustained media attention of the campaign up to that time because of a controversy over his alleged use of family influence to get into the National Guard during the Vietnam War (Dionne 1988b: 1).

The fact was, however, that most Americans had not yet begun to pay serious attention to the campaign. As Frank J. Fahrenkopf, Jr., former Republican National Chairman, noted at a news conference called to announce a commission to examine why the party nominating conventions had been ignored by the public: "Professional wrestling actually did better on some of the alternate channels than the Democratic and Republican conventions" (Schwartz 1988 : 14).

It might be countered that most voters are indifferent to the bottom of the ticket, which makes this degree of ignorance about the vice-presidential candidates less surprising and not so alarming. But other evidence, not included in Table 5-1, suggests that ignorance was not limited to the question of who the running mates were.

The September survey found too that large numbers of respondents were not aware of the basic power situation in the national government. Only 53 percent knew, for example, that the Democratic Party had a majority in the United States Senate; 46 percent either thought the Republicans were in control or reported being unsure. Fifty percent either thought the House of Representatives was in Republican hands or didn't know who had a majority.[2] The numbers improved in the second survey, but only slightly. The percentages still admitting ignorance or misidentifying the party in control of the Senate and House were 44 and 47, respectively. These findings call into question the assertion by some analysts that voters have a penchant for divided government, seeing to it that the White House is controlled by one party and the Congress by the other (Broder 1989a: 4) That, as Elizabeth Drew puts it, is "overintellectualizing their act" (Drew 1989 : 351). Voters may, as some polls suggest, prefer divided government in principle. But nearly half of the eligible voters in the Markle surveys didn't even know which party controlled Congress.[3]

The first survey also showed, in an "information test" to be reviewed in detail later (Table 5-7), that most Americans could not identify more than a few of the most heavily publicized candidate issue positions.

The great majority of Survey 1 respondents were aware, however, that George Bush was the incumbent vice president (88 percent), that Michael Dukakis was governor of Massachusetts (60 percent), and that the federal government's budget was out of balance (91 percent), all pertinent to assessing candidate qualifications and policy proposals. They were thus not totally without relevant information. But the things they did not know make it clear that the American people still had much to learn and were thus susceptible to being taught and otherwise influenced about the candidates, the issues, and the political situation as the stretch drive of the presidential campaign got under way.

It is also apparent from Table 5-1 that many people had changed their assessments of the presidential candidates by the close of Survey 2. For the numbers moved from near-evenly divided support for Bush and Dukakis in September to a clear preference for George Bush just before the election. These changes were accompanied by significant changes in fixed-response estimations of each candidate's character and competence (see Tables 5-10 and 5-11 below).

There is in addition clear evidence of learning—not only about who the vice-presidential candidates were, as Table 5-1 shows, but also about what the issue stands of the presidential candidates were (Table 5-7). Taken together, the various changes in sentiment and evidence of learning demonstrate the fact that influence was exerted.

Who or what did the influencing? What contributions did the media and the candidates make to the changes, either independently or in tandem with other forces? Answers from the surveys alone can only be inferential or speculative, but are considered as we delve further into the results.

Findings

The findings come in four clusters. Each reflects a body of information arguably necessary to any assessment of the status of the electorate's preparation to vote.

First is a group of results that get at basic orientations toward the tasks of what can be called presidential citizenship: the motivation to become informed and to vote, conceptions of the presidential role that voters must fill, and the general grounds for choosing between presidential candidates and the reasons for preferring one to the other.

Next reported are people's appraisal of the issues that confronted the nation in the fall of 1988, as they responded in their own words to questions like "What are the two or three most important problems the next president will face?"

Thereafter, voters size up the candidates. By telling us—in their own words—the most important things they learned about George Bush and Michael Dukakis in the course of the campaign, they reveal much about what did and did not influence their stocktaking.

Last come public attitudes toward the media, including reports on how much attention gets paid to media coverage, assessments of how much influence the media has, and of the fairness of the media's coverage of candidates and issues. Reactions to the biggest media events of the campaign—the three candidate debates—complete the picture.

Selecting the President: Basic Attitudes

The Motivation to Participate. It is indisputable that democracies require the informed and consistent participation of ordinary citizens to be viable. Both the theory and the practice of democracy require that citizens exert a relatively high degree of control over leaders, in the first instance by choosing them in free elections (Dahl 1956). This makes voting behavior a central concern (Wolfinger and Rosenstone 1980; Asher 1984). Yet students of rational behavior, as understood in economics, tell us that individuals in large populations have nothing tangible to gain from casting a vote (Downs 1957). The probability of any single vote affecting the outcome of a presidential election is so small as to be negligible, smaller than the probability of being run over by a car on the way to the polls. Thus, a rational voter ought not to bother with something like voting, where the costs outweigh the benefits.

The fact, however, is that people in large numbers go to the polls, in some countries actually at some risk to their lives. What motivates them to do so? The classic study of American voting behavior (Campbell et al. 1960) noted several fundamental attitudes that predispose a citizen to turn out to vote. Chief among them is the "sense of citizen duty." That is a belief, ingrained as the result of political socialization, that the good citizen "ought" to participate. A citizen raised with that belief will derive a personal satisfaction from voting and a sense of utility that even advocates of economic rationality cannot deny entirely (Riker and Ordeshook 1968).

Our two 1988 samples of eligible voters appear to be products of the same network of influence, for they felt compelled to express strong convictions about the importance of voting. The great majority in both surveys also claimed to have satisfied the legal requirements for eligibility. Seventy-eight percent of Survey 1 respondents said they were registered to vote, and 85 percent claimed to be registered in Survey 2. Since one cannot vote without being registered, these percentages, though inflated (a *New York Times* editorial entitled "A Chance to Expand Democracy" [1990] said that 61 percent of voters were actually registered in 1990), are important indices of eligibility as well as motivation. More than 80 percent of registered voters typically show up at the polls in presidential elections. Eighty-seven percent did so in 1980, for example (Squire, Wolfinger, and Glass 1987). But given that the 1988 voter turnout of 50.16 percent was the lowest in sixty-four years, it is clear that fewer of our respondents actually voted than said it was important to do so, or than claimed to be registered. But whether out of true conviction or just a feeling that one should voice the sentiment, Table 5-2 shows that these people said that voting in the presidential election was extremely important to them.

The questions in Table 5-2 are not complete measures of the motivation to vote, but they provide information that is clearly relevant to it. On a ten-point scale where 10 indicates greatest importance, the mean response to the importance question is near the top for both surveys. In the first survey, 65 percent, and in the second 69 percent, actually chose the number 10 as the best index of voting's importance to them. Clearly strong feelings of obligation underlie these responses. Most people feel they ought to endorse the importance of voting, even though many end up staying away from the polls. But the dictionary defines motivation only as something that prompts a person to act in a certain way. The definition doesn't require the act to be carried out. The feeling of obligation to vote is certainly a prompt in this sense, even when it doesn't actually result in the casting of a ballot.

Table 5-2. *The Motivation to Vote*

Survey	1	2
How important to you is voting in the presidential election?		
Mean response (10-point scale)	8.9	9.1
% positive (6–10 on scale)	90	90
% negative (1–5 on scale)	9	8
How interested are you in presidential politics?		
Mean response (10-point scale)	7.1	7.4
% positive (6–10 on scale)	72	75
% negative	27	24
Are you *now* registered to vote, or not?		
Registered (%)	78	85
Not registered (%)	21	15
Not sure (%)	1	1

Harris Survey 1; N=1,876; conducted 9/6–19/1988.
Harris Survey 2; N=1,875; conducted 10/18–11/4/1988.

Interest, defined as feelings of concern, involvement, or curiosity, is also relevant to motivation. What attracts one's interest can also be a prompt to act in certain ways. Interest in presidential politics is not as strong as is the perceived importance of voting to these respondents. Yet the mean interest scores on the ten-point scales suggest something significantly more than indifference. Since there is probably less social pressure to express interest in presidential politics than there is to acknowledge the importance of voting, we might reasonably construe the expressed levels of interest as less likely to be inflated by obligation, and thus more reflective of actual sentiment. To the extent that it is genuine, interest would contribute to the motivation to vote.

The steady decline in voter turnout in recent presidential elections, the often astonishing ignorance of important political topics, and most recently the polls showing disgust for the tenor of the 1988 campaign are often interpreted to indicate a growing public cynicism and alienation that imperil the electoral process (C. B. Gans 1988a; Drew 1989). Ominous though such trends may be, they must be set against the evidence in Table 5-2, which collectively implies still-strong public identification with the electoral process and—perhaps—a latent readiness to respond to calls for revitalized participation. At a minimum, these expressions of interest and obligation suggest that alienation has yet to reach irreversible levels.

Qualifications for the Presidency. We next look at how the people defined the job they were about to fill. The very first substantive question posed during the telephone interviews was an open-ended query about the job requirements of the presidency. The question (its exact wording appears in Table 5-3) was intended to get respondents to define their own terms "up front," before the interviewers had any opportunity to influence respondent word choice or frame of reference, the sort of thing that unavoidably happens in the process of posing a long series of questions.

The question sought to reveal how people conceive of what it would take in 1989 to be a good president. We wanted to know how they defined the requirements of the job, because from such ideals flow the standards and expectations that shape the context for the actual voting choice. We were also interested in learning just how thoughtful and sophisticated ordinary citizens were about the presidential role.

We expected that answers to this question and other open-ended questions involving evaluations of the presidential candidates would

Table 5-3. *Qualifications for the Presidency*

What must the winner of the (1988 presidential) election have within himself, and bring to the job, in order to be a good president?

Survey	1 (%)	2 (%)
Character	54	57
Honesty/integrity/trustworthiness	41	42
Strong personality	8	8
Moral values	4	4
Commitment/determination	4	3
Competence	41	40
Good/strong leadership	14	14
Intelligent/knowledgeable	11	11
Foreign-affairs experience	10	8
Experience	7	9
Good judgment/common sense	6	4
Good speaker	3	2
Issue position	36	34
Concern for needs of all people	15	17
Ability to reduce deficit/improve economy	7	5
Create/provide jobs	5	3
Concern for needy	5	3
Maintain strong defense	4	2
Miscellaneous	16	18

Harris Survey 1; N=1,876; conducted 9/6–19/1988.
Harris Survey 2; N=1,875; conducted 10/18–11/4/1988.

be classifiable into three primary categories: *character, competence, and issue positions.* These categories embrace the commonsensical grounds for thinking about the demands of the presidency and for comparing and contrasting the merits of presidential candidates.

Voters would want to know what kinds of people the candidates are, we thought, because they have notions of their own concerning the sort of person the president ought to be. They also want some assurance that the hopefuls have the ability to handle the job as they, the voters, understand it. And voters surely also want to know where, in policy terms, the candidates want to take the country, to check against their own visions of what ought to be done.

Having coders group the responses to Question 1 into their naturally occurring categories was the test of whether these expectations were accurate. Could this "character/competence/issue position"

(CCI) model accommodate the majority of responses given, or would other categories have to be created to meaningfully organize and summarize the responses?

The results appear in Table 5-3. They show that "miscellaneous" categories did have to be created for the answers, 16 and 18 percent in Surveys 1 and 2, that didn't fit expectations. Still, it is clear that the great majority of the spontaneous comments of our respondents about presidential requirements did fit into the expected categories. These are workable labels for the dimensions people use to make sense of the demands of the presidency.

Table 5-3 also lists several of the specific comments classified under each broad category. Open-ended questions posed to random national samples produce results that mirror the heterogeneous qualities of the electorate. They typically yield long strings of unrelated reactions. Forced to choose their own words and to formulate their own specific definitions and concepts of subjects to which they have had little prior common exposure, people tend not to converge on the same small cluster of ideas. As we will see later, it is not unusual for there to be ten or more specific attributes mentioned under a broad category like "character" or "competence." And few specific attributes are mentioned by more than 4 or 5 percent of respondents.[4]

In this light, we can appreciate how unusual it is that the character category—which Table 5-3 shows drew by far the largest body of commentary (54 and 57 percent in Surveys 1 and 2)—had within it an attribute cluster that generated as much agreement as it did on both surveys. That cluster was honesty/integrity/trustworthiness, mentioned by 41 and 42 percent in respective surveys. These were the highest percentages to emerge from any of the open-ended questions included in the Markle telephone surveys.

Nine additional character qualities were also mentioned, with little variation from one survey to the next. The top three are reproduced in the table.

Six of the nine responses fitting the Competence category (which drew 41 and 40 percent of respondent comments) are listed in Table 5-3.

In the issue-position category the table shows that the most frequently mentioned "issue" (generating only 15 and 17 percent support respectively) was the conviction that the next president in his policy actions ought to display concern for the needs of all the people, a kind of across-the-board fairness. Not depicted in the table is a long string of issues generating single-digit support.

Two of the presidential-qualifications findings deserve concluding emphasis. First, the basic concept of what the new president should bring to his job scarcely changed at all from the first to the second set of interviews. No new qualifications emerged between Labor Day and election day, and no specific qualification was mentioned by a substantially greater or lesser percentage of respondents from one survey to the next. The electorate's sense of what the new president ought to have within himself and bring to the job was therefore not materially affected by any agent of external influence in the closing weeks of the campaign. Few of the other open-ended questions prompted such stable cross-time responses.

Second, examination of the contents and the extent of the consensus within each of the three categories shows that Americans have the clearest conception and the greatest agreement in just one area— character—and within that area on just one specific constellation of desirable presidential character requirements: honesty, integrity, and trustworthiness. These were the only attributes a large proportion of our respondents independently asserted that the next president ought to bring to the White House.

The importance of character is not a new, but a well-established finding. It squares with the results of research showing that American citizens tend to emphasize personal attributes when evaluating presidential candidates (Campbell et al. 1960; Glass, 1985; Miller, Wattenberg, and Malanchuk 1986) and tend to give high priority to trustworthiness in assessing them (Kinder and Fiske 1986).

The desirable competence and issue-position qualifications generated much less consensus. Although the specific competence attributes mentioned—strong leadership, intelligence, foreign-policy experience—were reasonable, the small percentages mentioning each show that no clear, widely shared sense had emerged of the precise sorts of competence that would be particularly needed in the years just ahead. If there is a surprise here, it is that the frequently noted competence shortcomings of the departing Reagan administration— the president's storied inattention to detail and his general disengagement from the daily work of the presidency—did not much affect the wish list of capabilities desirable in the new president.

Evaluative Priorities. Although it took a character attribute to generate significant agreement on what the new president should bring to the job, when citizens are asked to rank-order the importance of various qualifications for the presidency, character winds up near the bottom.

Table 5-4 displays percentage responses to the following question: "Which of the following four key characteristics do you feel is most important to you in terms of deciding whom to support for president?"

The results offer snapshots of how respondents viewed their own decision criteria in the abstract at two points during the campaign season. The rankings are clearly subject to change, as the Survey 2 shift away from issue position and toward experience and competence shows. They are also subject to the influence of context, which is suggested by the comparatively low rank of character in both surveys. Character became an issue in its own right following Democratic presidential candidate Gary Hart's May 1987 withdrawal from the race because of adverse publicity surrounding his liaison with fashion model Donna Rice. Hart's character troubles were followed by those of Democratic candidate Joseph Biden and Republican candidate Pat Robertson, both of which also generated a great deal of unfavorable media attention.

Extensive media coverage eventually provoked a backlash. Europeans and others expressed amusement at the "exacting moral yardsticks" applied to those seeking high public office in the United States (Markham 1987:17). By November 1987, Americans were fed up with what they regarded as "media overkill" on candidate character, according to a Times Mirror–Gallup survey (Rosenstiel 1987:A4). Another survey conducted by the Gallup organization for the Times Mirror Company found that 49 percent felt a candidate's

Table 5-4. Evaluative Priorities

Which of the following four key characteristics do you feel is most important to you in terms of deciding whom to support for president?		
Survey	1 (%)	2 (%)
The candidate's position on the issues	40	31
The candidate's record of experience and reputation for competence	39	43
The candidate's personal qualities of character	15	17
The candidate's political party	6	6

Harris Survey 1; N=1,238; conducted 9/26–29/1988. (Mistakenly omitted during the Survey 1 Markle protocol, this question was asked as part of a separate Harris survey on these dates.)
Harris Survey 2; N=1,875; conducted 10/18–11/4/1988.

"ability to accomplish things" was most important, with 33 percent giving the highest priority to "stand on issues," and only 14 percent putting character first (Skelton 1987 : A7). That number is comparable to those for character in Table 5-4, suggesting that the backlash endured throughout the campaign.

An intriguing question is why competence displaced issue position as the top evaluative priority from Survey 1 to 2. For Table 5-4 shows that the percentage viewing issue position as the major basis for choice drops from 40 to 31, and competence moves from a second-place 39 percent to the first position at 43 percent.

One likely reason is that no collection of problems took root in the public mind as matters of compelling urgency once the campaign got under way in earnest after Labor Day. There were no crises—such as a shooting war or runaway inflation—that injected pain directly into the lives of millions of voters. The problems that did exist were real enough, but they were subtle–and, in the context of peace and prosperity, hard to paint in fearful colors. The candidates did not mount the sort of persistent crusade that would have been necessary to to instill—through drumbeat cries of alarm coupled with patient, repetitive explanation—a widespread sense of urgency about complex problems like the budget deficit or the need to reposition America in the international economic order. The media did manage to convince a sizable minority of the dangers of the budget deficit. But the candidates, mindful of their electoral prospects, avoided discussion of that and other serious priorities.

Too, both Michael Dukakis and George Bush, at different times and for different reasons, sought to focus attention on experience and competence. This is another likely explanation for the shift in Table 5-4. As early as his July acceptance speech at the Democratic Convention, Dukakis asserted that the election was about competence rather than ideology. And Bush, seeking to captitalize on his superior record of federal government experience, spent much of the campaign portraying his opponent as dangerously inexperienced, in the tradition of Jimmy Carter.

Are the abstract candidate choice priorities endorsed by respondents in Table 5-4 reliable guides to how the same voters would choose between the 1988 candidates? There is reason to be doubtful. Survey respondents can be expected to rank "socially respectable" response options highly. And both issues and competence currently have somewhat greater political legitimacy as grounds for choice than do character and party identification. Yet party identification remains a significant influence on voting behavior (Abramson

1983:85), and we have already considered the importance of assessments of candidate character in voting (e.g., Miller, Wattenberg, and Malanchuk 1986; Glass 1985).

By listing the factors respondents said would determine their voting decisions in 1988, Table 5-5 sheds clearer light on how abstract evaluative criteria get translated into specific candidate preferences. The open-ended question, "What is the most important reason for choosing (Bush/Dukakis) over his opponent?" was posed to the 1,299 people who said they had made their voting decision by the time of the second Markle survey. Respondents were free to give as many "important" reasons as they had for their preferences, and nearly fifty reasons were offered. Only reasons endorsed by 4 percent or more are included in the table, which reduces the list to sixteen.

We see that party identification emerges as one of the two most frequently mentioned bases for choice despite its low rank in Table 5-4. Experience, the top-rated Survey 2 criterion in that table, retains its importance in Table 5-5. Character, downgraded when respondents were asked to rank it in the abstract, is still adduced by 11 percent in the form of attributes like honesty/integrity/trustwor-

Table 5-5. *Reasons for Candidate Preference*

What is the most important reason for choosing (Bush/Dukakis) over his opponent? What other important reasons are there?

Reason	%
Party identification	16
Experience	16
Honesty/integrity/trustworthiness	11
Dislike other candidate	11
Continuation of Reagan's policies	11
Ability to reduce deficit/improve economy	8
Need a change	7
Aligned with my beliefs	6
Concern for working/lower classes	6
Concern for needs of all people	6
Foreign-affairs experience/knowledge	6
Maintain strong defense	5
Tough on crime	4
Oppose abortion	4
Conservative	4
Intelligent/knowledgeable	4

Harris Survey 2; N=1,299 decided voters; conducted 10/18–11/4/1988.

thiness when people reflect on why they prefer one specific candidate to another. Character-rooted preferences may also figure in the thinking of the 11 percent who say they dislike the other candidate.

Issue position also retains considerable importance in Table 5-5, both in the strong percentage claiming to base their choice on continuation of Reagan's policies and in the fact that many of the reasons given for candidate preference dealt with issues in one way or another.

Both Tables 5-4 and 5-5 suggest that voters' evaluative priorities are not abstract commitments that are permanently fixed in order of importance from one election to the next. They can instead be expected to change along with circumstances and candidates.

Appraising The Issues

The next group of findings are responses to questions that focus on the issues. Our effort to measure the state of the electorate's preparation on the issues took two forms. The first sought evidence of reflection on the nation's major problem priorities.

The Most Important Problems. In order to gauge how much and what kind of thought people had given to the nature of the problems the president would have to confront, we asked, "What are the two or three most important problems the next president will face?" The results, which also give evidence of the sources of the public's thinking on the major problems, appear in Table 5-6.

Respondents were free to mention more than one problem, which is why the sum of the issue category percentages exceeds 100. The table reports only the five most frequently mentioned issues under each major issue category.

As is usually the case in good economic times, domestic issues generated the largest amount of commentary, followed by economics and foreign affairs. Again we see evidence that no small cluster of issue priorities came to dominate the public mind in 1988. But it is also clear that two issues in particular—drugs and the federal budget deficit—had floated to the top of these long lists by the time of the first survey, stimulating the concern of the largest groups of respondents. Concern for both had increased by 5 percent at the time of the second survey. Here is clear evidence of change—increases—in issue salience. What brought it about?

The increase in the salience of the drug issue seems to have resulted primarily from the attention given it by candidates. Drugs had been ebbing and flowing as a public concern since the midterm

Table 5-6. *The Most Important Presidential Problems*

Survey	1 (%)	2 (%)
Domestic affairs	72	73
Drugs	16	21
Jobs	11	7
Education	10	9
Homeless	10	12
Environment	8	7
Economics	45	46
Reduce deficit	18	23
Control inflation	9	7
Trade deficit	6	5
Balance budget	4	5
Control taxes	4	4
Foreign affairs/national security	34	30
Arms control	9	9
Keep the peace	8	5
Keep strong defense	7	6
Keep negotiating with U.S.S.R.	6	7
Improve foreign relations	5	3
Miscellaneous	12	8

Harris Survey 1; N=1,876; conducted 9/6–19/1988.
Harris Survey 2; N=1,875; conducted 10/18–11/4/1988.

congressional elections of 1986. In August of that year, 13 percent of the public listed drugs as the most important problem. By October 1987, a *New York Times*/CBS News Poll showed the figure had fallen to 3 percent. But by early 1988, abetted primarily by the attention the Reverend Jesse Jackson gave the issue from the beginning of his presidential campaign, and secondarily by the drug-related indictment of Gen. Manuel Antonio Noriega, the Panamanian leader, the drug issue had again become important.

In May 1988, for example, some four months before the first Markle survey, a *New York Times*/CBS News Poll found that only one issue was named as the nation's most important problem by as much as 16 percent of the public. That issue was drugs (Dionne 1988a:14). Expressing its editorial surprise at the importance of drugs in an earlier statewide poll, the *New York Times* opined that it could only be explained by peace and prosperity, and that as the campaign heated up, more "presidential" issues would surely assume primacy (*Why There Are No Issues* 1988:26).

The results in Table 5-6 show otherwise. The issue joined the Massachusetts prison-furlough program and mandatory death sentences for drug dealers to become part of the heavily played Bush attack on the "liberal" Michael Dukakis (Drew 1989:332). This made drugs more rather than less important during the campaign. George Bush's debt to the issue is suggested by the fact that the only specific promise he made in his inaugural address was a ringing pledge to end the drug problem: ". . . take my word for it: This scourge will stop" (Transcript 1989).

The budget deficit, which the table shows attracted even more concern, can only have received its impetus from the media, since the candidates avoided the issue whenever possible. We saw in Chapter 4 that the media did indeed give it a great deal of coverage. The candidates refused to offer detailed, credible policies for addressing the deficit, even though the elite press freqently complained in print and on the air about their failure to do so (Taylor 1988:16). Only as his inauguration approached did President-elect George Bush begin referring to the budget deficit as a top priority (Kilborn 1988b).

The informal consensus among mainstream economists, as was widely and frequently reported in the print and broadcast media during the campaign, held the budget deficit to be the single most important problem facing the nation. A significant portion of the public absorbed this agenda-setting message. Table 5-6's 23 percent for the deficit is high for an open-ended question that presents no list of issue options to choose from. Other evidence suggests that the numbers were even larger when respondents were given a list of specific options from which to choose. In a survey of this kind conducted between September 9 and 11, 1988, by the *Los Angeles Times*, 45 percent said the deficit should be "the most important political issue in the presidential campaign," with drugs identified as such by 38 percent, making it the second-ranking issue in the poll (Los Angeles Times Poll 1988).

Table 5-6 shows that foreign-affairs issue-mentions actually declined in the final weeks of the 1988 presidential campaign. Arms control, which held steady at 9 percent in both surveys, is the issue generally thought—by presidents, journalists, and citizens—to be among the most durable and significant presidential priorities of the postwar era, and a crucial test of presidential mettle. It did attract the largest volume of commentary among foreign-policy/national-security issues. But the proportion mentioning it is modest; no doubt a reflection of comparatively less attention to foreign policy from the candidates and the media. In light of the changes in the

Soviet Union wrought by Mikhail Gorbachev and the post-election talk of the end of the cold war, the neglect of foreign affairs in the 1988 presidential campaign was remarkable.

Candidate Issue Positions. Large national-policy priorities aside, how well informed were people about what the candidates were actually saying on the campaign trail? And to what extent did people's store of information about such matters increase as the election drew near? Answers to such questions tell us something about how effectively the candidates were communicating, the media covering, and the voters following the candidates and the campaign.

An informed citizenry is a prized commodity in a democracy. Harkening back to ideals, democratic theory would have us expect citizens to be particularly well informed about what the two major candidates for the nation's highest office have to say about the issues. The results presented in Table 5-7 enable us to see how closely 1988's reality approximated this ideal.[5]

For both surveys, Table 5-7 lists the percentage of respondents attributing each issue position to the correct candidate (% Right) and the percentage unsure which candidate had endorsed each position (% Unsure). Subtracting the sum of these two numbers from 100 gives the percentage getting a particular answer wrong.[6]

The Problem of Norms. The American electorate is not routinely tested on its knowledge of candidate issue positions. Therefore no standards based on past performance are available to guide our interpretation of these results. Reasonable people will disagree concerning just how much general public knowledge of candidate issue positions is desirable or sufficient. Different standards yield different "grades."

For example, if we arbitrarily treat each issue position as having an equal chance of becoming known to individual citizens, and expect responsible citizens to become fully informed, we might look for something similar to the normalized testing standards of a grammar school (i.e., a majority of the "class" scores near the mean of around 70 percent, in this case fourteen correct answers). By these standards our respondents failed both administrations of the test. On only five questions did 50 percent or more get the right answer on the first test. The number of questions 50 percent or more could answer correctly increased only to seven on the second test.

The results are equally dismal if we look at the percentage of respondents getting as many as fourteen items—the number required

Table 5-7. *Candidate Issue-Position Test*

Survey		1		2	
Issue Position	Candidate	% Right	% Unsure	% Right	% Unsure
A					
Capital punishment	Bush	56	27	78**	10
Against Midgetman	Dukakis	54	30	63*	22
No new taxes	Bush	53	10	60*	9
Universal health care	Dukakis	47	35	58**	23
Tax as last resort	Dukakis	48	15	56*	11
No mandatory prayer	Dukakis	50	23	53	19
Good jobs/good wages	Dukakis	52	12	53	11
Gun control	Dukakis	40	24	49*	16
Get delinquent taxes	Dukakis	31	34	49**	22
B					
Still in cold war	Bush	44	31	46	31
Teacher fund	Dukakis	43	30	41	28
Line-item veto	Bush	34	48	39*	45
Soviet motives	Dukakis	33	27	39*	23
Voluntary pledge	Dukakis	38	18	38	14
Flexible freeze	Bush	30	41	36*	34
"100 days" program	Dukakis	35	46	35	42
C					
30 million new jobs	Bush	29	20	30	18
Conventional forces	Dukakis	24	25	30*	21
Education president	Bush	25	29	29	24
Day-care tax credit	Bush	28	25	26	25

Harris Survey 1; N=1,876; conducted 9/6–19/1988.
Harris Survey 2; N=1,875; conducted 10/18–11/4/1988.
*Five percent or greater Survey 2 increase.
**Ten percent or greater Survey 2 increase.

for an "average" letter-grade of C—correct. On the first test, for example, only about 3 percent of the sample did this well. The average
score was just under eight, improving to just over nine on the second test.

But if items are grouped by a "degree-of-difficulty" scheme which
does not assume that all issue positions are equally likely to become
known, the picture is different.

Table 5-7 separates the issues into three such categories. Type A issues, the first nine listed, are primarily those that received extensive coverage from the media and/or extensive attention in paid candidate advertising. The candidates' positions on taxes, capital punishment, and to a lesser extent school prayer were among the centerpieces of paid and free media attention. Too, several were "hot-button" issues salient to large numbers of voters. Others, like Dukakis's stands against the Midgetman Missile and his early campaign theme of "good jobs at good wages," did not get as much consistent attention as the campaign wore on. But they were relatively easy to guess along Democratic-Republican lines, which helps to explain their high percentages.

It is reasonable to expect people who watch television news and other programming regularly to be familiar with most of the Group A stands.[7] Indeed, by the second test, between 49 and 78 percent of respondents could link the right candidate to each position in this category.

The remaining categories (Groups B and C in Table 5-7) include issue positions that were less well publicized and generally of less immediate concern to voters. These stands were acknowledged by the candidates and occasionally repeated in response to questions. But they were not heavily stressed in campaign advertising nor given the quantity of free media attention accorded candidate positions on such issues as taxes and capital punishment. Familiarity with stands like Mr. Bush's flexible-freeze plan for cutting the deficit or Mr. Dukakis's belief that its own economic problems and not the U.S. military buildup motivated the Soviet Union to negotiate the Intermediate Nuclear Force treaty, would require closer attention to the campaign than would Group A issues.[8]

How Good Is Good Enough? These "degree-of-difficulty" breakdowns permit a more charitable view of the public's performance. They show that slender to substantial majorities became familiar with the most heavily publicized candidate issue positions as election day approached (Group A). The case can be made that it would be unrealistic to expect more. But there are also grounds for a more critical view.[9]

More than half of Survey 2 respondents remained unsure or wrong about thirteen of the twenty issue positions. An average of 61 percent on Group B positions and 71 percent on Group C positions could not identify who stood for what by the end of the second survey. Though few of the eleven lesser-known issue positions received extensive publicity, many—like Bush's stances on education and child care, or Dukakis's position on the motives of the Soviet

Union—were unarguably important, involving how the two presidential finalists conceive of vital national interests.

Information about all of these positions was consistently available—if not always on the nightly television news, then in news magazines and many newspapers. If a majority of voters were ignorant of them, it was clearly because they opted to remain so, and not because it was impossible or even particularly difficult to become informed.

Even those who are tolerant of public apathy would be unlikely to contend that these test results are reassuring. In Chapter 7, it is argued that they and other evidence signal a problem serious enough to require remedial action. That voters bear the primary responsibility for informing themselves, with an assist from the media and the candidates, was suggested earlier.

Evidence of Learning.   It remains to examine the evidence of learning, and to identify its probable sources. For despite the public inattention to issue positions just noted, there is still considerable evidence of significant issue-position learning in Table 5-7. Comparisons of Survey 1 and 2 percentages show that only four issue positions registered zero gains or actual losses in the percentage reporting familiarity. An additional five showed modest gains of between 1 and 4 percent. Knowledge of the remaining eleven issue positions increased much more significantly, as indicated by asterisks in Table 5-7. Eight became known by between 5 and 9 percent more respondents, and three by an additional 10 percent or more.

Of the three largest changes, two involved Dukakis positions. But it was Bush's endorsement of capital punishment, awareness of which already stood at a healthy 56 percent in late September, that grew a remarkable 22 points to 78 percent just before the election. This was far and away the best-known issue position, fully 15 percentage points better known than its closest competitor.

Why did this particular issue position attain such notoriety? Probably because it is the clearest representative on this list of twenty issues of the winning Bush campaign strategy of defining himself as a strong conservative and the lesser-known Dukakis as a weak liberal. The sharply increased recognition of the Bush capital-punishment position demonstrates that his campaign themes were among the most influential "educational" forces in the 1988 campaign.[10]

First articulated by the candidate on the hustings and in his paid television advertising, the Bush themes were picked up and reinforced by the pervasive media coverage of the attacks the candidates made on one another's qualifications described in the preceding chapter. Some 19 percent of the 7,574 television and newspaper stories we coded involved coverage of the "negative comparisons" the candidates made of their opponents with themselves. And most of those stories dealt with emotional issues like capital punishment.

This coverage was augmented, and its influence no doubt strengthened, by the even more pervasive media attention to the political horse-race dimensions of the the campaign (36 percent of coded story allocations) in which reporters, adopting the perspective of campaign managers, clinically dissected and discussed the merits of each candidate's political strategy and the ebbs and flows of the campaign.

Of course the media also covered Michael Dukakis's advocacy of a universal health-care system and his plan to expand federal efforts to collect delinquent income taxes. These positions registered very substantial 11- and 18-point increases, respectively. And since paid Dukakis advertising did not dwell on these stances, it was apparent that media coverage alone did much to increase their visibility. But when the dust had settled, there was a striking 15-point "familiarity gap" between the best-known Dukakis position and the Bush capital-punishment stance. What accounts for it?

Our coding showed that more candidate-qualifications stories dealt exclusively with Bush (541) than with Dukakis (329), while 454 dealt with comparisons of various kinds between the two candidates. Too, the best-known Dukakis issue positions in Table 5-7 clearly did not get as much attention in another area—the political horse-race story category—as did the Bush capital-punishment stance. Dukakis got plenty of attention in the political horse-race stories, but the bulk of it dealt with themes not captured in any of Table 6's issue positions: the furlough of Willie Horton, the unclean state of Boston Harbor, the Massachusetts governor's veto of a bill requiring schoolchildren to recite the Pledge of Allegiance, and the comparative ineffectiveness of his presidential campaign, among other things.

So the Bush capital-punishment position did get more net media coverage in one category or another. But that is not the whole story, for Dukakis positions got enough media attention to become familiar to anybody willing to pay attention. There was simply a larger audience primed to focus on Bush's position on capital punishment. Television and newspaper coverage matters. But as the Bentsen and Quayle recognition data in Table 5-1 make clear, the extent of public awareness of any bit of information is not a simple linear function of the amount of media coverage. Voters must be paying attention before any information, however accessible, can be registered in consciousness. And the tendency to pay attention is obviously related to the information's capacity to arouse voter interest.[11]

The eight additional issue positions in Table 5-7 that became increasingly familiar (to 5 percent or more respondents each) as election day approached are further evidence of influence and learning. For the most part, the origins of that influence are the same: media coverage of candidate pronouncements. The reasons for the variations in the size of recognition increases are also similar. Issues that matter most to voters—like taxes and gun control—got more mention from candidates, more coverage by journalists, and greater reaction from the audience—than less salient issues like the flexible-freeze proposal or the line-item veto.

The Candidates

Shifting the focus to questions about the candidates themselves, we found, predictably, that when voters were asked, "What do you see as the most important differences between what Dukakis and Bush plan to do if they were president?" the usual lengthy string of small response-clusters resulted.

Perched atop the string, however, is evidence of how the largest cluster framed the essential choice between the 1988 hopefuls. The theme is familiar: strength versus weakness. But this time it is national defense that distinguishes the candidates. The largest plurality—12 percent in Survey 1, increasing to 17 percent in Survey 2—saw the most important difference as Bush's strength versus Dukakis's weakness at defending the country.

Again, evidence of an effectively transmitted Bush theme leads the list: ". . . with clever commercials and tough campaigning, Bush managed to shift the debate . . . to strength versus weakness . . . [making] Dukakis's perceived weakness on defense a major campaign issue . . . " (Ornstein and Schmitt 1989:42). The sentiment would endure beyond the election and eventually force Democratic Party Chairman Ronald H. Brown to make his central priority overcoming the view that Democrats are soft on crime and defense matters (Dionne 1989).

The second most frequently mentioned distinction was the belief that Mr. Bush was dedicated to continuing President Reagan's policies, while Mr. Dukakis would change course. Both candidates sought to foster this view (it grew from 8 to 11 percent between

September and November) but it ultimately worked to the then-vice president's advantage. The third most mentioned difference was that Dukakis favored raising taxes. Again, advantage Bush.

Skipping past the dozens of other small clusters of substantive responses to the "don't know" category, we come to another familiar theme: evidence of voter indifference and apathy. Sizable percentages—45 and 35 in Surveys 1 and 2 respectively—were unwilling or unable to articulate any expected differences between Bush's and Dukakis's presidential plans.

What Have You Learned?   These findings, which are not reported in a table, are paralleled and extended by the results presented in Tables 5-8 and 5-9. In an effort to tease out evidence of the sorts of information about the candidates that was sticking in the minds of potential voters, we asked the open-ended question: "What are the most important things you have learned in this campaign about George Bush and Michael Dukakis?" These tables show clearly what was and was not getting through, and are rich with implications concerning the sources of the "learning."

The tables organize the learning responses into major categories

Table 5-8. *Learned about Bush*

Survey	1 (%)	2 (%)
Character	33	34
Strong personality	11	9
Dishonest/distrust him	9	9
Is a wimp	7	3
Issue position	22	28
Continue Reagan policies	10	9
Strong on defense	4	5
Tough on crime	0	3
Competence	22	24
Experienced	5	9
Miscellaneous	23	21
Quayle choice showed poor judgment	5	0
Negative campaign/mudslinging	0	5
Don't know/no answer	19	15

Harris Survey 1; N=1,876; conducted 9/6–19/1988.
Harris Survey 2; N=1,875; conducted 10/18–11/4/1988.

Table 5-9. *Learned about Dukakis*

Survey	1 (%)	2 (%)
Issue position	30	39
Weak on crime/prison furloughs	5	9
Liberal	4	7
Concern for needs of all	4	5
Miscellaneous	29	31
Dislike him	2	5
Negative campaign/mudslinging	2	4
Competence	26	24
Good political record	6	4
Would be good president	6	5
Character	24	28
Honesty/integrity/trustworthiness	12	12
Dishonest/distrust him	5	5
Good personality	2	5
Don't know/no answer	21	14

Harris Survey 1; N=1,876; conducted 9/16–19/1988.
Harris Survey 2; N=1,875; conducted 10/18–11/4/1988.

like "issue position," "character," and so on. Only the two or three largest response clusters are included under each category, and most of these are single-digit percentages. But remember that as few as 3 percent of either Harris sample can represent as many as 5 million eligible voters. Since the popular vote difference between George Bush and Michael Dukakis was less than 7 million in 1988, the small percentage shifts displayed in Tables 5-8 and 5-9 were potentially quite important.

The clear pattern discernible in Table 5-8 is of candidate Bush eliminating or overpowering his negatives, while sustaining or adding to his positives. Thus, the percent regarding him as a "wimp" drops from 7 to 3 and the notice of his "poor judgment" for choosing Indiana Senator Dan Quayle as his running mate literally disappears by the second survey. The percentage perceiving him as "strong," a synonym for "presidential" in many minds, holds at a robust 9 percent in Survey 2. This, plus increased recognition for his toughness on crime and his national government experience (not to mention his commitment to the basic Reagan direction), apparently offset the sharp increase in those taking note of the negative tone of his presidential campaign. These things also helped outweigh the endurance of a significant percentage expressing distrust of Bush.

The Dukakis portrait in Table 5-9 was also painted by the Bush campaign. Aided by the fact that 21 percent of the Survey 1 respondents said they knew little or nothing of Dukakis as a person, the Bush forces managed to implant an unflattering definition of the Massachusetts governor in enough voters' minds to damage his prospects.

Virtually every instance of cross-survey change in Table 5-9—whether an increase in the number who disliked Michael Dukakis or a decrease in the percent that thought he would be a good president—worked against the governor's political fortunes. The two most significant increases in "learning"—Dukakis's weakness on crime and prison furloughs and his liberal status—were direct results of Bush advertising or stump speech attacks. Other learnings not listed in the table—1 percent who said the governor "lacked concern for the environment" because of his failure to clean up Boston Harbor, and the 3 percent who took note of his support of gun control—fit the same pattern.

Despite having initiated the negative tone of the campaign and deployed the more aggressive attacks (Boot 1989:28), the Republican camp profited from an increase in the perception that Dukakis was also engaged in a negative, mudslinging campaign. Though we saw in Table 5-3 that the largest consensus on desirable presidential character centered around honesty, integrity, and trustworthiness, Dukakis's consistently high marks on these attributes were insufficient to overcome his negatives in other areas. Neither did the few other learnings favorable to him, such as the notice of his "good personality" or his "concern for the needs of all" help him. Being respected for your strength is obviously more helpful than being admired for your virtue if it is the presidency you seek.

It is noteworthy that none of the candidate issue positions discussed in Table 5-7 was among the most frequent responses to this open-ended learning question. Nor was media coverage of national problems like the budget and trade deficits, competitiveness, the homeless, and other issues (9.7 percent of the 7,574 stories coded—see Table 4-1) enough to stimulate significant mention of candidate positions in these areas. The issues mentioned frequently enough to be included in Tables 5-8 and 5-9 deal with general qualities, not concrete specifics like issue positions. It was clearly the candidates and not the media that had the most control over the issue agenda that reached the public. And candidate Bush was more successful than candidate Dukakis at setting the agenda, framing the issues, and winning voter acceptance for his definition of the decisive grounds for choice.

Changing Perceptions of the Candidates. Tables 5-10 and 5-11 together present a detailed map of the changes in public perceptions of the candidates that took place between Labor Day and election day. Each table contains twelve fixed-format statements that probe several dimensions of the candidates' personal qualities (character) and capabilities (competence) relevant to success in the presidency. Respondents were asked to rate the candidates on a scale of 1 to 10, with 10 the most favorable rating. The results—expressed as mean responses to each question for each survey, and as net positive and negative changes—reveal both candidates' patterns of strength and weakness in the public's estimation.[12]

The rating patterns show that by the time of the first survey, most respondents had a good sense of who the candidates were, and a quite accurate feel for their comparative strengths and weaknesses as portrayed by both the media and the candidates themselves. Dukakis had an average rating of 6.5 for all twelve attributes, received his highest rating of 7.1 for being a man of honesty and integrity and his lowest (5.7) in the area of foreign-policy knowledge.

Bush's overall rating was 6.6. His high rating of 7.2 for his foreign-policy knowledge came precisely in Dukakis's area of greatest weakness, which was an area of traditional importance to voters in choosing presidents. His low rating of 5.9 as an "inspiring leader" reflected longstanding problems of leadership image that had already begun to improve as a consequence of his aggressive campaign and highly regarded August 1988 nomination acceptance speech.

The comparative patterns also show that despite the closeness in the polls at the time of the first survey (see Table 5-1), Bush enjoyed important early advantages over Dukakis. Tables 5-10 and 5-11 show that these advantages existed before the Bush advertising effort, which began in earnest in most markets in late August, had had much time to work. This important fact was often overlooked by those who attributed Bush's eventual victory largely to negative advertising. In addition to his first-survey 1.5 point advantage in foreign policy, he bested the Massachusetts governor 7.0 to 6.1 as "someone who knows how to get things done in Washington, D.C." He was rated half a point better at knowing "enough about problems in the U.S. to make intelligent presidential decisions." And he was perceived as somewhat better able to withstand presidential pres-

Table 5-10. *Changes in Evaluations of Michael Dukakis*

	Mean Response		
Survey	*1*	*2*	*Change*
How would you rate . . .[a]			
Character			
1. Dukakis as a likeable person	6.6	6.1	−0.5
2. Dukakis as a trustworthy person	6.6	6.2	−0.4
3. Dukakis as strong enough to stand presidential pressure	6.7	6.5	−0.2
4. Dukakis as an inspiring leader	6.3	5.9	−0.4
5. Dukakis as a man of honesty and integrity	7.1	6.9	−0.2
6. Dukakis as someone who would be firm and resolute in a crisis	6.7	6.5	−0.2
Competence			
7. Dukakis as having the ability to be a good president	6.7	6.4	−0.3
8. Dukakis as someone who knows enough about problems in the U.S. to make intelligent presidential decisions	6.5	6.3	−0.2
9. Dukakis as someone who knows enough about economic policy to make intelligent presidential decisions	6.5	6.2	−0.3
10. Dukakis as someone who knows enough about foreign policy to make intelligent presidential decisions	5.7	5.3	−0.4
11. Dukakis as someone who knows how to get things done in Washington, D.C.	6.1	5.8	−0.3
12. Dukakis as someone who would manage the government well	6.6	6.3	−0.3

Harris Survey 1; N=1,876; conducted 9/6–19/1988.
Harris Survey 2; N=1,875; conducted 10/18–11/4/1988.
[a] Scale of 1–10; 10 highest rating.

Table 5-11. *Changes in Evaluations of George Bush*

	Mean Response		
Survey	*1*	*2*	*Change*
How would you rate . . .[a]			
Character			
1. Bush as a likeable person	6.1	6.4	+0.3
2. Bush as a trustworthy person	6.1	6.1	0.0
3. Bush as strong enough to stand presidential pressure	7.1	7.4	+0.3
4. Bush as an inspiring leader	5.9	6.2	+0.3
5. Bush as a man of honesty and integrity	6.4	6.4	0.0
6. Bush as someone who would be firm and resolute in a crisis	6.7	6.9	+0.2
Competence			
7. Bush as having the ability to be a good president	6.7	7.0	+0.3
8. Bush as someone who knows enough about problems in the U.S. to make intelligent presidential decisions	7.0	7.3	+0.3
9. Bush as someone who knows enough about economic policy to make intelligent presidential decisions	6.9	7.1	+0.2
10. Bush as someone who knows enough about foreign policy to make intelligent presidential decisions	7.2	7.5	+0.3
11. Bush as someone who knows how to get things done in Washington, D.C.	7.0	7.2	+0.2
12. Bush as someone who would manage the government well	6.6	6.8	+0.2

Harris Survey 1; N=1,876; conducted 9/6–19/1988.
Harris Survey 2; N=1,875; conducted 10/18–11/4/1988.
[a] Scale of 1–10; 10 highest rating.

sure and slightly more knowledgeable in economic policy, another area of traditionally special importance to voters.

Not that Dukakis was without leads of his own in the first survey. Not only did respondents rate him higher than Bush on integrity, they also perceived him as more likeable, trustworthy, and inspiring. And he managed a tie with the vice president on three key assessments: firmness in crisis, having the ability to be a good president, and the ability to manage the government well. Still, the earlier ratings make it clear that it was more of an uphill struggle for Dukakis than usually realized. All of the Dukakis ratings advantages were in the area of character rather than competence. And since Bush's lower character ratings were still in the acceptable range, his competence advantages became that much more significant.

The consistency of the change patterns from the first to the second survey is striking. Every single Dukakis change was downward; all of Bush's, upward. The Dukakis reductions ranged from half to two-tenths of a point. The fact of variation—some evaluations dropped farther than others—can be taken as evidence of discrimination. This implies some degree of selective influence on perceptions of Dukakis, even though the fact that every single category declined suggests indiscriminant downgrading.[13]

The largest Dukakis reductions involved likeability (-0.5), trustworthiness (-0.4), inspirational leadership (-0.4), and knowledge of foreign policy (-0.4) Do these particular declines have specific origins? The foreign-policy decline can be plausibly linked to a recurring Bush campaign theme underscoring the Massachusetts governor's lack of foreign-policy experience. The drop in perceived trustworthiness, especially when contrasted with a smaller decline in his honesty/integrity rating, suggests the effectiveness of branding Dukakis as a decent man who couldn't be trusted to be strong enough on crime and national defense.

The likeability and inspirational-leadership drops were more likely than others to have been self-inflicted. Throughout the fall campaign, polls and interviews showed people having difficulty warming up to Mr. Dukakis, whose manner struck them as wooden and unemotional. This assessment was crystallized by the Democratic nominee's response, during the second presidential debate with Mr. Bush, to CNN anchorman Bernard Shaw's hypothetical question about Mr. Dukakis's likely reaction to the rape of his wife. Dukakis's response struck viewers as unfeeling and insensitive, convincing many that he lacked the human empathy needed for effective presidential leadership.

The Bush increases in Table 5-11 are more homogeneous, all being either two- or three-tenths of a point. The absence of stand-out changes similar to those in the Dukakis ratings invites suspicion that the changes were driven primarily by the sort of indiscriminant upgrading that follows a decision to support a candidate, rather than by selective external influence like media coverage or paid advertising.

The burden of the evidence in the four candidate tables is that voters absorbed more impressions than facts about these two men, and that they increasingly "learned" to regard Bush as strong, knowledgeable, and experienced, and Dukakis as weak, liberal, hard to like, honest, but naïve about crime and criminals, and dangerously ignorant of foreign policy.

Evidence found in this book and elsewhere can be taken to imply that much of the credit for the movement toward Bush goes to the Bush campaign strategy.[14] The Bush organization managed to sidestep many Republican vulnerabilities and convert the election into a "referendum on the failed policies of the governor of Massachusetts, especially in his first term more than a decade ago, rather than on the performance of the incumbent administration or the leadership or judgment of the G.O.P. nominee" (Ornstein and Schmitt 1989:44).[15]

The Media

We have drawn inferences about the impacts of print and broadcast journalism on what people know and how they perceive candidates and issues throughout this chapter. Such effects are often subtle and can go unrecognized by those who are influenced. Good examples of this are what have been called the "agenda-setting" and "priming" effects, whereby television news, through its coverage patterns, subliminally influences the priorities the American public assigns to national problems and the standards by which governments, presidents, policies, and candidates for public office are judged (Iyengar and Kinder 1987:63).

But unaware as they may be of precisely how television and newspapers influence them, most Americans acknowledge some degree of reliance on the media and say they pay increasingly close attention to media coverage of the presidential campaign as election day approaches. Table 5-12 displays the responses to three fixed-format questions dealing with media coverage of the 1988 campaign. The first shows that nearly three-quarters of respondents to both surveys acknowledged some dependence on television and newspaper coverage in deciding which candidate to support.

Table 5-12. *Attitudes toward Media Campaign Coverage*

Survey	1 (%)	2 (%)
In deciding who to vote for in this election, how much do you depend on what you see on television or read in the newspapers?		
A lot	34	35
Some, but not a lot	38	39
Not much	16	15
Hardly at all	10	9
Not sure	2	1
How closely do you follow the media coverage of the election campaign?		
Very closely	16	25
Somewhat closely	42	43
Not very closely	27	21
Not closely at all	15	11
All in all, do you think the media (television, newspapers, magazines) have been fair or not in their coverage of all the candidates for president and vice president?		
Fair	60	60
Not fair	32	34
Not sure	8	6

Harris Survey 1; N=1,876; conducted 9/6–19/1988.
Harris Survey 2; N=1,875; conducted 10/18–11/4/1988.

The second question deals with attention, and the results show that the percentage claiming to follow media coverage somewhat or very closely grew from 58 to 68 by the time of the second Harris survey. Meanwhile, those who said they followed "not very closely" or "not closely at all" declined from 42 to 32 percent. The opportunities for media influences like agenda-setting and priming can only increase along with the size of the audience. And these figures show that the audience got larger as the time for decision neared.

The third question, on fairness, speaks to media credibility, another core determinant of openness to influence. The results show that healthy majorities continued to believe in the essential fairness of candidate coverage throughout the fall campaign season. This finding is consistent with other research demonstrating that the public believes most of what it hears, sees, or reads in the press (Robinson and Kohut 1988; Sudman 1987).

If the media can shape people's beliefs about problem importance and their evaluative dispositions (Iyengar and Kinder 1987) can they also transmit simple information relevant to voting decisions, such as the issue positions of presidential candidates? Does attention to news media coverage of the campaign increase familiarity with candidate issue positions? The data in Table 5-13 suggest a positive answer.

The sample drawn for the second Harris survey was divided into three groups according to performance on the issue-position test reported in Table 5-7. These are the "high," "medium," and "low" groups under "Candidate Issue-Position Knowledge" on the horizontal axis of Table 5-13. The "medium" group was largest (N = 1,256; 67 percent of the sample) and consisted of those scoring between one-half of a standard deviation above and one-half of a standard deviation below the mean. The "high" group was comprised of all those scoring more than half a standard deviation above the mean (N = 262; 14 percent of the sample). The "low" group included those scoring more than half a standard deviation below the mean (N = 266; 14 percent).

Clearly, greater attention to news media coverage is associated with greater knowledge of candidate issue position. Although the data do not permit precise specification of the causal direction, the likelihood is that following media coverage closely "causes" greater knowledge of candidate issue position, rather than vice versa. "Some voter [sic] may glimpse a presidential candidate for a half hour in their hometown," writes David Broder, "but most will get almost everything they know about those candidates indirectly through the media" (Broder 1987a: 274).[16]

Media Fairness. How do groups differ in perceptions of media fairness? Interestingly, those who followed media election coverage

Table 5-13. *Media Attention and Issue-Position Knowledge*

	Candidate Issue-Position Knowledge		
	High (%)	Medium (%)	Low (%)
Follow media coverage			
Very/somewhat closely	89	71	35
Not very closely/not closely at all	10	29	63

Harris Survey 2; N=1,875; conducted 10/18–11/4/1988.

Table 5-14. *Why Are News Media Unfair?*

Survey	1 (%)	2 (%)
Quayle issue overblown	42	24
Biased	25	25
Dig too deep into candidates' past	13	6
Focus on trivial, irrelevant issues	13	11
Media blow things out of proportion	11	10
Focus on the negative	7	8
Gary Hart issue overblown	6	2
Dishonest	3	5
Debates: unfair questioning	—	5
Overemphasis on polls	—	4

Survey 1; N=595; conducted 9/6–19/1988.
Survey 2; N=639; conducted 10/18–11/4/1988.

closely and scored in the top category on the issues test recorded higher percentages in the unfair category than less attentive, less knowledgeable groups (not reported in tables). Forty-five percent of the high-knowledge group said coverage was unfair, compared to only 34 percent of the medium-knowledge group and 20 percent of the low-knowledge group. And 38 percent of those who said they followed media coverage closely regarded that coverage as unfair, compared to only 26 percent of those who didn't watch closely. Larger percentages of conservatives and Republicans (41 and 40 percent, respectively) perceived coverage as unfair than Democrats and moderates (29 and 30 percent). Only 30 percent of liberals said the media was unfair, while 35 percent of Independents said so.

Why did significant percentages of our two samples continue to regard the media as unfair from one survey to the next? Table 5-14 summarizes the responses to an open-ended question, "Why do you feel the media have been unfair?" All those who said the media were unfair—595 people in the first and 639 in the second survey—were asked this question. No fewer than sixteen reasons were offered. The ten that generated the most supporters are included in the table.[17]

The Debates

The last body of survey data we will consider has to do with reactions to the presidential and vice-presidential debates held in 1988. Presidential debates are major media events that are of crucial importance in the preparation of the electorate to vote. Not only do they generate by far the largest audience for a campaign event; they are also unique in affording the opportunity to watch the candidates' minds at work in circumstances that are less scripted and controlled than usual. Debates offer voters a level of contact with candidates unmatched in spot ads and news segments—the longest and most intense view of the hopefuls available (Jamieson and Birdsell 1988). Those who watch debates acquire and remember more information about candidates and issues than those who don't (Becker et al. 1978). Debates also enable voters to test their personal reservations about candidates. In 1960 and 1980, for example, the debates put to rest reservations that enabled their winners to reach the White House (Jamieson and Birdsell 1988). The same might be said of the second 1988 debate between George Bush and Michael Dukakis.

According to the Associated Press, about 60 million people watched the first debate between Bush and Dukakis on September 25, an estimated 50 million tuned into the October 5 Bentsen-Quayle debate, and some 62 million watched the final presidential debate on October 13. Our second survey asked people whether they had watched or heard the debates. We also asked them to rate—on a 1 to 10 scale—the extent to which each debate influenced their decision concerning whom to support for president. The results appear in Table 5-15.

Responses to questions like those in Table 5-15 may misrepresent reality. For example, fewer than claimed to may actually have watched or listened to the debates. If 48 and 45 percent of the 169,963,000 U.S. citizens eighteen years and older (1989 *World Almanac*, p. 322) had actually watched the two presidential debates, as the table suggests, then 81 and 86 million viewers, rather than the 60 and 62 million estimated by the Associated Press, would have been tuned in. Too, people may underestimate the extent to which they were influenced by what they saw or heard of the debates.

These cautions notwithstanding, vast numbers of citizens did watch the debates. Particularly noteworthy is the fact that 45 percent admitted to being influenced by the second presidential debate, a 12 percent increase over the first. The second presidential debate, which most polls suggested was won by George Bush, was memorable for CNN anchorman Bernard Shaw's question to Dukakis about whether he would favor an irrevocable death penalty for the killer if Kitty Dukakis were raped and murdered. Dukakis's impersonal response reinforced the perception that he was stiff, emotionless, and not in tune with mainstream American values (Drew 1989:311).

The second debate was also the setting for a telling candidate criti-

Table 5-15. *1988 Presidential and Vice-Presidential Debates: Audiences and Impacts*

	September 25	October 13
Did you watch or listen to the debate between George Bush and Michael Dukakis?		
Watched debate (%)	48	45
Listened to debate (%)	2	2
Neither watched nor listened (%)	49	52
Not sure (%)	1	1
How much did this debate influence your decision concerning whom to support for president?		
High influence (6–10 on scale) (%)	33[a]	45[b]
Low influence (1–5 on scale) (%)	64	54
Mean score	4.7	5.3

Did you watch or listen to the debate between Lloyd Bentsen and Dan Quayle?	
Watched debate (%)	44
Listened to debate (%)	2
Neither watched nor listened (%)	54
How much did this debate influence your decision concerning whom to support for president?	
High influence (6–10 on scale) (%)	40[c]
Low influence (1–5 on scale) (%)	56
Mean score	5.1

Harris Survey 2; N=1,875; conducted 10/18–11/4/1988.
[a] Percentages based on the 913 who watched/heard this debate.
[b] Percentages based on the 862 who watched/heard this debate.
[c] Percentages based on the 845 who watched/heard this debate.

cism of media campaign coverage policy. Isn't it true, George Bush was asked, that Jimmy Carter, Richard Nixon, and Barry Goldwater have all said how awful the campaign has been and how little time has been given to the issues? Yes, responded Bush, but consider as an example what happened on my recent swing through Illinois, where I spoke extensively and even issued a position paper on the farm problem. The networks paid no attention to what I said about that issue. Instead, they concentrated on the slightest disparagement of me by Dukakis, of Dukakis by me, and most attention to the alleged disqualifications of Dan Quayle. Senator Goldwater reports from Arizona that we should be discussing the issues. Well, how does he know I have not been discussing the issues? If he watches the television news he will never discover that I have been talking about the issues (Buckley 1988:14A).

Did ABC "Prime" the Audience? If, as Table 5-15 suggests, television coverage of the second presidential debate represented the most-watched and perhaps the most influential event of the 1988 presidential campaign, then it is important to ask if anything about the coverage—whether organization, content, tone, or post-debate analysis—affected public assessments of the candidates.

The candidates themselves had placed tight restrictions on how the networks could operate, including who could pose questions, where the press would be seated, what kind of camera angles would be permitted, and the like. The restrictions were so pervasive that they prompted the League of Women Voters to withdraw its sponsorship of the debate. Said league president Nancy Newman, "The League of Women Voters is announcing today that we have no intention of becoming an accessory to the hoodwinking of the American public" (Curry 1988:1).

Restrictions notwithstanding, network news organizations remained free enough to take steps that many critics believed improperly influenced the debate audience. The first concerned the competitive balance between the candidates. On the eve of the October 13 debate, ABC gave extensive coverage on its evening newscast to its own fifty-state Electoral College poll that showed Dukakis trailing badly in the Electoral College, despite being relatively close in the popular vote polls. The message was visually reinforced with a large U.S. map in the background coloring most of the nation as Bush territory. Many observers felt that the timing of that poll not only discouraged potential Dukakis voters but also raised the stakes of the second debate dramatically, making it necessary for Dukakis to land a "knockout" punch in order to be judged the winner (Dionne 1988e:1)

The second step was to reintroduce the practice of picking debate winners and losers. The networks, stung by criticism in previous years that they had crossed the line of journalistic propriety by engaging in "instant analysis" of debate performances, had consciously avoided choosing winners in the first two 1988 candidate debates. But after the final presidential debate, NBC and ABC did call Bush the winner, while CBS and CNN were more reserved. Why the change in policy? Network journalists said that one reason was that the result seemed more obvious than debate outcomes usually do. It was also the case that ABC News was able to produce the results of an "instant poll," its own telephone survey, that gave the debate to Bush by a 49 to 33 percent margin (Andrew Rosenthal 1988a:8).

The ABC News "instant" poll was featured in newspapers around the country and helped to spread the perception that Bush had won the debate and most likely the election. The *Wall Street Journal/ NBC News* poll published five days later found that respondents were picking Bush as the debate winner by a better than 3-to-1 margin. Observed the author of the *Wall Street Journal* poll story: "[Our poll found] a wider margin than some surveys taken immediately after the debate, suggesting a 'ripple effect' as more and more news reports crown the vice president the winner" (Jaroslovsky 1988).

Conclusion

This chapter used the results of two random national telephone surveys to describe the state of the electorate's preparation to vote in the 1988 presidential election. To facilitate the evaluation that was the purpose of the research, normative questions about voters, candidates, and the news media, implicit in democratic theory, were raised wherever it was apparent that the survey evidence could be used to address them. The chapter's contents can be summarized by using its findings to address three major questions about the performance of the electoral triangle.

Did voters become sufficiently well informed about candidates and national priorities to make intelligent decisions? Tables 5-1 through 5-11, which together provide a detailed picture of what people knew, felt, and learned about these matters, suggest a negative answer. Voters knew little of the complex agenda that would face the next president and even less of what the candidates proposed to do about national problems. Their reports of what they had "learned" about the candidates suggest an inability to distinguish facts from self-interested candidate distortions. Only on the comparative strengths and weaknesses of the candidates as prospective leaders did voters seem to have developed informed impressions.

Did the presidential candidates use their platforms responsibly, clarifying national priorities and suggesting how they would address them? Data showing what voters did and did not learn (Tables 5-6 through 5-9), permit inferences about what candidates contributed to their enlightenment. Though both candidates took numerous positions on the issues, our evidence suggests that the most influential candidate messages had little or nothing to do with the next president's agenda.

Did the major print and broadcast news media operate both to inform the voters about issues and priorities and to protect them from candidate distortion and misinformation? Inferences from tables already mentioned, voter reactions to media coverage and the presidential candidate debates (Tables 5-12 through 5-15), and content-analysis data reported in Chapter 4 all signal important shortfalls in the media's collective contributions to an informed electorate.

Up next are the results of depth interviews conducted in the weeks preceding the 1988 election with small groups of voters in four states spanning the nation.

6. CITIZENS IN GROUPS

 A core feature of the new political technology is something called a "focus group." Eight to fifteen people gather around a table with a moderator who poses a series of questions about political topics of interest to whoever assembles and pays for the group. The result is a conversation that sheds a certain kind of light on what the voters are thinking.

What these group discussions do is put "a face and a voice to the often sterile and disconnected findings of large-sample surveys, as well as to illuminate hidden issues and suggest the 'why' behind commonly held beliefs or opinions" (Morin 1988a). Democratic pollster Stanley Greenberg elaborates: "In an age when voters are so fluid on matters of ideology and party, so much of getting the message right becomes a matter of tapping the right emotions and using the right language ... That's what focus groups get you that polls don't. You get the texture" (quoted in Taylor 1989:7).

For those who doubt whether much of value can be learned from such groups, consider this brief story. It is May 1988 in Paramus, New Jersey, a middle-income suburb near New York City. Five men—Bush campaign manager Lee Atwater, media consultant Roger Ailes, pollster Robert Teeter, chief of staff Craig L. Fuller, and senior adviser Nicholas F. Brady—huddle behind a one-way mirror that affords them a view of a group of ordinary citizens seated around a table. In search of ideas for the fall stretch drive of the presidential campaign, they are watching one of two focus groups of fifteen blue-collar and white-collar Democrats—all former Reagan supporters—assembled to talk about the probable issues of the fall campaign.

Bush campaign manager Lee Atwater reports that all thirty of the participants initially planned to vote for Dukakis. But after they were told about the Massachusetts governor's veto of a 1977 Pledge of Allegiance bill and the prison furlough program that let Willie Horton, a convicted murderer, escape to commit rape and assault, fully half became adamantly opposed to Dukakis. That was one of those "ah-hah!" moments, Atwater said later. "I realized right there that we had the wherewithal to win . . . and that the sky was the limit on Dukakis's negatives" (quoted in Taylor and Broder 1988). The winning themes for Campaign '88 had been discovered (Boyd 1988).

Purposes

This story illustrates the most clearly demonstrated value of focus groups, a technique invented in the private sector as a market research tool. It is to learn what works, and how it works, in the effort to sell a product. Whether the product is toothpaste or a presidential candidate, the principles are the same.

Understanding Influence

The Markle Commission used focus groups to learn more about how political influence worked in 1988. We sought a better understanding of the relationships between what the media covered (Chapter 4), what the candidates said, and what the mass electorate came to know and believe about the candidates and issues (Chapter 5).[1]

Content analysis showed that the media covered the political horse race and the ongoing war of words between the candidates, with lesser attention to qualifications, issues, and other matters. Our surveys suggested that, abetted by saturation media coverage of the strategic side of the contest, the most influential source of voter "learning" was the Bush campaign itself.

What could focus groups tell us of why this was the case? Why did some messages, like Bush's, get through, while others, notably Dukakis's, didn't, as paid candidate advertising, free media coverage, and daily interactions with others competed for the attention of our participants?

A related aim was to see if we could disentangle, impressionistically if not scientifically, the impacts of the different sources of influence from one another. We wanted a feel for the difference each made by itself, something that might emerge from careful listening.

Assessing Citizens' Potentials

Driving our efforts to understand political influence were several urgent questions about our discussants themselves. How seriously did they appear to take their civic responsibilities? Did they seem equal—in such terms as intelligence, preparation, and concern—to the demands made on citizens in the theory of democracy? Would they be able to handle increased civic demands? Under what conditions might they be willing to do so?

If improvement in the way Americans manage their democracy is to be seriously contemplated, then the "improvability" of ordinary citizens, often regarded as limited by pundits and analysts, deserved some rare, explicit attention.[2]

Another aim was to identify the kinds of assistance—more or better information, clearer or more thorough explanation, or simply exhortation and encouragement—people seemed to need from outside sources if they were to function at a level approaching their full capacity. This too required a sensitivity to how—and how well—group participants seemed to be coping with and using the campaign information that was bombarding them from all sides.

Finally, we kept in mind the classic focus-group question: what would it take to sell these people something? If the Markle Commission were to include citizens in a call for revitalization, what would it take to "sell" ordinarily disengaged Americans on the idea of getting a bit more politically involved and concerned? And what could the groups teach us of how to go about it?

Clearly, then, we brought a crowded agenda to the sessions we had convened to discuss the election. But group settings seemed especially promising places to explore these interconnected questions.[3] In the same sense that watching presidential candidates "think on their feet" during debates reveals much of relevance to their fitness, so, it seemed, would observing citizens grapple with questions about the presidential campaign. As will be apparent after a brief methodological digression, we were not disappointed.

The Research

The use of focus groups here differs from typical practice in two important ways. First, we conducted sixteen groups instead of just one or two. We wanted sufficient geographic and demographic diversity to support a claim that our findings are, while in no sense statistically representative, at least substantially more characteristic of the American electorate as a whole than results drawn from a single group conducted in one location could hope to be.[4]

Even more important, we wanted our exposure to people to be sustained and varied enough to protect against overreaction to particular individuals or groups as we sought answers to our questions.

Table 6-1. *Markle Focus Groups: Sites, Dates, and Participants*

Wave[a]	1	2	3	4
Westchester, N.Y.	12	12	9	12
Sacramento, Calif.	12	9	12	12
Houston, Tex.	12	[b]	11	[b]
Chicago, Ill.	12	12	12	12
(Total participants=161)				

[a]Wave dates: 1=9/19–22/88; 2=10/3–6/88; 3=10/17–20/88; 4=10/31–11/3/88.
[b]The first and third Houston group participants also participated in Waves 2 and 4, respectively.

Second, our research questions made it necessary to schedule our groups over a period of time, rather than all at once. Only thus would it be possible to examine how the succession of emergent events or influence attempts—candidate debates, political advertising, candidate gaffes, unexpected disclosures—affected people. And only by meeting with some groups more than once could we get any cross-time perspective on the learning capacities of our participants.[5]

Sixteen group sessions were conducted in four waves of four each, every two weeks, between Labor Day and election day, in all four major regions of the country, and involving a total of 161 people.[6] Table 6-1 gives the dates, regions, and number of participants for each of the groups.[7]

Results

The analysis and presentation of qualitative results does not build on numbers, graphs, and charts. It builds on questions, in this case about how citizens are, and might be, influenced. Our approach is to blend insights harvested from the groups with other information relevant to our questions.[8]

Some Preliminary Facts about Citizens

We start with certain baseline facts, observations, and truisms about people, as human beings and as political actors, that affect how they are influenced.

First is the obvious: people are creatures who simultaneously think, feel, and believe. That is, they display mental (thinking, analysis, logic), emotional (feeling, sensing, intuition), and ideological (valuative, preferential, judgmental) orientations toward politics as toward other life experience.

This complex human wiring influences how media and candidates fashion their messages. It affects how receptive people are to particular messages. And it also clearly affects the nature and quality of decision-making about important topics like the choice between presidential candidates (Hogarth 1987).

Democratic theories, theories of human development, and theories of educational practice have all concluded that the optimal mode for important decision-making is rational-cognitive (cold reasoning) and that emotions (hot reasoning) and ideological beliefs (coded reasoning) reduce the accuracy of information processing to the detriment of objectivity and other rational analytic virtues.[9]

But strong emotions and beliefs will usually prevail unless there is some commitment to "responsible" analysis prior to judgment.[10] Perhaps the clearest example in our focus groups of how thinking and feeling got mixed together in practice came in response to the question, "What have you learned about Michael Dukakis and George Bush?"

Despite being carefully prompted to do so, people rarely distinguished what they had "learned" about the candidates from what they "felt" (i.e., liked or disliked) about them. In group after group, the learning question evoked lists of feeling-tinged reasons for preferring one over the other: "I dislike Dukakis on abortion," or "Bush raises no issues, he just slams Dukakis on harbor pollution and the ACLU," to cite just two examples from the final Chicago group.[11]

Beliefs figured prominently as well. Their power to orient and simplify was especially evident in the prominence a great many of our discussants gave to party identification. Apparent in the results of the surveys as well (Table 5-5), party identification remains a pervasive influence that cuts across age, education, and styles of political reasoning.

Party's significance as an influence varied from a lightly held value preference that did not inhibit reason or responsiveness to new information, on the one hand, to a mindless kind of dogmatism that rendered all information but the party affiliation of the candidate virtually irrelevant. Barbara (NY2)[12] illustrates the first: "I'm not a die-hard Republican [but I like] lower taxes, lower unemployment . . . If Democrats are in, it's goodies for all. Taxes will go up either way . . ." Thelma, of the second Chicago group, is an example of the second: "I'm a Democrat . . . I follow the party line . . ."

Even those who did not avow partisanship used such labels to make sense of the voting choice. Said, for example, C4's Vickie: "I dislike both [candidates] but will support Dukakis because he talks about small persons, and because Bush is too conservative . . ." As Nancy (NY4) sagely put it: "We see through the eyes of our preferences."

Our second baseline observation concerns the people in our groups. They tended to fall into three broad "types" according to how they used information and responded to influence attempts. Each type seemed to assign slightly different priorities to thinking, feeling, and believing. And each also differed in awareness of and efforts to correct for their own biases.

These differences matter here because varying approaches to reasoning and using information lead to differing degrees of hopefulness about democracy. Thus, the greater the proportion of citizens who fit the "judicious" type (whose characteristics are implicit in the label, though described in detail later), the better; and the more that fit the "closed" category, the less the prospects for any significant improvement. Toward the end of the chapter we look at the types and speculate about how their distribution in the voting population might affect the prospects for upgrading the electorate's civic preparation.

The third baseline fact concerns a well-established attribute of the American people that was apparent even in groups made up of the better-educated, as ours were. Most Americans simply do not care very much or know a lot about government and politics. Many group participants conceded that they were not paying continuous, intense attention to the campaign or to public affairs in general. Indifference to such matters is in fact pervasive among all but a small slice of the population. In sociological language, it is a problem of "unsupportive norms."

Americans are locally rather than nationally oriented.[13] This is well illustrated by the typical group answers to our question "What are the most important changes the next president will need to make for the good of the country?" Many people mentioned the need to reduce the budget deficit, which news reports were trumpeting as what the experts agreed the next president needed to do first. But most did not respond in terms of a national agenda for which the president is uniquely responsible. Instead they spoke in terms of the problems most visible to them in their local settings.

The list drawn up by the third Houston group makes the point: "attack the drug problem . . . force educational policy down to the local level . . . concentrate on early education . . . give us back the jobs and benefits we used to have . . . encourage a revitalized family . . . put criminals to work . . . do something for those without medical coverage . . ." Such lists were typical. The discussions that produced them made it plain that most participants had no sharply etched concept of what were and were not federal-level problems, or where and how the presidency fit into the problem-solving process.

Localism and political indifference have several major consequences. The immediate result is that most Americans are astonishingly ignorant of basic facts about the national government and of their rights and responsibilities as citizens in a representative democracy.[14]

A related consequence is that political candidates can and do exploit public ignorance with misleading advertising and appeals to emotion, as was obvious in 1988.

Still another impact is on the contents of the media's political coverage. News organizations respond to the public's lack of political interest by moving election (and other political) coverage away from the policy issues and factual details the audience finds boring, and toward those aspects of the contest—conflicts, contests, and personalities—ordinary Americans find more interesting.[15]

A final result is that in the absence of crisis, Americans are generally unresponsive to calls for political attention, sacrifice, or improvement.[16]

How could people with such characteristics ever be persuaded to invest time and energy in civic retooling and upgrading? Attention to that question is saved for last. But we can bring this opening review of the basics to a close on a hopeful note.

There is a growing body of evidence that Americans feel affectionate toward the nation and dutiful toward their obligations as citizens. Herbert J. Gans (1988:61–62) summarizes the evidence suggesting the existence of an idealized "love" of the nation.[17] Voting studies since The American Voter (Campbell et al. 1960) have uncovered a "sense of citizen duty" that leads even those who report minimal concern about elections and low political interest to vote in respectable numbers. High percentages of the respondents to our national surveys and our focus-group questionnaires (see Tables 6-3 and 5-2) said that voting was important to them and expressed interest in presidential politics. And compared to citizens in other industrialized democracies, Americans are better educated, more interested in politics, and more likely to engage in political discussion and volunteer work (Powell 1986:19).

Politicians from George Washington to George Bush have recognized and manipulated the emotional power of patriotic symbols like the flag. Evoking and harnessing usually latent patriotic sentiments to civic improvement projects (instead of some candidate's political fortunes) has rarely been tried outside of crisis circumstances. But should the need be perceived, the potential is there.

Sources of Political Influence

The *Random House Unabridged Dictionary* defines *influence* as "The capacity or power of persons or things to be a compelling force on or produce effects on the actions, behavior, opinions, etc. of others." How, then, do politically inattentive but generally patriotic citizens, whose thinking is as often driven by feelings and beliefs as by logic, respond to political influence?

The Media. It is often assumed that the media can have dramatic impacts on the evaluative dispositions of voters. For example, a front-page *New York Times* story about a 1988 poll showing George Bush to have overtaken Michael Dukakis opines: "the findings illustrate the powerful effect the nationally televised conventions have in influencing public opinion, even in a case such as this where Mr. Bush's strong acceptance speech and other upbeat events had to compete for attention with the controversy over his selection of Mr. Quayle" (Oreskes 1988a).

Directly and indirectly, the media dominate and saturate the political stimulus field. David Broder's previously quoted words bear repeating: "Most of the campaign is out of the voters' sight. Some voters may glimpse a presidential candidate for a half hour in their hometown, but most will get almost everything they know about those candidates indirectly through the media" (Broder, 1987a:274).

The people we talked to almost invariably believed that media had a pervasive impact on how they viewed the campaign and the political world. Many echoed Broder's point that media are the sole source of information available to most. As Loren of S3 put it: "If all we know is media, we have to rely on it and tend to believe it . . ." And Ruth, H2: "All I know is what I read or see. The media thus *dictates* what I know." The second Houston group vote was typical. By a margin of 11 to 1 they concluded that media have various important impacts, including influencing votes.

There was, however, no sense of alarm that their views of the world were being subtly influenced by forces beyond their control. The media's influence was generally seen as random and unplanned, rather than systematic and ideological; side effects of an effort to supply the news in a way that attracts readers and viewers.

DETERMINANTS OF MEDIA AND OTHER INFLUENCE

Media and other influences have selective impacts. The 1988 campaign was filled with examples of selective public attention and influence. Some things, like Bush advertising, or media coverage of the budget deficit, clearly got through to the general public (Chapter 5). Other things, like most candidate issue positions, media horse-race coverage (discussed below), or Dukakis advertising, had much less impact.

In one way or another, these differences can be traced to the complex human wiring discussed earlier. Factors like party identification, political interest, knowledge, uncertainty, and emotional salience have all been suggested as plausible explanations for variations in influence. The clarity of an influence attempt can also make a difference, as in the contrast between crisp Bush and confusing Dukakis advertising. So can the public's readiness to hear a particular message, clear or not.

A public generally content with the political and economic status quo may simply have been more responsive to the messages of its representative, George Bush, than to the messages of his less familiar challenger. That appeared to be the case in the groups. Such receptivity may operate independently of the content of the message. That would help explain why such seemingly peripheral matters as Bush's stand on capital punishment became so widely known, while the Dukakis position on a matter of presumably more direct concern to average voters, like universal health care, was far less familiar (Table 5-7).

ATTITUDES TOWARD MEDIA

Similarly, attitudes toward the media might affect the influence media exert, particularly if people regard media coverage with suspicion. That was not the case here, however, as group participants' overall dispositions were positive. Opinion ranged between mild dissatisfaction and clear satisfaction. Even the most critical groups took pains to conclude that American media are as good as any, or that given the constraints they face, they do as well as could be expected. Every group produced a majority show of hands indicating belief that the media were doing a generally good job. There was no sense of a special need to be vigilant against media influence.[18]

That is not to say they didn't have criticisms. Most focused on sensationalism, excessive prying into candidates' private lives, and frivolous coverage. Participants were asked for examples of "good" and "bad" coverage. Examples of "bad" coverage included staking out Gary Hart's house and similar personal intrusions, network stories about hecklers at a campaign speech rather than coverage of the speech itself, overkill coverage of Bush's selection of Dan Quayle as his running mate, and extensive coverage of media-commissioned polls and of staged "photo opportunities" like Bush's visit to the flag factory and the Dukakis tank ride.

Also criticized was the preoccupation with candidate conflicts. Said one man, pointing to the extensive media attention given to Democratic vice-presidential candidate Lloyd Bentsen's unfavorable comparison of Dan Quayle with John F. Kennedy: "They seem excessively interested in who can sling the most mud and make the other guy look worse."

Participants complained frequently (although specifics were almost never given) about the mixing of fact and opinion in media coverage. There was a widespread sense that all journalists let at least some subjectivity creep into their work, but that there are no ideological conspiracies, and the media do not lean systematically one way or the other. The few participants who did see systematic bias suggested it was politically to the left. Almost all agreed that media coverage of the campaign was "fair." Some suggested that it was necessary to consult a variety of sources so that the various points of view could be weighed.

A strong minority view was that television journalists in particular too often overstepped the bounds of neutrality, as when Dan Rather debated George Bush, or when Sam Donaldson editorialized on the remarks of one or the other candidate. Relatedly, many people did not like being told what to think, or how to interpret what they had seen, as with post-debate "spin doctors."

GROUP CONCEPTS OF THE MEDIA'S ROLE

The foregoing prompted criticism because the people in our groups turn to newspaper and television accounts of the campaign primarily to get information about what is happening. When we asked our groups what the media should try to do during a presidential campaign, the most frequent response was "provide well-rounded, thorough, and unbiased coverage." Many said they did not like it when the facts were glossed with interpretation or opinion. Some even argued that newspapers should not endorse candidates on their editorial pages because doing so compromises their objectivity.[19]

In light of Chapter 2's solemn discussion of media responsibilities for informing and protecting the electorate in a democracy, these are surprisingly limited expectations. Concepts of the press as "democracy's watchdog" figured only marginally in the expectations expressed by the people in these groups. More frequent were tolerant comments suggesting that the media covered what they covered in order to attract viewers or sell newspapers, or because of manipulation by the candidates and their handlers. There was no evidence of a deeply rooted, widely shared conviction that the news media had any special obligations to educate, uplift, inspire, or protect voters.

For example, one media service most ardently approved in the theory of democracy is vigilance against the misstatements of candidates. There was a limited amount of such coverage in the final months of the '88 campaign (see Chapter 4). One study found that in the 126 network news broadcasts that excerpted political commercials in 1988, the television reporter addressed the truthfulness of the commercial's claims less than 8 percent of the time (Broder 1989e). If our focus groups were any indication, such surveillance was not expected and little noticed. Only two men, one a participant in the second Houston group, the other in the final New York group, mentioned having seen and been impressed by television tapes showing the candidates contradicting themselves.[20] The New Yorker balanced his praise with a little criticism: "The side-by-side comparison of false ads was a service the media provided. [But] their daily coverage doesn't come to grips with issues. You really have to dig to learn the candidates' positions. This *should* be a media responsibility."

EVIDENCE OF MEDIA INFLUENCE

We assessed the extent of media influence by watching for indirect evidence of it while other matters were under discussion, and also by asking about it directly near the end of each meeting. The use of facts obtained from the media was the clearest evidence of media influence the groups displayed. Every participant made use of facts or examples that could only have come from exposure to television or newspapers. Too, there was frequent use of specific media stories as authoritative support for a particular argument or point of view someone was pressing. Mike (NY3), for example, used a *Newsweek* story showing that Quayle and Bentsen had voted the same on thirty-one of forty issues to buttress his argument that Bentsen's debate attack on Quayle for, among other things, the latter's voting record, was not persuasive. Earnie (H3) made similar but less specific use of a *Time* magazine background article on Dukakis that he avowed had "turned him off" the Massachusetts governor.

Other effects were likely to be more subtle. But since the daily exposure of most individuals to television and newspaper election coverage is fairly extensive, and since campaign coverage does fall into certain repetitious patterns (e.g., horse race, conflicts, qualifications, etc., Table 4-1) they figured to be substantial.

Our search for media and other influence focused on areas related to the aspirations of democratic theory. What, for example, did our discussants know and believe about issues and candidate qualifications? And from where did such knowledge and beliefs seem to come?

AGENDA SETTING

Knowledge of the policy agenda facing the nation is something responsible citizens are supposed to have. The role of the media in general and particularly television news in communicating an agenda had already been suggested by experimental research (Iyengar and Kinder 1987). What such research had not clarified, however, is how media agenda-setting power compares with, or interacts with, alternative sources of influence. Our findings on agenda setting, which make use of group votes, were interesting for the light shed on such competing influences.

We asked every group to formulate a list of the next president's most important problems, and to identify (by vote) a small handful of top priorities. The most frequently mentioned presidential priorities in the combined groups were the budget deficit, drugs, health care, education, and avoiding taxes, in that order.

The interesting fact is that the different influences at work in the Campaign '88 political environment—media, candidates, and the grass roots—were all sending somewhat different agenda-setting messages.

The news media gave substantial attention to the budget deficit, repeatedly trumpeting the bipartisan consensus among economic experts that it was the nation's most pressing problem. The candidates ducked the issue because it spotlighted choices—cut popular spending and/or raise taxes—inimical to their chances for victory (see Chapter 4). Since ordinary citizens heard little from the candidates and had no direct experience with deficit pain in their daily lives to increase the issue's salience, it is clear ipso facto that media coverage was the source of the top priority the groups attached to the deficit.

As for drugs, the elite media initially sniffed at the issue, regarding it as a sub-presidential problem (Why There Are No Issues 1988).

News organizations were, however, eventually compelled by public opinion polls and by the candidates—first Jesse Jackson and eventually George Bush—to cover drugs as a major campaign issue. That coverage, plus televised candidate advertising, helped keep the issue's priority high in the public mind. But it was citizen alarm at highly visible drug abuse at the grass roots level that put the issue on the agenda in the first place.

Health care and education, the third and fourth priorities in the groups, were also highly visible issues in the daily lives of many voters that candidates and media began to emphasize in response to public concern. The fifth priority, avoiding taxes, was a perennial political winner with voters that Vice President Bush's repetitious "read my lips, no new taxes" pledge turned into perhaps the campaign's biggest cliché.

The obvious conclusion is that no single source of influence set the entire priority agenda for these people. Instead, candidates and media, together with personal observation and experience, all seem to have played important parts in driving one or another of these five issues to the top of the list. With only one exception, it is hard to disentangle or rank order the impact of particular influences on the perceived importance of particular issues.

That exception is the media's impact on the perceived importance of the budget deficit. This is one of the clearest illustrations of media influence to emerge from the groups and from our national survey results as well (see Table 5-6). Media influence on this issue can be isolated because no other influence center was pressing to keep the deficit alive in the public mind. The media taught the public to regard the deficit as the most important problem facing the nation.

Interestingly, very little paid political advertising dealt with any of these issues. Of the five, only the drug problem figured significantly in ad campaigns. Heavily advertised issues, such as crime, pollution, and liberal permissiveness, were indeed mentioned in the groups as worthy of presidential attention. But none was as frequently voted among the top priorities by the group as the five issues above.

That reveals something important. While advertising was noticed and certainly had some impact on our participants (see below), it did not wield enough power to push an issue to the top of their priorities. Like the saturation media coverage of the Quayle selection discussed in Chapter 5, then, the advertised agenda does not automatically overpower or even necessarily "register" with the audience. It will be noticed. But to be powerfully influential, it must reinforce dispositions already at work in people's minds.

PRIMING

A phenomenon called "priming" is regarded by some researchers as "more insidious and perhaps more consequential than agenda setting" (Iyengar and Kinder 1987:4). They explain it this way: ". . . when evaluating complex political objects [such as] the promises of a presidential contender . . . citizens do not (because they cannot) take into account all they know . . . What they do is consider what comes to mind, those bits and pieces of political memory that are accessible. And television news . . . is a most powerful force determining what springs to the citizen's mind and what does not. *By priming certain aspects of national life while ignoring others, television news sets the terms by which political judgments are rendered and political choices made*" (ibid.:4; emphasis in original).

The authors go on to show (in experiments with Yale undergraduates) that when a news broadcast encouraged viewers to regard the president as responsible for a particular problem, that problem figured prominently in their assessments of the president.

These researchers do not explicitly address it in their experiments, but one of the most important potentials for priming during American presidential election seasons is the pervasive media coverage of the political horse-race aspects of the campaign. We saw in Table 4-1 that more than half of 1988's post-Labor Day media campaign coverage dealt with the ongoing strategic contest between the candidates, while only about 30 percent of the coverage centered on issues and candidate qualifications for office.

Horse-race coverage concentrates on who is winning or losing and not on who is qualified to be president. But it might easily be misconstrued as somehow relevant to deciding who ought to be elected. Its very pervasiveness and prominence could lead readers and viewers to assume that the strategic political contest is a worthy test of suitability for office, and that the shrewdest campaigner with the most effective strategy, advisors, and advertising is best equipped to govern.[21] If we found that a sizable portion of group participants tended to appraise candidates in such terms, it would suggest a political horse-race priming effect.

It is noteworthy, then, that this was not a prominent feature of the evaluative commentary we heard. Assessments of Bush and Dukakis only rarely focused on how well or poorly each man's campaign was going. There were occasional remarks showing that the horse-race coverage had penetrated the speaker's thinking. Said, for example, Barbara, at the final Sacramento group: "[Dukakis's] California campaign is not well managed . . . He hasn't used [his] opportunities to score against Bush." Or another woman's comment (Donna, NY3) that "[the] media goes with the winner . . ."

Much more common were assessments of character, competence, and issue position: the very criteria discussed in Chapter 2 as most relevant to an appraisal of presidential candidates. In the case of George Bush, the two most frequently mentioned evaluative criteria involved his prior government experience and the light shed on the Bush character by his selection of Dan Quayle as running mate. As for Dukakis, it was his issue stands, particularly on crime and abortion, that attracted the most attention (a demonstration, no doubt, of the power of Bush advertising), although his lack of charisma was frequently mentioned as well.

The horse-race coverage was noticed, inasmuch as complaints about the media's preoccupation with campaign hoopla were numerous. But as with other input they deemed irrelevant to their needs, people seemed impervious to its influence.

This is not to say there were no indications of priming or related influences. Our direct questions about media influence yielded numerous examples. A few people actually complained of being "brainwashed," in ways that hint at priming, by the media. For example, Denise, NY2: "I came to hate Gary Hart because I heard about him [i.e., his imprudent behavior with Donna Rice] so much . . . The media made that an issue . . . that made me hate Hart . . . [they] made me believe character was the issue." Or Gloria, NY2: "[Media coverage constitutes a] slow brainwash when they show it over and over on purpose."

Such recognition of the influence power of repetition was quite common. One clear instance of this power noticed by some and evinced unintentionally by others involved implanting and reinforcing stereotypes. Stereotypes are cognitive simplifiers. All people seek simple and fixed ways of understanding things that reduce the demands for analysis. And media, by frequent repetition of certain conventional wisdoms, offer what amounts to a stereotyping service.

Houston participant Jerry (H4) advanced a plausible explanation of how the process works: "The media create stereotypes with adjectives." The "experienced Bush," and the "unemotional Dukakis" are examples of media-reinforced stereotypes about the candidates that were encountered repeatedly in the groups.

Also apparent was the influence power of suggestion. Merely hearing or seeing something, not even necessarily from a particularly credible source, can plant an idea that hadn't occurred before, but that takes root and exerts influence. Suggested Marg (S3), a random comment or interpretation "can sway your thinking ... get you thinking in a new way, when at first you didn't take it that way ..." But the more credible the influence, the greater, perhaps, the suggestive power. As Faye (NY3) put it, "If you like a political commentator, you may take on [his] views ..."

Our discussants unknowingly echoed various findings of social psychological research in noting that other nonrational media influences were also significant.[22] "Camera angles, tall versus short, all might influence ...," continued Faye. Or (Steve, NY3) someone may "vote for who Clint Eastwood likes ..." Said Tony (NY3), "TV lets you be swayed by looks and personality ..." And Sheila (NY3), "People are easily swayed by glitter ..." Loren (S3) entered a vote for the emotional power of media entertainment: "I love to watch a liar squirm on TV."

Why are such seemingly irrelevant factors capable of exerting influence? One reason was suggested by Syl of S3: "Influence depends on audience and topic ... [many can be affected] *emotionally*, especially with negatives ..." It is true that television offers a unique opportunity to make what are essentially emotional decisions about candidates. As Alton (S4) put it, "[TV is] a vehicle we use to determine if we like someone or not."

Under what conditions will nonrational factors be influential? People in a state of indecision may be particularly susceptible. "The press has a lot of power because there are so many undecided people," said Jerry (H3). Too, people who lack information have been shown to be influenced more—by political advertising as well as by the sort of random, nonrational influences described above—than the better informed (Joslyn 1985).

Many if not most participants conceded that they were not paying close attention to the campaign, tending instead to tune in and out sporadically. Such attention patterns favor nonrational influences, and particularly emotionally evocative ones. "You just absorb it," suggested a Houston man.

Political Advertising. Except for an understandable interest in what does and doesn't attract readers and viewers, news editors and producers do not seem to dwell much on how their news products affect the audience. Media influences like priming, agenda setting, or stereotyping are significant but unintentional byproducts of news coverage managed with other ends in mind.

This is in striking contrast to the deliberate and highly specific persuasion attempts built into political advertising. Ads are carefully targeted to evoke the urgent concerns of specific voting groups. And they are crafted to generate emotional momentum away from one candidate and toward another. These design characteristics are important reasons for the influence power that ads can wield.

THE POWER OF REPETITION

Still more important, however, is the fact that ads are repeated relentlessly. Because of this, exposure to them is for all intents and purposes involuntary and unavoidable. Every member of our groups had seen or heard about the Bush furlough and Boston Harbor ads. Most had seen many other ads as well. Discussants were well aware, as a Houston man put it, that "political ads hit home by repetition." Said a New Yorker (Eric, NY2): "Boston Harbor . . . I see it so much it sticks in my head . . ."

The first paid television appearance by a presidential candidate was made by Harry S. Truman in 1948, but the kind of paid television advertising seen in 1988 did not emerge until the 1960's (Jamieson 1984:35). Research on the effects of political advertising is still developing, but that available finds what would be expected: that citizens' awareness and perceptions of candidates' policy preferences are positively related to frequency of viewing spot ads, and that citizens with low political interest may be affected by such ads more than those with high political interest, who may already know something about the candidates and their policy positions (Joslyn 1985:195–205; Atkin and Heald 1976). One canny focus group participant, C4's John, put it simply: "The less you know, the more ads will influence you."

Experimental research from the 1988 campaign has shown what less scientific observers already knew: that Bush ads had more impact than Dukakis ads. One study found, for example, that Bush political advertising influenced subjects' attention, memory, and laboratory decision-making significantly more than did Dukakis advertising (Schleuder, McCombs, and Wanta 1989).

BUSH ADS DOMINANT

Unquestionably, Bush campaign ads, and particularly the negative ads dealing with Massachusetts prison furloughs, Dukakis's weaknesses in national defense (the tank ad), and Boston Harbor pollution, had a dramatic effect on the people in our groups. This was most apparent in responses to the question we posed about each

candidate early in every group session, well before any explicit discussion of campaign advertising was introduced: "What have you
learned about (name of candidate) that may affect how you will
vote?" Most striking was the proportion of negative things "learned"
about Dukakis that could be traced to Bush advertising.

Content analysis of focus-group audio tapes showed that 155 of
430 "learning" comments about Dukakis (some 36 percent) were
negative. Of the 155 negative comments, 88, or 57 percent, were
traceable to (or at least consistent with) Bush campaign advertising.
These included statements like "Dukakis would slow the development of national defense," or that he was "responsible for the foul
state of Boston Harbor." Denise of NY2 said she'd learned that the
prison furlough matter was a liability for Dukakis and (like Donna
of NY4) that Dukakis had failed to clean up Boston Harbor.

Other such comments featured the American Civil Liberties
Union, the Massachusetts furlough program, capital punishment,
crime, Dukakis's veto of a Pledge of Allegiance measure, gun control, and liberalism. Tony (NY3) summed it up just as George Bush
did in his campaign speeches: "Dukakis is very liberal . . ."

Of course the free media, which in 1988 paid unprecedented attention to campaign advertising (see Chapter 4) reiterated many
Bush themes, thereby magnifying their influence. David Broder reports that Harvard media researcher Kidu Adatto found that "although excerpts from candidates' commercials appeared on the network evening news programs three times in the 1968 presidential
campaign, such excerpts were shown 126 times" during the 1988
campaign (Broder 1989e).

But the point to be made here is that the themes originated in paid
political advertising. Repetitive advertising plus media coverage
was enough to insure their "sticking" sufficiently to be mentioned
in response to our questions. This evidence plus the survey results
found in Table 5-9 show clearly that Bush advertising was the
most influential educational force at work in the 1988 presidential
campaign.

The evidence of advertising's influence supplied by the "learning"
question was unobtrusive. That is, people were not reflecting on
whether advertising had influenced them, but instead were unconsciously and unintentionally demonstrating it in the process of discussing what they thought was something else, well before the subject of advertising came up for explicit discussion.

But 1988's political ads were eventually subjects for discussion
in each of the groups, and many people acknowledged advertising's
impact on themselves or those close to them. Said, for example,

Steve (NY2): "TV is unbelievably powerful . . . If [a] commercial [is] well-done, I'll remember . . . Bush Boston Harbor debris influenced me . . . unbelievably persuasive . . ."

Even children took note. One young father (David, C4) reported being shocked when his four-year-old son came to him and said that "Dukakis is bad."

"Why?" asked David.

"Dirty river," replied the son.

After reflecting a while on her earlier testimony that she had learned that Dukakis was a liberal and an ACLU member, Stephanie (C4) ruefully concluded: "We're victims of TV ads."

SOME FOUND ADS USEFUL

Not everyone felt victimized. A few of our participants made cogent arguments about the relevance of ads to assessing suitability for the presidency. A Houston man, for example, said he had supported Dukakis originally, but changed because the furlough of Willie Horton showed Dukakis to be *stupid*, capable of a degree of innocence not to be countenanced in the presidency. Another man (Richard, NY4) took Bush advertising about Dukakis's failure to support the Pledge of Allegiance as evidence of Bush's concern for national unity and for the values of America's children. To him, the pledge was a fine thing. In the final Chicago group, no less than seven of twelve participants said they had learned something useful from ads.[23]

DO ADS UNDERMINE THE PROCESS?

On the whole, however, group participants regarded campaign advertising, and particularly negative advertising, as a net minus. Opinions about the negative tone of the campaign in the groups paralleled what national opinion polls were showing at the time. Discussing the results of a *Washington Post*-ABC News poll of 1,009 likely voters conducted October 26–31, 1988, Richard Morin notes: "More than 80 percent of voters surveyed said Bush and Dukakis spent more time 'attacking each other' than discussing the important issues . . . Three out of four Republicans and Democrats agreed that the current campaign had been more negative than previous presidential contests. Three of five said Bush had waged a 'dirty' campaign, while two of five said the same of Dukakis" (Morin 1988b).

Participants in focus groups conducted by the *Wall Street Journal* expressed sentiments similar to those in the Markle groups: "One thing that both men and women in the groups agree on . . . is a strong dislike for the negative tone adopted by the candidates of late. Both groups implore the contenders to ease off on the personal criticisms and focus on more substantive issues" (McQueen 1988).

A good many of the Markle group participants expressed sympathy with the idea of restricting or banning negative ads. This sentiment squares with communications research, where a consistent finding has been that people don't like negative ads, whether they "work" or not (Shapiro and Rieger 1989; Garramone 1984). Interestingly, this is just as true of commercial as it is of political advertising. Specialists on managing corporate images say that when competitors tear each other apart in comparative advertising, as for example Burger King and Wendy's (Where's the Beef?) have done for years against other fast-food chains, it tends to hurt the reputation of the whole industry (Schwadel 1989). "Consistently for the last decade, two thirds of a national sample of consumers have agreed with the statement that commercials are insulting to the intelligence" (Thorson 1989:195).

The impact of campaign advertising on actual voting is notoriously hard, if not impossible, to demonstrate unequivocally. Still, like our focus-group participants, politicians, political consultants, and journalists believe that ads influence votes. And most of the books and articles on the 1988 election published before this book show their authors to be convinced that negative advertising played a large role in the election's outcome.

OTHER RELEVANT RESEARCH

But at what price? An interesting study conducted by Michael A. Shapiro and Robert H. Rieger of Cornell University sheds relevant light. These researchers attempted to isolate advertising's impacts by conducting an experimental simulation in which people were exposed to contrived "positive" and "negative" political advertising campaigns and asked to "vote" by evaluating the candidates associated with the advertising. This experiment was the first to directly compare similar positive and negative ads.

The situation was unrealistic, in that participants in the experiment knew nothing of the fictitious "candidates," who were invented for the research, except for the information presented in two parallel sets of television ads. But the study's results suggest interesting possibilities concerning how advertising may affect the attitudes and behavior of voters in the real world.

In one version of the ads, the sponsoring candidates stressed their own positive qualifications. In the other version, the ads featured an attack by their sponsor on the opponent. Some positive and negative ads featured substantive issues, while others (also including both positive and negative ads) focused on image and personality.

The results showed that when the negative ads dealt with substantive issues, the ad sponsor came out ahead of the ad target in the voters' judgment. This finding is consistent with what political practitioners believe: negative advertising that deals with what voters regard as a relevant campaign issue can work to the advantage of the sponsor.

But even though the sponsor obtained a comparative advantage, participants in the experiment rated *both* candidates lower when the sponsoring candidate used a negative ad. And when the negative ad featured a personal attack rather than a substantive issue, the voters rated the sponsor lower than the target (Shapiro and Rieger 1989).

These findings suggest the downside of negative advertising both for those who use them and for the larger political process. Negative advertising can backfire on the sponsor if voters perceive the attack to be too personal, or otherwise unfair. But even when, as in the 1988 presidential race, the negative ad buys one candidate a comparative advantage, the net reduction in respect for both candidates may trigger a corresponding disenchantment with the larger political process.

This scenario offers a plausible explanation for the results of a *Wall Street Journal*-NBC poll conducted about two weeks before the 1988 election. The poll, which began on October 14, documented an almost "exact reversal" of earlier public sentiment in showing that by a 57 to 38 percent margin, likely voters had become displeased with the choice between Bush and Dukakis, and with the campaign itself.

What had happened to create voter dissatisfaction with the choice of candidates and with the campaign? GOP attacks on his liberalism and policy record had succeeded in tarnishing Dukakis to such an astonishing extent that "substantially more voters now have an unfavorable opinion of him than have a favorable one 50 to 36 percent" (Jaroslovsky 1988). Bush had come from behind to gain a significant advantage. But the attack strategy that helped make the turnaround possible also alienated significant portions of the electorate from the campaign as well as the candidates.

The consensus testimony of all the Markle groups converged on three similar conclusions: First, that Bush and Dukakis were not the best candidates either party had to offer. Many agreed with Mike (NY3): "I can't believe these are the two best candidates!" Second was disenchantment with the tone of the campaign. Said Judy (NY4): "Bush lacks integrity [in that he permitted] a mudslinging campaign." Or Pat (NY4): "Bush panders to superficial issues." Third was the tendency to avoid the tough issues. Phil (NY4) put it well: "Bush shows a great concern for the tangential."

An outspoken minority of our focus-group discussants also expressed great disdain for attack advertising. Phil (of NY4) may have been the most eloquent: "Ads suspend all rules of fairness and integrity. The whole notion of dealing with complex issues in thirty or sixty seconds is absurd." Agreed Nancy, seated across the table: "Ads are selling, and that's bad."

Candidate Debates.   The three 1988 candidate debates drew the opposite reaction. Judging from the enthusiastic response of our focus groups, they were the high point of an otherwise uninspiring campaign. People often referred to them as the single most relevant and valuable source of information about the candidates. Many asserted that things they had learned in the debates would be decisive in their voting decisions. What did the debates offer that people found so valuable?

Most frequently mentioned were insights into various personal qualities of the hopefuls. Said Marvin (NY4), for example: "Bush impressed me in the debates . . . he's not afraid of a fight." And Carol (S4): "I'm a Democrat, but the debates turned me [toward Bush] . . . Bush appeared more honest."

Mike (NY3) felt he had learned enough to form both personal and policy conclusions about Michael Dukakis: "Two things in the last debate turned me off . . . when asked what he would do if his wife were raped, [Dukakis showed] no emotion . . . [and] he'd give up too many military weapons . . ."

Stephanie (S4) got a sense of which was the most realistic candidate ("The debates showed that Bush was more informed, and that Dukakis was too 'pie in the sky.' Where would he get the money . . . ?"). She also expressed the view that the debates offer a more credible source of information than the media: "The media knew about [John F.] Kennedy's shenanigans, but they didn't tell us. That is frightening . . . The debates are all we can trust."

The debates as political spectacles seemed to enliven others, and to heighten their interest in the election: "I found the Bentsen-Quayle debate entertaining . . . should have more debates" (Steve, S4).

And they offered something otherwise nearly unattainable during a campaign season: "I liked the debates because they gave me a chance to compare [the candidates]" (John, C4). They not only afforded the chance to compare the candidates directly, but to do so in the least rehearsed, least edited, and least controlled setting of the campaign ". . . because you see them live, unrehearsed, and on-the-spot" (Steve, NY3).

Debates and long, one-on-one interviews like the one Dukakis gave to Ted Koppel on "Nightline" near the campaign's end are particularly important sources of intuitively relevant data, given people's unavoidable tendency to emphasize rapport and trust in appraising candidates (see Chapter 5).

A few people, like Dennis of the final Sacramento group, criticized the debates for being too tightly controlled: "The debates were phoney. Nothing but a dual forum. There should be real give and take." But most felt that even sanitized debates afforded a priceless opportunity to watch the candidates "think on their feet" with the pressure on, something otherwise unavailable in 1988.

Social Influence in the Groups. This effort to assess the political influence that touched Markle group participants in 1988 would not be complete without some attention to the ways in which these people influenced one another in the process of exchanging thoughts and ideas. For whenever citizens discuss politics with other citizens, the stage is set for the politics of one or more discussion partners to be affected (Huckfeldt and Sprague 1988).

Influence of this kind is strongest in social settings that are more permanent than focus groups: settings that encourage regular interactions among people over long periods of time. This fact sharply limits what could be learned of interpersonal influences by watching these groups. Nevertheless, two bits of evidence emerged that are interesting and important enough to report.

The first came from comparing group responses to the pre-session questionnaire (see Table 6-3) with the voting intentions expressed in the groups themselves, usually by a show of hands. The questionnaires gave Dukakis a 51 to 49 percent edge over Bush. But listening to the discussions and counting heads within the groups always showed Bush in the lead. Why? In part, no doubt, because the groups moved toward Bush as the election approached along with the rest of the country. But occasionally, a particular group would endorse Bush with a voice vote, though later review of the questionnaires showed that Dukakis had begun the evening with a majority. In these cases there hadn't been time for any influence to operate other than that exercised within the group itself.

The logical explanation—that Dukakis support was soft, and the outspoken Bush support heard in the groups was more fervent and thus somewhat intimidating if not actually more influential—is the most plausible. Bush supporters, though lukewarm in ways suggested earlier, still liked Bush more than Dukakis supporters liked Dukakis. They had also formulated stronger, more persuasive arguments for their stand.

They could, for example, truthfully argue that Bush had more federal-government and especially foreign-policy experience, was a much more familiar and thus "safer" political figure, had made a credible pledge to continue the perceived peace and prosperity of the Reagan years, and was vocally more respectful of mainstream social values. A typical Dukakis supporter could only cite party loyalty, the abstract "need for change," or a generalized notion that "Democrats are more for the little guy." The clincher may have been the fear, expressed by foes and admitted by Dukakis supporters, that Dukakis might turn out to be "another Jimmy Carter," well-meaning but lacking the experience and skills to carry off a new agenda without wreaking havoc.

Dukakis supporters might conceivably have responded more effectively, but the candidate himself was finding it difficult to do that out on the hustings, so better Dukakis arguments were not plentiful at the time. In any event, the group debates were always lively, and Bush supporters were consistently able to out-argue, and in some cases convert, many Dukakis supporters, if only for the duration of the session.

This kind of conversational influence was undoubtedly duplicated all around the nation, featuring the same arguments pro and con, right up until election day. Such discussions had more to do with the real qualifications of the candidates than did the television advertising or the campaign rhetoric. For this and other reasons, they may have had as much or more impact on the outcome of the election.

The second bit of evidence about political influence was testimonial in nature and suggested something of its limits and scope. We asked people whether they engaged in much discussion of the election among their friends, family, and coworkers. The responses of the members in the third New York and Sacramento groups are illustrative. Seven of nine participants in the New York group indicated that they discussed the campaign with others fairly regularly, as did nine of twelve in the California group. But the range of the political culture was best illuminated by the small number who either loved or hated to talk politics.

Those who loved it were like *aficionados* discussing their favorite sport or soap opera. But the nontalkers said they avoided politics as a contentious and unpleasant subject for conversation, especially among family members and other close associates. Doesn't this cut down on learning and reflection about the voting choice? "No," said Donna of NY3: "I learn on my own. Discussions become [unpleasant] debates." Steve, seated a few places down the table, didn't need to spend time discussing the candidates, because "my opinions are now pretty much formulated." And said Paul (S3), in an effort to deflect further probing by the moderator: "I [just] don't discuss politics with anybody."

If, as some argue, there can be no democracy without talk (B. Barber 1984:268), then a wide sharing of this view would constitute a threat. In fact, however, most of our participants seemed eager for political conversation and became increasingly absorbed as the discussion proceeded. In and outside the groups, nontalkers are clearly less plentiful than nonvoters, who are considerably more threatening to the health of the democracy. And even the self-described nontalkers got involved and held their own in the group discussions, where the interlocutors were strangers and thus not likely to become recurring sources of unpleasant disagreement.

Some Conclusions about Political Influence. Before leaving the subject of influence, it is worth highlighting certain postulates about the influence process that emerge from this discussion of the groups and from the surveys reported in Chapter 5. We have seen that influence may stem from various sources—media, advertising, social interactions—and is evidenced in various ways, such as learning, attitude change, and voting behavior.

One clear indication is that citizens are not influenced in direct proportion to the ubiquity or repetitiveness of the influences to which they are exposed. The Bentsen/Quayle recognition data in Chapter 5, the failure of the focus-group discussants to evince much of a priming response to the extensive media campaign horse-race coverage, and the comparatively low priority ranking of issues featured prominently in paid advertising, are illustrative.

Nor, it seems clear, are people always influenced in the intended ways by the information or persuasion attempts they do selectively admit to consciousness. That is, they may give evidence of having been influenced in some ways—e.g., learning from ads, or being affected by the negative tenor of the campaign—that may increase cynicism, or reduce the motivation to vote, but do not necessarily influence actual candidate preference. Many people said, for example, that they planned to vote for Bush despite being anxious about his running mate Dan Quayle, irritated and disgusted at the Bush campaign strategy, and not overly impressed with Bush himself.

These response patterns imply a measure of independence and inner-directedness. They suggest that many people are not manipulable in simplistic ways. We can speculate that when persuasion attempts like negative political advertising do appear to "work," it is because they push in directions that the audience already wants to go for reasons of its own, reasons that may well differ from those offered in the advertising.

Does this reflect favorably on the capabilities of ordinary citizens and the prospects for democracy? Perhaps. But there is additional evidence to consider.

The Capabilities of Citizens

Numerous polls, together with voting turnout statistics, point to apathy, indifference, and ignorance among ordinary citizens of representative democracies in the United States and abroad (Dalton 1988; see also chapters 4, 5, and 7). Liberal democracy's idealized expectations of citizens are quite demanding, and never met in practice (Margolis 1979). The gap between ideal and reality is so large that the scholarly writing on democratic theory has gradually revised expectations downward.

Abandoned are the ideals of such theorists as Rousseau and Mill, who expected citizens to invest real time and energy in the role in order to be worthy and capable of democracy. In their place now stands the "modern" view, illustrated in the writings of Schumpeter (1947), Berelson, Lazarsfeld, and McPhee (1954), Dahl (1956), and Sartori (1987), that accepts perfunctory candidate evaluation and minimal majority turnout at the polls as sufficient evidence of workable representative democracy (Pateman 1970).[24]

Even these reduced expectations are increasingly honored in the breach, as suggested by the 1988 presidential election turnout, the lowest in sixty-four years. Nevertheless, exhorting Americans to take citizenship more seriously is rare. Anything smacking of criticism is virtually absent in the writings of journalists, pundits, and scholars who are regularly forced to confront evidence of what idealistic democratic theory regards as citizenly irresponsibility. Neither politicians nor journalists like to talk about the most basic problem—the lack of public interest. Perhaps it is because they fear alienating their constituency (Oreskes 1989). It is as if they believe that little more can be expected; that we must simply accept the mass public as we find it.[25]

Is this implicit consensus based on a fair and accurate reading of the American electorate's current potential? Or are ordinary people better equipped to meet the larger expectations of democracy than voting statistics and prevailing assumptions suggest?

These questions reflect an ancient debate whose grounding in value conflicts makes it unresolvable by empirical evidence alone. The American version of the debate is traceable to the divergent opinions of human nature and potential held by Alexander Hamilton and Thomas Jefferson.[26] The existence of persuasive evidence on both sides of the debate is a vexing fact. At different times in his distinguished career, for example, America's foremost political columnist, Walter Lippmann, was moved to embrace flatly contradictory views about the capacities of ordinary people.[27]

The debate continues, and assumes fresh urgency whenever some new event brings questions about the capacities of citizens back to the center of attention. The prominence in 1988 of negative presidential campaign advertising, and particularly its apparent success with voters, is an example. It raises such questions as why people tolerate, let alone respond to, attack advertising. Why is there no forceful expression of public indignation? Why don't citizens refuse to reward such methods at the polls? Why don't they insist that candidates discuss important issues and make policy commitments, thereby restoring campaigns to their status as referendums on future national policy? The power of the ballot to compel such changes is absolute. Why don't people use it? Does the fact that they passively tolerate such abuses of the political process imply that they are incapable of thoughtful collective action in pursuit of the democracy's well-being, except, perhaps, when some palpable disaster threatens?

These questions reflect a broader conviction that the quality of political practice in a representative democracy can never exceed the innate potential of the citizenry. If that is the case, then what is the innate potential of the American electorate? As noted in the introduction, we sought to use these group discussions to shed light on the state of the voters.

Potential Defined. "Potential" is here defined as that combination of attributes needed to support the kind of "good democratic practice" required of citizens in Chapter 2's normative model. It is clear, for example, that a reasonable degree of intelligence is required to grasp the information needed to assess candidates and issues. Also needed is enough time and energy to devote to nonwork, nonfamily issues like study and participation in civic business.

Equally important is a certain collection of motives and beliefs associated with maturity, self-discipline, and altruism. These include a belief in the importance of voting, a feeling of personal obligation to the larger common good, and an ability to temper one's passions in the interests of clear thinking about alternative candidates and arguments.

Most important, however, is a certain understanding of the special place of citizens and presidential campaigns in this representative democracy, and of the related obligations of media and candidates. As described in Chapter 2, that understanding involves a concept of the citizen as proprietor and sovereign, and of the campaign as a process created for the benefit of citizens, in order to help prepare them to choose representative leaders responsibly. The role of the media and candidates in this view is subordinate and pedagogical. Selling and persuading are tolerated, but not at the expense of the primary educational mission.

Assessing Potential. How did the focus-group participants stack up against these standards? Concerning native ability, the foregoing pages give ample evidence that virtually all of the 161 people who took part were easily intelligent enough to meet the cognitive demands of citizenship. A glance at Tables 6-2 and 6-3 shows that the gap between them and a representative sample of the entire electorate on matters of education and political interest is not so great as to make the groups utterly unrepresentative.

My feeling, after listening to thirty-two hours of group discussions, was that the general level of discourse was not an embarrassment to democracy. These people were eager to give one another the reasoning behind their various opinions—so much so that they sometimes obviously invented reasons they hoped would seem plausible rather than admit to operating on impulse or instinct alone. The widespread inventiveness at rationalizing opinions was itself sufficient evidence of adequate intelligence. The group comparisons of Bush and Dukakis, summarized earlier, buttress this conclusion.

Individual Differences. There were, however, important individual differences apparent in the groups, and they pertain to the cluster of citizenly virtues that features maturity, self-discipline, and altruism. We noted earlier that three broad reasoning styles and ways of integrating thought, emotion, and belief in reactions to the campaign gradually became apparent to those who watched more than a few of the groups. The perception of types emerged gradually and unexpectedly; therefore no procedure had been established for classifying each participant into one or another of the types. Consequently no figures are available to specify the distribution of percentages fitting each type. Many participants emitted ambiguous signals and would have been very difficult to classify in any case. But since the possibility of distinctive reasoning styles among the larger citizenry is not farfetched (readers will have encountered similar variations in daily life), and since the distribution of styles could affect the prospects for improving democratic practice, admittedly preliminary impressions seem worth discussing here.

JUDICIAL REASONERS

The reasoning style that reflects the greatest maturity and self-discipline, and that is most supportive of democratic norms is here called the "judicial." Judicial people in the groups had a tendency to verbally review and weigh the evidence before expressing their opinions. They showed by their commentary that they felt obliged to stay open to new evidence that might be relevant to their voting choice even when, as was often the case, a preference was clear. They seemed concerned with being fair, and with letting each side have its "day in court." They were good-natured, with a greater tendency to express humor than anger or other strong sentiment. When asked what he was "looking for" to help him make up his mind whom to support for president, for example, S1 participant Michael, a clear judicial processor, replied with tongue in cheek, "divine guidance!"

The reasoning behind a candidate preference usually had the ring of common sense and of respect for the general interest. Thus, George, responding to a comment that Bush would be good for Houston, made a point of saying that he didn't believe in "selfish voting," because "the president better be for the whole country." Another Houston man agreed that Bush was the choice, but had an equally unselfish rationale: "[choosing Dukakis would] force you to start all over from square one . . . We're beginning to see a turnaround . . . let's not stop that and start over . . ." And Vince (NY4) found a homespun way to express his own reasoned conclusion: "Bush has been there, and it doesn't make sense to put a cold egg into a warm nest."

Such people were generally quite intelligent, although it was clearly attitude toward their responsibilities and toward information, rather than intelligence alone, that distinguished them from the "closed" or "reactive" types discussed below. Judicial reasoners often reached the same conclusion (i.e., support for George Bush or Michael Dukakis—although all three reasoning styles gave a majority to Bush) as the other types, as would be expected in a choice limited to two candidates. Again, it was reasoning style, not conclusion, that distinguished them.

Young to middle-aged and generally well informed, these were the kinds of people who left observers feeling confident about the potential of ordinary citizens and the prospects for upgrading American-style democracy. It is noteworthy that the consensus that usually emerged concerning various discussion topics had usually been endorsed by judicial group members. Thus the modal position most often had judicial support, although it is unclear whether force of numbers (judicials did seem more numerous than the other types) or force of argument best explains why.

CLOSED REASONERS

Closed reasoners, who were nearly as plentiful as judicials, were much more likely than other types to see the candidate evaluation process through some particular, highly selective lense. They were, in short, believers. Beliefs, backed by strong feelings, took obvious and often freely acknowledged precedence over cold reasoning as evaluative tools. Many made it clear that their minds were made up, and that they had no use for any new information about the candidates or the issues.

Closed reasoners included strong identifiers with both political parties. Others were ideologues: fervent liberals or conservatives. Still others were single-issue proponents—of nuclear power, the death penalty, pro-choice, right-to-life, and the like—who regarded the candidates' stand on their issue as a litmus test.

A somewhat extreme example of fervent commitment to a single decision-value (in this case self-interest) was provided by Leo, of the second Houston group, who said: "Forget all the issues . . . I've blocked it out . . . you want some wild-eyed Northeastern liberal? . . . Let's look out for ourselves . . . Get a guy [George Bush, whose Texas residence is Houston, located in Harris County] who cares about Harris County . . . He's local, that's all [we need to know] . . ."

Leo had another characteristic not underrepresented in this category: a resourceful intelligence. Despite his advice to "forget all the issues," he was very well informed and had fashioned some sophisticated arguments to support his position. This made him an effective spokesman for his point of view. He courteously but firmly dismissed as naïve and misguided arguments that voting and other political decisions are, or should be, shaped by unselfish values.

Other closed reasoners were less polished and more self-righteous about their commitments than Leo. They were also more intense and emotional, often becoming impassioned. This, and the closed reasoner's special tendency to "learn" that which supports ideological or other preconceptions, are illustrated by two Sacramento 2 responses to the question, "What have you learned about Michael Dukakis?" Said Don: "[That he's a] liar, a sneak, and I don't trust him . . . He put his state into debt . . . has done nothing to stop welfare, or help the environment." Said Ben, an avowed Democratic loyalist: "[Dukakis has shown me] the ability to choose a running mate to pull the party together . . . the ability to pick who he wanted despite Jackson pressure . . . he came through . . ."

Another man, Mike of NY3, was intensely pro-Bush and found ways to interpret incoming information that permitted him to stay that way: "[the fact that Bush seems goofy] shows that he's human . . ." Mike was the man whose use of a *Newsweek* article was cited earlier as an instance of media influence. Here, the same episode illustrates how a man with a strong point of view can use evidence to sustain it. "I was at first anti-Quayle . . . when Bentsen jumped on him [saying] you're no John Kennedy . . . But a *Newsweek* article [showed that Bentsen] didn't know Quayle . . . On thirty of forty-one issues, Bentsen and Quayle voted the same . . . As Bush said, why run against my vice president? . . . Bush jumped on the press for distorted coverage, and that increased my confidence."

This same man showed his familiarity with the tendency to notice or not notice information according to its effect on one's preferences in his later criticism of television news anchors: "Today Rather, Jennings, and Brokaw all said it was very unfair to run polls, because it sways the public . . . [but only because Michael Dukakis] their guy was behind . . ."

REACTORS

Reactors, who made up the smallest of the three groups, were the most easily swayed by the opinions of others. They lacked both the impassioned sense of direction typical of closed reasoners and the commitment to fair and responsible evidentiary procedures characteristic of the judicial processors. Their remarks suggested a tendency to respond to the influence of the most recent strong stimulus—whether a television ad, an impassioned statement by someone in the group, or an event like the debates—that they had encountered.

Reactors were neither particularly interested in, nor very well informed about, the campaign, national problems, the government, or politics generally. They were more often undecided than either of the other types.

And they were often confused. Many seemed to find the process of deciding whom to vote for a trying one. Said Mike in S2: "[First I] hear one thing, [then I] hear another . . . campaigns are tough on me . . ." And Robbie (H3): "I'm getting lost . . . [It's all so] confusing . . ."

There may also be a stronger-than-average tendency among reactors to rely exclusively on impulse or intuition, as implied in Pam's (H3) remark: "I'm waiting for a story to break to make up my mind . . . can't vote on one issue . . . I'll trust my instinct on voting day . . ." And Geary (H3): "I'm waiting for something to move me . . . probably something negative . . ."

These examples of significant variations in approaches to political reasoning suggest something of why there are grounds for much hope and some concern about the state of the electorate. They also show why intelligence alone is not enough for effective citizenship; that attitudes, values, and concepts of civic responsibility have as much or more to do with the prospects for democracy in America.

But even if the most basic democratic requirements of citizen will and ability are adequately met, there is inevitably room for improvement. What changes could enhance the practice of citizenship during presidential campaign seasons? Impressions of the groups suggest the following possibilities.

What Citizens Need

ROUTINIZED DISCUSSION OPPORTUNITIES

Political theorists have suggested the value of discussion in the development of civic competence (e.g., B. Barber 1984:268). Our experience with the focus groups suggests that with an agenda and a format designed to facilitate learning, political conversation could indeed improve the practice of citizenship.

Our participants frequently said that they had enjoyed and benefited from the group discussions. The two Houston groups each met twice, but participants were not informed that they would be invited back until shortly before the second meetings. In the second meeting of the first Houston group, nine of twelve people said that participating in the first meeting had led them to pay more attention.

Apart from such direct testimony, the involvement and animation apparent at most meetings suggested that many people relished the opportunity to discuss such matters. Watching initially guarded people become interested, engaged, and productive discussants made it seem plausible that if routinized civic discussion opportunities were easily available, they could do much to bring out the best in citizens.

The discussions seemed to stimulate interest even in those who professed indifference to the election or distaste for political argument. People naturally enjoy and learn from interacting with one another, particularly (as the experience of sensitivity-training groups has suggested) when participants begin as strangers gathered for the purpose of discussing a topic they find interesting and important.

Reconvening election discussion groups one or more times would likely serve as incentive for participants to pay more attention to the information needed to evaluate candidates and to contribute to the next discussion.

BETTER PREPARATION ON THE ISSUES AND THE CANDIDATES

The evidence of voter ignorance presented in Chapter 5 plus that indicating a preoccupation among focus-group participants with local rather than national or international problems presented earlier in this chapter argue for repeating this familiar suggestion.

Although citizens have routinely been found, since the advent of regular polling in the 1940's, to know less of public matters than they should, it remains necessary to point out that such ignorance is at odds with even the modest expectations of representative democracy, which require that citizens at least be aware of the important differences between candidates and able to hold candidates accountable for the plausibility of their policy claims and the accuracy of their charges against one another.

We saw in Chapter 4 that citizens willing to search could find topflight policy-analysis journalism, both print and broadcast, relevant to the 1988 choice. But the group discussions suggested that few had done much searching or studying.

To be sure, candidates have some obligation to discuss the state of the nation. And media organizations might conceivably do more to clarify (through such "agenda-setting" cues as stories about the national agenda, story positioning, amount of column inches or air time, and repetition) what the consensus of informed opinion is concerning the next president's most urgent priorities.[28] But the responsibility for acquiring information ultimately rests with the individual citizen.

AN AWARENESS THAT CITIZENS "OWN" PRESIDENTIAL CAMPAIGNS

A noteworthy if not surprising fact is that none of the groups generated any explicit discussion or debate on the meanings and implications of citizenship. There was an implicit awareness in all the groups that responsibilities for gathering information and voting were incumbent upon people like themselves. But at no time did such issues become salient enough to break into the discussion. In their various comments on the candidates and the media our participants conveyed the sense (again, without anyone ever explicitly saying as much) that those agencies, not the voters, were the major players, with considerably more at stake in the upcoming election than any of those present.

People like themselves, who stood at considerable physical and psychological distance from the heat of the electoral battle, seemed content to limit their input to rather formulaic expressions of opinion and to the act of voting. The steady decline of voter turnout shows that nearly half the eligible electorate outside the groups did not even view casting a ballot as essential.

We noted earlier that recent democratic theorists see voter detachment as a sign of trust in government and an indicator of democratic stability (Lipset 1963; Almond and Verba 1963). Whatever the merits of that view, such detachment is also the major reason why these and other citizens tolerated, even as they deplored, the negative, largely issueless presidential campaign of 1988.

Yet this very tolerance, rooted in vague understandings of the rights and responsibilities of the major actors in national elections, was itself a principal explanation for the unsatisfying quality of the campaign. Whatever candidates or media organizations might seek to do to improve the process, the fact remains that only the electorate has the right, and wields enough power, to demand a significant and enduring change in the way American presidential elections are conducted. As noted in Chapter 2, for example, a citizenry that regarded itself as sovereign, viewed elections as devices for meeting its needs for information and guidance, and expected candidates and media to service those needs, would demand and get a different kind of presidential campaign.

Those who would upgrade the quality of presidential elections, then, must ultimately address the understanding and definition of citizenship that is accepted by the electorate.

REVISED EXPECTATIONS OF CANDIDATES AND MEDIA

Relatedly, certain common understandings of the obligations of the news media and of candidates for high office were not shared by our discussants, who expected relatively little of either. People in the groups did not generally regard the news media as the public's surrogates, agents, or protectors against the abuses of candidates as of governments, a view of the press as "democratic watchdog" that is held by many journalists (cf. Graber, 1988:123).[29] Instead, people in the groups saw the press as a business whose product (and major responsibility) is simply to provide accurate, factual information.

Neither were candidates seriously expected to do anything other than what they perceived as necessary to win. People were resigned to the preeminence of self-interest as the driving force behind the conduct of campaigns by candidates. Like many political professionals, some of these citizens gave evidence of regarding it as naïve to expect otherwise.

But for reasons already suggested, it seems clear that people like our discussants would be better served if they and their counterparts in the mass electorate *expected* the media to tailor coverage to suit their needs for information and protection against candidate distortions. And they would also be better served if they were known to *expect* candidates to explain the state of the nation and the relevance of their campaign proposals to the national agenda. Such expectations would surely stand as incentives to improvement. They would be respected by media and candidates because they are enforceable in the marketplace and at the polls.

Selling Democracy to Citizens.   What would it take to "sell" ordinary Americans on the idea that they should assert their ownership of the political process? This version of the classic focus-group selling question was kept in mind as we observed the groups. The traditional answer in advertising circles is to portray what is being sold as somehow necessary to the well-being or happiness of the buyer. If people can be moved to endure the discomforts of crowded department stores in search of consumer products advertising has persuaded them they need, then they can be focused on new concepts of politics and motivated to act in ways now thought unlikely or impossible.

The largest barrier, and the first obstacle to overcome, is the lack of motivation. Why should people care about political matters they correctly perceive as very distant from their most pressing personal concerns? They also feel politically insignificant as individuals, another important barrier. As Vince (NY4) put it: "I don't follow as closely as I should, [but then] my vote hardly matters."

The fact is that self-interest motives cannot be the decisive factors in reintegrating citizens into the political process. Neither can the opportunity to wield significant personal influence on political outcomes. Instead, anyone who would seriously address the motivational barrier to change must begin with the demonstrated and durable sentiment of civic obligation noted earlier, first measured in the classic *American Voter* study, and demonstrated again many times, most recently in our Harris surveys.

This motive is much closer to altruism than self-interest, and it is latent in every social and economic stratum. It is clear that a significant proportion of Americans care about and love an idealized vision of the country (H. J. Gans 1988). There is a measure of civic passion in ordinary citizens. It erupted in our groups during discussion of matters like negative ads and media hype. It was also apparent in public reactions to the "flag patriotism" of the 1988 election and post-election flag-burning debate, although those expressions illustrate manipulation of civic sentiment for political gain.

This is not the place to detail a nonpartisan consciousness-raising strategy for citizens. But a carefully wrought "social marketing" effort (Kotler and Roberto 1989) is precisely what would be required to awaken the electorate as a corrective force in presidential and other campaigns. If millions of Americans can be dissuaded from smoking because of a publicity campaign to acquaint them with the health risks, and if America's diet can be changed in response to the cholesterol threat, then citizens can be taught that the health of their democracy requires yet another kind of change in their habits. Like the earlier changes, this change would also result in a reward. But the new reward will be the enhanced self-regard that comes from helping to improve democratic practice in America.

Conclusion

The Markle focus groups did not alter the major findings discussed in Chapters 4 and 5. Instead, they enliven and intensify—with human faces and voices—the themes of political persuasion and public response. The groups disclosed something of the selectivity of media and candidate influence, citizen indifference to things political, the variety of reasoning styles, the latent feelings of obligation to the polity, the ignorance of issues and government, the confusion about national priorities, and the disgust with the candidates and the campaign that summarized the state of the voters' thinking in America during the fall of 1988.

Appendix

Demographic Comparisons

Table 6-2 offers a comparison of several demographic characteristics of the 161 individuals who took part in the Markle focus groups with the 1,875-person random national sample drawn for the second Harris survey reported in Chapter 5. The comparison enables us to

Table 6-2. Demographic Comparisons: Focus-Group Sample versus National Sample[a]

	Focus-Group Sample	National Sample[b]
	% (N=161)	% (N=1,875)
Occupation		
Professional	26	12
Manager	9	10
Clerical	11	6
Skilled craftsman	5	17
Age		
18–29	17	28
30–44	39	30
45–74	44	42
Education		
Some high school	5	25
High school graduate	19	39
Some college	42	18
College graduate	19	10
Post-graduate	14	7
Ideology		
Conservative	27	36
Moderate	48	41
Liberal	16	18
Unsure	10	5

Table 6-2. *(continued)*

	Focus-Group Sample	National Sample[b]
	% (N=161)	% (N=1,875)
Party identification		
Republican	30	30
Democratic	47	38
Independent	19	28
Not sure	4	4
Voted in 1984		
Yes	90	69
No	9	30
Unsure	1	1
Who supported in 1984?		
Reagan	57	64
Mondale	39	33
Other, unsure	4	3
Registered to vote?		
Yes	100	85
No	0	15
Income		
$7,500 or less	1	9
$7,500–15,000	7	14
$15,001–25,000	16	21
$25,001–35,000	23	19
$35,001–50,000	24	17
$50,001–75,000	17	9
$75,001–100,000	8	3
$100,001 and over	2	2
Not sure/missing	2	7
Race		
White	79	85
Black	16	11
Other	5	4
Hispanic?		
Yes	8	6
No	92	94
Sex		
Female	47	52
Male	53	48

[a]Percentages may not sum to 100 because of rounding.
[b]Harris Survey 2; N=1,875; conducted 10/18–11/4/1988.

gauge with some precision the degree to which this focus-group "sample" differed from a representative sample of American voters.

As is apparent, focus-group participants were more often white-collar workers, somewhat older, decidedly better educated, a bit less conservative, included fewer independents and more Democrats, were more likely to have voted in the last presidential election, and were more likely to have been registered to vote in 1988.

On the other hand, the two samples had comparable racial and sexual diversity, and large majorities of both groups said they had voted for Ronald Reagan in 1984. The distribution of incomes was broadly comparable, in that the largest clusters of both samples were concentrated in the $15,000–75,000 range.

Still, the focus-group sample included significantly fewer people in the two lowest income brackets. And, by design, the focus-group participants were consumers of media products, and their educational and occupational characteristics reflect it. This and their greater than average rate of political participation make them better described as "attentive" rather than "average" citizens. Their like can be found in every community in America. But they are more likely than the less informed to be opinion leaders.

Table 6-3. *Attitude Comparisons: Focus-Group Sample versus National Sample*

	Focus-Group Sample	National Sample
	% (N=161)	% (N=1,875)
Preferred candidate of decided voters		
George Bush	49	54
Michael Dukakis	51	45
How important to you is voting in the 1988 presidential election?		
Important or very important	97	90
How interested are you in presidential politics?		
Interested or very interested	90	75
How closely do you follow media coverage of campaign?		
Very, somewhat closely	88	68

Selected Attitudinal Comparisons

The focus-group participants also completed briefer paper-and-pencil questionnaire versions of the Harris telephone interview protocols prior to each group session. Table 6-3 reports selected comparisons that reveal the comparability of the two samples with respect to attitudes toward the presidential candidates and the campaign.

The differences in attitude are what might be expected given the demographic dissimilarities reported above. Focus-group participants were on average more interested in presidential politics, followed the campaign more closely, and ascribed greater importance to voting than did survey respondents. In the aggregate, they gave Michael Dukakis 51 percent support in Table 6-3, although the groups in Houston and California were never pro-Dukakis, and groups in all regions were moving toward Bush as election day neared.

7. 1992 AND BEYOND: THE MARKLE COMMISSION RECOMMENDATIONS

We come finally to the business of taking stock and looking ahead. Mindful of the foregoing research findings, and of the practices most likely to sustain and improve the healthy functioning of the presidential campaign process, the Markle Commission issued in May 1990 a report containing its recommendations for 1992 and beyond (*Report* 1990).[1] Those recommendations are reproduced in this chapter, along with evaluative commentary on the 1988 performance of each component of the electoral triangle.

The State of the Electorate

Assessment

The single most disturbing feature of the 1988 presidential campaign was the evidence of public indifference and ignorance implicit in our research results and in the national statistics on voter turnout. As for turnout, only 50.16 percent of eligible voters actually voted, the lowest presidential election percentage in 64 years. In the non-Southern states in which three-quarters of Americans live, the 54.1 percent turnout rate of 1988 is the lowest in 164 years (Burnham 1989 : 28). Even as enthusiasm for democracy ignites around the globe, it is waning in the very nation whose political traditions inspire others.

As for indifference and ignorance, such facts as the unfamiliarity of Republican vice-presidential nominee Dan Quayle to as many as one-third of our survey respondents (Table 5-1), the relative ignorance of candidate issue stands (Table 5-7), and the fact that half the respondents to our polls weren't sure which party controlled the House of Representatives are illustrative.

Evidence of political apathy and ignorance among American voters is, of course, far from unusual. It has been commonplace since the advent of scientific survey sampling in the 1940's and 1950's.[2] What is surprising is the relative scarcity of real concern, then or now, about this state of affairs. Our more recent evidence of public ignorance and indifference is no less troubling for its similarity to previous findings, nor any less indicative of a need for remedial action.[3]

More disturbing even than ignorance of particular facts, however, are the signs we uncovered that citizens do not realize that the presidential campaign process belongs to them.

As noted in the second chapter, democracy places citizens in the sovereign position. It does so both because individual human beings are seen as intrinsically worthy and deserving, and because the people are regarded as collectively the safest repository of ultimate power. Sovereignty in a representative democracy is expressed primarily by means of the ballot. Elections are thus crucial to the legitimacy of such democracies. And campaigns for office represent the principal opportunity for citizens to acquire the insight and information needed to vote responsibly.

If, as in 1988, candidates make no serious effort to enlighten citizens about the real national problem agenda and their plans for addressing it, and if the media, as in 1988 and before, devote more of their coverage to the political horse race and candidate conflicts than to the national agenda or the qualifications of candidates, then the campaign has not served its intended purpose.

Many, perhaps most Americans realize that something has gone wrong. Our focus-group research (Chapter 6) showed clearly that people were not satisfied with the negative tone or the issueless nature of the 1988 presidential campaign. But instead of expressing their disapproval by asserting their sovereignty—that is, by demanding candidate behavior more respectful of their needs for information and guidance—they expressed it with verbal cynicism toward politics and politicians and by staying away from the polls.

Voters presently see themselves as distant participants with little at stake, rather than as proprietors of a leader-selection process who share responsibility for its successful operation. They show potential for greater involvement by their claim that voting is quite important to them, and by expressing more than a little interest in presidential politics (Table 5-2). But our surveys and focus groups show that it simply does not occur to voters to insist upon respect for their sovereignty or to demand special efforts of candidates and media to fulfill their needs for information and guidance.

Plainly, American voters do not now hold themselves to sufficiently high standards of preparation. Nor are they demanding enough of the other major actors in the electoral triangle. They do not, for example, expect candidates to put explaining the issues on a par with winning. Nor do they perceive the news media as having any particular "democratic watchdog" responsibilities to voters. As one observer put it (Morrison 1988:254): "The public does not see the press as its tribune."

Our evidence also makes it clear that most citizens were not sufficiently well informed to recognize candidate disinformation. This is particularly disturbing in light of the fact that, as shown in Chapter 5, the public got most of its information about the candidates in 1988 from Bush campaign rhetoric and advertising (see Tables 5-8 and 5-9). When asked what they had learned about the candidates, it was not unusual for participants in our focus groups to repeat uncritically the contents of paid candidate advertising. And among the things occasionally repeated were the inaccurate contents of two particularly misleading ads (the Bush tank ad misrepresenting Dukakis's positions on weapons systems and the Dukakis ad inaccurately charging Bush with voting for Social Security cuts). Voters cannot hold either candidates or leaders accountable if they do not themselves know enough to distinguish fact from fiction.

Other evidence, however, casts citizens in a more favorable light and offers reason for hope. It suggests that although voters were influenced, they were not controlled by the demagoguery and negative advertising of Campaign '88. The case can be made, for example, that:

(1) The election outcome might have been the same had neither candidate given a speech or aired an ad. Researchers predicted the outcome of the election with uncanny accuracy well in advance of the fall campaign, suggesting that economic conditions had more impact than the campaign or media coverage of it (Morin 1989:37).

(2) Despite ignorance of factual material like issue positions, most eligible voters had quite accurate impressions of the general strengths and weaknesses of both candidates, and had already formed impressions favorable to Bush before campaign advertising began in earnest (see Tables 5-10 and 5-11).

(3) The Bush victory had more to do with the electorate's desire for continuity and continued prosperity with a more experienced president (Table 5-5) than with the impact of the Bush campaign on what voters "learned" about Dukakis "negatives" (Table 5-9).

(4) People chose Bush despite considerable poll evidence showing that a majority of the electorate was unhappy with the tone of his campaign, did not like his vice-presidential choice, and believed Bush was lying about his no-tax pledge. To many of his supporters, our focus-group participants suggest, Bush was simply the better of two unattractive options.

These things argue, as political scientist V. O. Key maintained in a famous study of the American electorate, that voters are not fools (Key 1966). Many did manage to respond to their own visions of the big picture. But even though it can be argued that the negative campaign did not determine the election result, it surely influenced many votes. And it just as surely contributed to an erosion of public respect for the electoral process and to diminished voter turnout. In this sense, democracy's "capital" was depleted—something potentially more damaging to the political process than the outcome of any particular election.

The most desirable public response to negative, evasive campaigns is not disenchantment and withdrawal from the process, as was evident in 1988, but indignation. Mistreatment of one's property would normally excite such indignation. But most people do not think of political campaigns as "citizen property." There is a widespread failure to recognize this fundamental fact of sovereignty in a representative democracy: that citizens have a "property right" to all campaigns for office; that it is the sovereign-voters, not the candidates, who collectively "own" the electoral process. This misperception is the largest single barrier to significant improvement, and thus the principal focus of Markle Commission concern. As long as voters are not aware of their vested right to demand good campaign practice, they are unlikely to get it. The initial commission recommendations sought to identify ways to change public perceptions and increase participation.[4]

Recommendations for Citizens

1. **Establish an "American Citizens Foundation"—a permanent, nonpartisan organization devoted to improving democratic practice in American electoral politics.**[5]

A non-partisan, not-for-profit organization, the "American Citizens Foundation," should be created to help return citizens to the center of electoral politics. It would signify that the electoral process belongs to the citizens and that they owe it their participation in identifying and defining national choices and issues. Funding should come from an automatic tax form check-off unless specifically declined by the individual citizen.

The Foundation should monitor American political conduct and practice, commission research, and communicate findings to the American people. The following two programs are central:

(a) **Create a national advertising campaign for democracy and the electoral process.**

We recommend using advertising techniques to revitalize public participation in Presidential elections. Under the aegis of the Foundation, the Advertising Council would be asked to volunteer to create a print and broadcast public-service campaign designed to encourage political participation by all citizens. The media would be asked to volunteer space and time for the ads. The campaign would employ the same power to motivate political participation in our democracy as any of today's best advertising exerts to gain favor for commercial products.

(b) **Establish a national education program to improve understanding of the individual's stake in the political process.**

An educated electorate is essential to a successful democratic society. This program would assign highest priority to education about the media's, the candidates' and the citizens' roles in the process. It would involve civic and professional organizations as well as state school officials and college and university teachers. Materials already exist for pursuit of this purpose. Additions might include a syllabus based on this Markle Commission Report, video material from the Advertising Council campaign, and other specially produced films and articles suitable for distribution and broadcasts that reach the schools.

Needed: A "New American Citizen"

Representative democracy cannot be more than pro forma unless there is a serious commitment to education for citizenship. Each new generation must undertake anew the intellectual groundwork needed to keep democratic processes viable. If this does not happen, an uninformed and unsophisticated electorate invites and perhaps deserves the sort of contemptuous manipulation implicit in "attack" television advertising, the hallmark of the 1988 presidential campaign.

Basic education for citizenship has traditionally taken place in families, schools, and political parties, with the educational assistance voters need to prepare for each successive election supplied, for better or worse, by the candidates (and, increasingly, as political parties have declined in significance) by the news media. Their 1988 work in this connection is evaluated below.

But additional, remedial work needs to be done—by the recommended American Citizens Foundation and other institutions— with voters outside of the confines of particular elections. A renewed national commitment to fundamental civic education must be the point of departure for a serious effort to re-engage the American electorate in its own most important political role. Detailed plans for such an effort are beyond the scope of this chapter, but the outlines can be sketched.

The initial task is to mobilize the relevant communities. Representatives of those organizations that share responsibility for the preparation of citizens—educational associations and institutions, the political parties, academics, journalists, and others—should examine the Markle Commission's contention that the business of citizenship needs revitalizing. If civic educational leaders agree that "the tired old academic workhorse 'civics' " needs updating and restoration to its once-honored position in the curriculum,[6] then other questions rapidly loom.

First is the question of motivation. As argued elsewhere in this book (e.g., Chapters 5 and 6) most Americans want to contribute to the nation's well-being. But they need to be given compelling new reasons to care personally about matters many now regard as distant and irrelevant to their lives.

Next come problems of definition. Just exactly what are the responsibilities of citizens, candidates, the media, and political parties during a presidential campaign and at other key moments in the life of a representative democracy? New thinking and intensified discussion of these matters, updated to incorporate the new realities of a mass electronic democracy, are badly needed. A contribution to that discussion was offered in Chapter 2.[7]

Only when responsibilities have been clarified and persuasive arguments for their acceptance made ready can the business of equipping citizens to function effectively in the age of television begin in earnest.

The Candidates

Assessment

By any standard higher than self-interest, the presidential candidates, and particularly the winning candidate, performed poorly in

1988. None of the candidate responsibilities outlined in Chapter 2 was adequately met. Neither man, for example, made any serious effort to educate the electorate about the state of the nation or the priorities facing the next president. In the effort to "move the numbers," candidates instead experimented with various themes largely unrelated to what most analysts regarded as 1989's likely presidential priorities. As David Gergen put it at a Kennedy School election postmortem: "the day after the election we faced a totally different set of realities" (Runkel 1989: 266). To the extent that 1988 campaign issues like flag patriotism did survive the election, they continued to divert legislative and executive attention away from more pressing matters.[8]

Both candidates took a number of specific issue stands (e.g., Table 5-7). But neither sought to prepare the ground for governing by presenting significant proposals for addressing such obvious priorities as the budget and trade deficits, declining U.S. economic competitiveness, the savings and loan crisis, or how the United States would respond to U.S.S.R. leader Gorbachev and otherwise position itself in a post–cold war world. To their credit, the print and broadcast media took repeated note of these candidate evasions (see Chapter 4). And what little the public did absorb of the real national agenda came from the media rather than the candidates (Chapter 5).

One candidate, Michael Dukakis, displayed what political reporters sometimes call a "goo-goo" (i.e., good government, elevated) attitude toward the electoral process by refusing at first to respond in kind to the relentless negative attacks of the Bush campaign. In so refusing, it might be said that he acted to encourage citizens' respect for the political process, as good democratic practice requires. But some in the media, and many members of his own party, interpeted this as evidence of naïveté, incompetence, and stubbornness rather than an effort to sustain good practice. Refusing to compete in the increasingly ugly game of negative politics is enough to brand one a loser in the eyes of the *cognoscenti*.

For his part, George Bush, a man with a reputation for integrity, decency, and respect for the political process, was nevertheless persuaded to use misinformation and negative emotional appeals on the grounds that it was the only way to overcome 17-to-25-point Dukakis poll leads and his own high personal "negatives" in the polls (Edward Rollins, quoted in Runkel 1989:267).

The evidence shows clearly that the Bush campaign was the instigator of the ugly tone of the campaign which the voters found so distasteful (Boot 1989:28). This fact was noted by some commentators, who argued that such campaigns undermine respect for the political process (e.g., Oakes 1988; A. Lewis 1988). Particularly deplorable was the emphasis placed by the Bush campaign on the case of a black prisoner, Willie Horton, who raped a white woman while he was on leave from a Massachusetts prison. The cynical exploitation of this tragic incident epitomizes the sorry state of contemporary presidential politics.

The Horton case had been characterized to reporters by Bush campaign manager Lee Atwater in the summer of 1988 as "one of those gut issues that are values issues, particularly in the South, and if we hammer at these over and over, we are going to win." Vice President Bush made frequent references to Mr. Horton in his campaign speeches as symbolizing and representing "the misguided outlook of my opponent when it comes to crime." Hundreds of thousands of Republican party campaign fliers that were mailed to voters in New York and other states featured a photograph of Horton and the headline "How Serious Is Dukakis about Crime?"

Bush spokesman Mark Goodin denied that the Bush campaign "had any control" over such independent Republican Party efforts. Television spots on the prison-furlough issue run by the Bush campaign did not include Horton's photograph or mention his race. But Bush's frequent reference to the Horton case often led to his picture appearing in newspapers and on television. Horton's picture did appear in television advertising sponsored by the Committee for the Presidency and paid for by supporters of the Republican ticket but not, under federal law, subject to the campaign's control (Andrew Rosenthal 1988b).

Months after the election, former Dukakis campaign manager Susan Estrich observed: "Perhaps President Bush and his aides never intended to inject race into the campaign. But the man they chose to symbolize the crime issue was Willie Horton . . . Independent groups of Bush supporters arranged for television tapings and publicity tours for Horton's victims. And day after day, month after month, in sound bite after sound bite, the man who is now president of the United States told Willie Horton's story . . . Conceivably George Bush never intended to start a [racial] fire . . . But one thing is certain: Not once in the campaign did he stand up and try to put it out" (1989:10).

The Democratic candidate should certainly have responded more forcefully than he did to deflect these scurrilous tactics. Michael Dukakis would later admit as much, saying "I made a lot of mistakes in the '88 campaign . . . But none was as damaging as my failure to understand this phenomenon [campaigning by 'phraseology,' '10-second sound-bites,' 'made for TV backdrops,' and 'going negative'] and the need to respond immediately and effectively to distortions of one's record and one's positions" (Butterfield 1990). The opposing candidate is generally in a better position than the news media or anyone else to combat such practices. But the Republican candidate did the political process the greater disservice by engaging in them in the first place.

A positive note was the occurrence of two debates between the 1988 presidential contenders. In light of the fact that debates between presidential candidates have taken place in only four previous elections (1960, 1976, 1980, and 1984) this was noteworthy and laudable. Markle research (Table 5-15) shows that as many as 80 million people may have watched portions of each debate; there were far and away the largest audiences for any campaign events. Especially noteworthy is the fact that between 30 and 45 percent of our survey samples said that they were influenced by the debates. Since the data show that some 47 percent remained undecided between Dukakis and Bush before the first debate on September 25 (Table 5-1), it is clear that people were still open to influence.

Some critics have suggested that the 1988 debate format allowed too little informal exchange between the candidates (Markey and Graham 1989). The experience of other nations, such as France, shows that less structured verbal contests between presidential candidates can be much more evocative than our own 1988 format of the real thinking of the candidates. There is always room for improvement.

But as had happened only twice before (in 1960 and 1980), the 1988 debates, and particularly the second presidential debate on October 13, would put to rest reservations about the debate winner, thus enabling him to reach the White House. For both candidates and voters, then, these were high-stakes events. Most important, the 1988 debates were the least scripted and controlled opportunities the voters had to watch the candidates' minds at work. Citizens cannot learn all that should be known about candidate qualifications by watching debates. But the unedited exposure to the candidates the debates offered was enough to make them the two most genuine and significant educational opportunities for citizens during the 1988 campaign.

It is hard to find other good things to say about the candidates' use of their respective campaigns. The public respect accorded their status as the finalists for the nation's highest leadership position, their control of enormous financial resources and extraordinarily talented advisors, plus their monopoly on information the media need in order to cover the campaign, all conspire to situate presidential candidates in the strongest, most commanding position with respect to the operation of democracy's greatest ceremonies. This is increasingly unfortunate, for candidates and their advisors show less and less regard for political civility or for the needs, rights, and sovereign status of the people whose support they seek.

In their book on the 1988 election, Jack W. Germond and Jules Whitcover entitled their last chapter "Anything Goes" (1989:456). The phrase nicely captures the spirit of an ethos that places winning above all else. The cynical value structure of the new insider's game is symbolized by the "handlers" of the winning campaign—Roger Ailes and Lee Atwater. These men, like most of their campaign and advertising colleagues across the political spectrum (e.g., Robert Squier), regard it as both necessary and legitimate to ignore the needs of voters and what they see as overly romanticized notions of good democratic practice in pursuit of victory for their clients.

At post-election conferences like that held at Harvard's Kennedy School in December 1988, handlers are surprisingly frank about how they manipulate candidate issue positions and attempt to push voter "hot buttons" in search of votes (see Runkel 1989:267–270). The clear implication of their frankness is that the candidate's real policy positions and intentions are none of the voters' business. It is *caveat civis* (let the voter, like the buyer, beware!) in the political marketplace. They show their conviction that the campaign process is for candidates and their handlers to manipulate at will unless and until somebody can muster the clout to make them stop. These are precisely the attitudes and values that give the public the impression that politics is such a cynical, unsavory business.

The handlers are also unpersuaded by arguments that "hardball" tactics were not necessary to produce a Bush victory in 1988 and will rarely override economic and international conditions as determinants of presidential election outcomes in any case. And they are defiant and unrepentant in the face of a growing chorus of criticism of the precedent they are accused of setting for political campaigns to come. Roger Ailes, for example, argues that the whole basis for his reputation as a master of "gut punching negative ads" is unfounded: "I probably make more positive ads than anybody . . . I won the top award for a positive ad from the Political Consultants Association last year, the spot where Bush is picking up his granddaughter at the end. How come nobody reports that?" (Reid 1989:14).

Students of political advertising corroborate Ailes's claim that he has produced more positive than negative ads. But Ailes sidesteps the point that matters: his contributions to the negative political arts—because of their perceived effectiveness and because of the widespread media publicity they have received—have come to symbolize an ethos that has done far more to influence public impressions of the political process than has his positive work, however plentiful.[9]

Recommendations for Candidates

The Markle Commission offered three recommendations specifically to candidates. They were:

(1) **Candidates pledge to conduct clean campaigns.**
We believe Presidential candidates must accept responsibility for helping the electorate prepare itself for informed choice. Their proposals, priorities and policy statements should be made clearly, and should be responsive to voters' questions and concerns. They should pledge to conduct themselves and their campaigns in ways that encourage citizens to respect and support the political process. We call upon Presidential aspirants to reject misleading advertising and to accept formal public responsibility for all advertising deployed in support of their candidacies. And we invite future victims of distorted commercial attacks to join us in proclaiming that such advertising prostitutes the electoral process, trivializes democracy and shows contempt for the people it seeks to mislead.

The trivialization of the campaign process with pseudo-themes and attack advertising completely distracted public discourse and diverted too much media and public attention away from the actual issue agenda and the qualifications of the candidates in 1988. It had similar impacts on the state and local races that followed. "Attack" campaign commercials in particular have come to symbolize the "state of the art" of public office seeking in America. Too infrequent condemnation and unchallenged repetition of such calumny has allowed it to establish a strong foothold and a claim to normalcy in American politics. This is deplorable, for it breeds public cynicism and distaste and almost certainly discourages voting.

The treatment for this disorder, however, cannot be imposed from without. Constitution and law prevent that. Thomas Jefferson's admonition, in his first inaugural address, still stands: "error of opinion" should be tolerated wherever reason is left free to combat it. But misleading advertising deserves vigorous condemnation as a violation of the spirit of American political ideals and as fundamentally disrespectful to voters.

Getting elected has always been the primary objective of presidential candidates and their organizations. Even textbooks of American politics, which generally pay some attention to ideals as well as hard-nosed realities, portray candidates as single-minded seekers of victory (e.g., Wilson 1986:179). Political professionals regard it as naïve to expect candidates to disavow what they euphemistically term "comparative" (instead of the more accurate labels, "attack" or "negative") advertising or to address "no-win" issues like the budget deficit when to do so might reduce the chances of victory. The 1988 presidential campaign struck most outside observers as less issue-oriented and more mean-spirited than usual. But defenders like those cited in Chapter 1 point to its consistency with well-established American political traditions, plus the naïveté of expecting candidates caught up in the heat of battle to do other than seek ways to prevail.

The 1988 campaign may indeed have been no more than the latest expression of political business as usual. But this kind of status quo alienates the American electorate and widens the chasm between campaigning and governing. Future presidential and other candidates must be persuaded to join in the effort to reintegrate the electorate into the campaign process. They can do so by acknowledging that they have responsibilities to the political order that go beyond the single-minded pursuit of victory, as suggested by the Markle Commission.

The insiders' norms of "victory at any price" have become unacceptably destructive to the American political process at every level. The time has come for political professionals—candidates and their advisors—to face and acknowledge responsibility for these costs. However contrary to the self-interests of office-seekers, ways must be found to revise the corrosive political status quo, so that candidates no longer feel compelled to cheapen and otherwise diminish the very system they seek to lead.

(2) *Make four Presidential debates permanent and condition public campaign funding on candidate participation.*

Research shows that the public pays more attention to the debates than any other campaign event. Therefore, the format and content of the debates should be designed to inform the voters of the comparative qualifications of candidates for the Presidency, including their records, their political alliances, their stands on other vital concerns of the citizens. The Commission recommends that public funding of campaigns be conditioned on candidate commitment to participate and that the debates become permanent future fixtures of Presidential campaigns.[10]

To improve direct candidate participation in the public dialogue, back-to-back appearances in discussions of the great issues should be considered.

We also suggest the debates be organized by a national committee of citizens in consultation with the political parties. And we strongly recommend that the debates be set a year in advance and be built into the media and political calendars.

Markle research suggests that the 1988 debates were the most significant learning opportunities available to voters. That is why presidential candidate debates should be institutionalized. We note that this was also the recommendation of the Commission on National Elections in 1986, and of a Harvard study sponsored by the Twentieth Century Fund in the same year. Debates are too important to the public interest to depend entirely on the vagaries and uncertainties of each successive election for their existence. It is understandable that candidates should seek a measure of control over such make-or-break events. And each nominee must ultimately decide whether to take part. But the public interest requires that the process of institutionalization begun in 1987 with the formation of the Commission on Presidential Debates should continue.[11]

It is true that the interests of parties and their candidates, who seek to win elections, are not precisely the same as the interests of citizens who watch debates, and who want unedited access to candid information about the hopefuls. Both major party nominees will usually favor more restrictive and protective debate ground rules than nonpartisan observers would prefer. As a practical matter, however, it is unlikely that any candidate will ever accept a debate format deemed harmful to the candidacy. Because of its sensitivity to this reality, a party-sponsored organization may have a better chance to institutionalize debates than would another organization that insisted on dictating the format to the candidates. Institutionalization must be the first priority, however, because even restrictive formats are better than no debates at all.[12]

Finally, the commission felt that candidates should be encouraged to shorten the campaign season to avoid demotivating voters because of overexposure.

(3) Make available matching funds for campaign expenditures only during the calendar year in which the election occurs.

There is a growing feeling that the electoral process from primaries to election takes too long thus discouraging voter turnout and increasing costs. Therefore, in an effort to shorten the candidate selection process and prevent voter apathy and boredom from becoming voter frustration and distaste, the Commission recommends that matching funds be provided for campaign expenditures only during the calendar year in which the election occurs.

The Media

Assessment

Three things were identified earlier (Chapter 2) that a democratic society might reasonably expect of private-sector news organizations upon whom it has conferred unique constitutional protections and near-monopoly control of the public information space. That they

(1) make available to the public information and analyses of the problems facing the nation and the qualifications of those who would be president;

(2) seek to protect the public from misinformation and self-interested distortions purveyed by candidates; and

(3) continually rethink and refine political coverage practices in response to the evolving methods of candidates and the changing needs of the electorate.

We found, in connection with item 1, that the media did make relevant information about candidates and issues available during the Labor-Day-to-election-day time period covered by our study. Our content analysis showed that the print and broadcast news media together devoted just under 30 percent of their coverage to the problems facing the nation and to the qualifications of candidates (Chapter 4; Tables 4-1, 4-4, 4-6). Readers and viewers willing to search could find topflight policy-analysis journalism, from which they could piece together their own assessments of the state of the nation and the next president's agenda (and, parenthetically, could increase their familiarity with candidate issue positions; see Chapter 5, Table 5-13).

We note also that the two C-SPAN channels attempted to become the "networks of record" for the 1988 campaign, devoting some 1,200 hours of original programming to campaign coverage between April and November (Lamb 1988:6). A great deal of relevant information, then, was made available.

But did the public make use of it? Only to a limited extent. We found, on the one hand, that media issue coverage was largely responsible for convincing a substantial number of Americans that the budget deficit, generally ignored by the candidates, was the nation's most important problem (Table 5-6). But other evidence shows that little additional substantive knowledge of national problems or candidate qualifications was taken in by the electorate (Chapter 5; Tables 5-1–5-11). This cannot be blamed entirely on the media, as attention to their coverage is not mandatory. But news organizations can do more to make relevant information appealing and useful, as suggested in the commission recommendations below.

The distribution of coverage across the categories shown in Table 4-1 raises familiar but important questions about media coverage policies. Does 30 percent constitute sufficient attention to issues and qualifications? Arguably not. Does the devotion of nearly 57 percent of post–Labor Day media coverage to the political contest and to candidate conflicts divert too many resources from providing information more directly relevant to the voting choice? It surely does. The heavy weighting on horse-race and candidate-conflict reporting shows a clear need for a greater balancing of policy-issue and candidate-qualification coverage. But on this as on other counts a distinction must be drawn between television and newspaper election coverage.

Television has become the central focus of the modern presidential campaign, for both candidates and citizens. Candidates design their campaigns and their speeches to produce visuals and "sound bites" that television producers will deem worthy of broadcast on the evening news. Reagan media specialist Michael Deaver, widely perceived as an architect of televised political image crafting, argues that he simply adapted an existing television news technique that was already widely used (Deaver 1988 : 34). And Bush media director Roger Ailes maintained that since television news would cover nothing but "polls, pictures, mistakes and attacks," a candidate had no choice but to feature such things as the price of getting on the all-important nightly newscast. Ailes also expressed surprise that "network news [led] in the evening with the new ads" during the 1988 campaign (McCarthy 1988 : 70).

In a book on the 1988 election, two veteran reporters suggest how well the Bush team harnessed television: "The three major television networks—NBC, CBS and ABC—contributed to Dukakis' lot by allowing their coverage, day after day, to be dictated by an agenda carefully prepared by the professionals managing the Bush campaign" (Germond and Witcover 1989 : 400).

Serious television coverage of presidential campaigns began only in 1952, and extended coverage only in the 1960's (Stanley and Niemi 1989 : 46). As recently as the 1984 presidential campaign, the print press still set the pace and the tone for coverage of the race, with television network reporters turning to the pages of the leading newspapers for help in planning their own coverage. By 1988, however, the tables had turned. Leading newspapers increasingly gave prominent attention in their own campaign coverage to the advertising and news-broadcast video wars between the candidates (see, for example, Table 4-7).

Newspapers covered the TV wars, then, but they still devoted more space in 1988 than did television news to the issues, as our findings in Table 4-2 show. By then, however, most voters were getting their campaign news from television (Stanley and Niemi 1989:48). And as Table 4-2 shows, the horse race was the dominant election story on every network except PBS.

The unfolding drama of the daily contest between the contenders is surely news, as journalists traditionally define that term. The first thing most voters want to know about the election each day is who is winning and losing. But an undue preoccupation with the race itself, to the exclusion of more substantive reporting, can influence the process by conveying to voters the notion that shrewd campaigning by a candidate with slick staging is an adequate test of suitability for office.

Recommendations

The dominance of television and the comparative neglect of issues and candidate qualifications coverage during the 1988 campaign led the Markle Commission to this initial recommendation to the media:

(1) *During Presidential campaigns, implement in one vital way the responsibility of broadcasters to act as public trustees. Congress should direct the FCC to call upon the networks regularly to offer public service airtime during Presidential campaigns to educate the electorate on the Democratic process.*

The United States government allocated the public airwaves free to a limited number of short-term license holders. Many more groups want broadcast licenses than there are available frequencies or channels. Under this existing scheme, the broadcaster is a trustee for all those not able to speak over the air, and agrees to render public service to its community and not simply strive to maximize profits.

The Supreme Court has therefore held that in the unique case of broadcasting, the First Amendment rights of the viewer/listener are paramount, and not second to those of the broadcast licensee. For 60% of viewers/listeners, according to Roper, the primary source of news and information is television.

Several constructive approaches together would greatly improve television service to the public and the dependable availability of informative political programming.

In order to reach the widest possible audience, from Labor Day to Election Day Congress should suspend Section 315(a) of the Communications Act mandating equal time, as was done in 1960. The intention is that the networks will devote a substantial amount of free time to the major candidates during prime time. In 1960, over 35 hours were scheduled when Section 315 was lifted.[13]

Such campaign coverage should include back-to-back or rotating candidate and party presentations, extended and more open debate and interview formats, background pieces on national issues and reviews of candidate qualifications.

Non-commercial broadcasting or another broadcast group might choose to become "The Election Channel," devoting sizeable un-edited blocks of time for campaign coverage and for in-depth exploration of candidates and issues and for use by the political parties. Such programming would greatly benefit the electorate and the political process.

We also suggest that local stations are in the best position to involve the public directly in discussions of campaign issues. Interactive programs that give citizens closer contact and encourage fuller understanding of the issues and the candidates are most desirable. Cooperative efforts in this respect with local cable television systems should be undertaken.

Turning to media expectation number 2, we find that leading news organizations did indeed call attention to candidate misrepresentations and inconsistencies in the late stages of the 1988 presidential campaign (Grove 1988; A Closer Look 1988; Broder 1989c). Most such distortions occurred in paid candidate advertising, and media coverage of that subject amounted to a major portion of the 4.4 percent allocated to media stories in Table 4-1.[14] But according to one close student of American presidential campaign advertising, "Only when the Bush 'tank' ad rumbled into the World Series did its obvious distortion of Dukakis' defense posture prompt ABC, and then the other networks, The Washington Post and the other major papers to set the record straight" (Jamieson 1988). This suggests that candidate distortions should have been publicized earlier.

They might also have been given more extensive coverage. For our research showed that the bulk of media stories about candidate advertising in 1988 did not scrutinize veracity, but instead emphasized the strategic guile of Republican ads and the political ineffectiveness of the Democratic advertising. In this sense, it overlapped with the political-horse-race coverage category and reflected what seemed to be a fascination among reporters with the evolving technology of presidential campaigning. Opposing candidates and an attentive public share responsibility with the press for "blowing the whistle" on candidate inaccuracies and distortions. Still, it seems clear that closer and more consistent media attention to how well candidate assertions square with the facts would benefit the public. Thus, the following commission recommendation:

(2) *Broadcasters and publishers assume a more substantive role in seeking the truth of candidate claims in advertising—both claims made in candidates' own statements and in those made by others in their names.*

So that the candidates will have direct and clear responsibility for all print ads and commercials, we recommend that print and broadcast advertising carry identification of the candidate in whose behalf it is run and, where appropriate, include verification that the candidate has seen and approved it. Also, the media should be alert to calling controversial ads to the attention of the candidates, and ask whether they stand by them.

We further urge that, at the least, media owe the same duty here as in the commercial product area and, therefore, must be diligent to verify the truth in these claims where advertisements are subject to broadcaster control.

As for expectation number 3 above, serving the public interest arguably requires a continuous process of rethinking, updating, improving, and fine-tuning coverage practices in response to changing campaign technology and strategy, and to the evolving needs and interests of the public. Just as new circumstances (e.g., more sophisticated and aggressive campaign strategies) became apparent in 1988, others will emerge in 1992 and beyond.

The press has a record of adaptation to changing public needs and political circumstances. When political parties yielded to primaries the task of screening candidate qualifications, for example, the media's role in scrutinizing candidates greatly increased (Patterson 1989).

The changes continue. The 1988 campaign was scarcely over before one major television network announced plans to alter its coverage policies in response to increased candidate emphasis on controlled staging of campaign events. When their 1988 election postmortem concluded that candidate efforts to manipulate the nightly news (e.g., the flag factory, the tank ride, etc.) were reaching egregious levels, ABC News said it would no longer cover staged events without the opportunity to ask the candidate questions (Apple 1989). It is to be hoped that the other networks will follow suit.

Additional 1988 innovations deserve note as well. The practice of juxtaposing false or distorted candidate claims alongside the disconfirming facts, point by point, was an extremely valuable service provided by at least one network and several print publications. By the time of the 1990 elections, this procedure was fast becoming a staple of media campaign coverage (see endnote 9). Efforts to help the general public make sense of the nation's problems and priorities, such as the ABC News American Agenda feature, should also be increased. The series of one-on-one interviews conducted by Marvin Kalb with 1988's pre-convention candidates and broadcast over public television and radio were illuminating and valuable, as were the lengthy one-on-one network television interviews with Michael Dukakis (Bush declined similar invitations) just before election day.

The excellent Public Broadcasting System telebiographies of Michael Dukakis and George Bush (broadcast on a program called "The Choice") were major highlights of the media campaign coverage season. In-depth biographical information about the candidates is crucial to citizen preparation for the electoral choice. Biographies could usefully become standard media coverage fare during all campaign seasons, much as horse-race coverage is now. The popularity of such publications as *TV Guide* and *People Magazine* suggest that there is potentially a vast audience that is eager for detailed information about the lives of presidential candidates as well as of entertainers and other public figures.[15]

Such examples highlight an experimental journalistic tradition worth expanding. In addition to calling upon communications-industry leaders and professional organizations to consider shifting journalistic resources away from the campaign horse race and toward issues, qualifications, "truthsquadding," and biography, the commission also invited them to consider expanded commitments to experimentation of the sort mentioned above, with special attention to counteracting the abuses of candidates. Thus, the third and final media recommendation:

(3) *Create internal initiatives within the news media to re-examine and refine the traditional methods of Presidential campaign coverage to counter the cynical misuse of media susceptibilities in order to manipulate the public's perceptions.*

Reflecting their serious concern, throughout the spring of 1990 much journalistic self-examination has centered on a group of sophisticated, media-wise political handlers who sought with consid-

erable success in 1988 to put a tilt or spin on campaign events. Their activities were deliberately designed to distort fact, misrepresent meaning and manufacture happenings to favor their side and to injure their adversaries. These manipulators exploited such susceptibilities as television's reliance on the short sound bite, and provision of colorful action for the cameras, or the print press' dependence on photo opportunities and captivity within the candidate's agenda. The political parties who might have served to verify information for the press were largely absent from the field.

To protect itself as well as the public from misuse, the press would well serve the democratic process by pursuing and sustaining a thoroughly systematic examination of the unhappy 1988 phenomenon through debate among news professionals to find effective remedies for 1992. Far from wearying of or abandoning this search, we urge such organizations as the American Newspaper Publishers Association, the American Society of Newspaper Editors, the National Association of Broadcasters and the Radio/Television News Directors Association, to use their leadership positions and their foundations to sponsor more internal dialogue on their convention platforms and in other ways. We urge such training, educational and research institutions as the American Press Institute, the Poynter Institute, the Joan Shorenstein Barone Center, the Gannett Center and the Thomas Jefferson Center for the Protection of Free Expression to seek new approaches for direct action. And we urge individual writers and thinkers in political science as well as political journalism to engage this issue before it takes root as a malignancy on the political process.

Conclusion

The Markle Commission concluded its report with three general recommendations concerning election mechanics that require no elaboration. They were:

(1) **Institute simultaneous poll hours throughout the 50 states by establishing a 20-hour election day.**

Presently, each state establishes the times at which polls open and close for all elections. However, in Presidential general elections, announced results from eastern states, after their polls have closed, may have an adverse impact on voters in western states. This has been an issue of growing importance for 20 years.

Unlike other election day intrusions, which expose voters to the influence of last-minute claims or charges by one side or the other in an election, current practice confronts voters with "facts" from an independent source; i.e., the news media, announcing projections made from exit polls. Those "facts" reveal the results of an election—who won and who lost—in which some voters have not even had the opportunity to participate.

Organizing election day so as to treat uniformly the opportunity to vote of citizens in all 50 states should be undertaken. Network commitments and press cooperation to refrain from "short-circuiting" the process with premature prognostication should be obtained as well.

(2) **Congress should act upon the broadcasters' good-faith commitment and elicit publishers' cooperation not to make public projections or announcements of winners in any elections in any state so long as any polls remain open in the 50 states.**

(3) *Simplify voter registration.*

Voter registration barriers discourage voter turnout. One way to simplify and ease the procedure would be to use as voter registration sites such accessible public agencies as libraries, post offices and other state and local institutions, thus allowing people to register in the course of using the service offered. In this vein, the Commission supports recently introduced "motor-voter" and postcard legislation. Social service agencies in particular can readily reach and enroll voters in a population that is disproportionately unregistered.

Taken together, the ten Markle Commission recommendations comprise a workable plan of action that, if implemented, could begin to realize Campaign 88's most important lesson: ownership of democracy's greatest ceremony must be restored to the American electorate.

NOTES

1. What Was Wrong with the 1988 Election?

1. According to *The 1989 Media Guide* (Wanniski, ed. 1989:50) the daily circulation of the *Wall Street Journal* is 2,025,176. Its editor is Robert L. Bartley.

2. The most carefully documented argument in support of the view that politics is appropriately concerned more with values than economics is that of Michael Barone (1990:xi), who argues: ". . . in the United States politics more often divides Americans along cultural than along economic lines . . . region, race, ethnicity, religion, or personal values . . . politics has often been a struggle to define who is really an American . . ."

3. The campaign waged by the Republicans in 1952 featured both negative attacks and distortions of the truth. "Taken all in all," writes Stephen E. Ambrose, "1952 is remembered as one of the bitterest campaigns of the twentieth century, and the one that featured the most mudslinging" (1987:298). "Terrible things were said . . . especially by Nixon about his opponents. Even Eisenhower's closest advisors regarded Nixon's charges against Truman, Acheson and the Democrats as 'Too strident, too loose, too exaggerated'" (ibid.:268). Bad things were also said about Stevenson by Joseph McCarthy and about Eisenhower by Truman.

The themes of "C2K"—Communism, Corruption, and Korea—set the tone of the Republican campaign, which was spearheaded by Richard Nixon while Dwight Eisenhower stayed above the battle. Only the loser, Adlai Stevenson, "could take some pride in his performance. Witty, thoughtful, intelligent, concerned, he envisioned an America that would build on and extend the social gains of the New Deal" (ibid.:296–299).

4. The 1988 campaign spawned a period of soul-searching about the state of American politics. "Is American politics so brain-dead," asked one politician, that such challenges as the economic integration of Europe in 1992, America's international competitiveness, second-rate domestic education, homelessness, and other problems cannot provoke a "vigorous, honest and

substantive debate between and within both parties about how they should be met?" Instead, "we are reduced to having political shysters manipulate symbols" (Oreskes 1990a:16).

5. Table 4-2 shows that television and print coverage patterns diverged, with television devoting more coverage than print to the political horse race.

6. The drug issue percolated up from the grass roots and became a campaign theme first of Jesse Jackson, who demonstrated the issue's importance to voters. Elite media such as the *New York Times* initially regarded the drug problem as a local and not a presidential issue. But they were eventually forced by the candidates and voters to acknowledge its importance in the presidential race. It was then adopted as a priority by George Bush during the fall campaign, and became a part of his attack on Michael Dukakis, forcing the latter to respond. The five-point increase from one survey to the next in the percentage regarding drugs as the most important presidential problem is therefore due to some combination of candidate attention, growing media attention, and continuing grass-roots awareness of the problem.

7. This was certainly true of our survey and focus group participants. The groups identified as presidential priorities the budget deficit, drugs, health care, education, and avoiding taxes, in that order. Health care and education, the third and fourth priorities, were (like drugs) highly visible issues in the daily lives of many voters that candidates and media began to emphasize in response to public concern. Avoiding taxes was a perennial political winner with voters that Vice President Bush's repetitious "read my lips, no new taxes" pledge made even more familiar.

8. Another bit of evidence concerns the impact of media coverage of candidate issue positions on public awareness of those positions. Table 5-13 shows that people who said they paid close attention to media campaign coverage did in fact display greater familiarity with candidate issue positions. And the old assumption that people pay more attention as the election draws nearer also appeared to be true. We found a 9 percent increase from one survey to the next in the number claiming to watch the media "very closely" (Table 5-12). The media also maintained a fairly high degree of credibility during the fall stretch drive. The portion of our two samples that regarded media coverage as "fair" remained stable at 60 percent.

9. Additional evidence of the impact on voters of the Bush campaign can be found in Table 5-7, which shows that learning about candidate issue positions generally favored the Bush candidacy. For example, by far the best-known issue position was the Bush stand in favor of capital punishment. It increased from 56 to 78 percent by the time of our second telephone survey. Our focus group discussions (Chapter 6) also provided abundant evidence of pervasive Bush influence on voters' perceptions of both candidates.

10. Before the Bush advertising campaign intensified after Labor Day (and at a time when our initial telephone survey showed the race virtually even, with Dukakis ahead of Bush 50 to 48 percent; see Table 5-1), first survey evidence in Tables 5-10 and 5-11 shows that voters had already formed what

proved to be stable impressions of the strengths and weaknesses of each presidential candidate. These impressions were of candidate attributes that were not directly mentioned in any campaign advertising, but that were quite clearly relevant to either candidate's suitability for the presidency, and of traditional importance to American voters.

In both our Labor Day and early November polls, for example, Bush was regarded as more knowledgeable and better able to make presidential decisions in foreign, economic, and domestic policy, and also better able to get things done in Washington, than Dukakis. The Massachusetts governor initially received higher "trustworthiness" ratings and was rated even or better in other areas as well. But none of the perceived Dukakis strengths involved attributes traditionally as important to voters in selecting presidents as those favoring Bush.

11. Key used election data from 1936 to 1960 to argue that voters are moved by concern about the relevant questions of public policy, of government performance, and of executive personality. He also commented on the use of manipulative campaign strategies, concluding that voters get what they will respond to: "because of the development of tricks for the manipulation of the masses, practices of political leadership in the management of voters have moved far toward the conversion of election campaigns into obscene parodies of the models set up by democratic idealists. They point to the good old days when politicians were deep thinkers, eloquent orators, and farsighted statesmen. Such estimates of the course of change in social institutions must be regarded with reserve" (1966:7). "If leaders believe the route to victory is by projection of images and cultivation of styles rather than by advocacy of policies to cope with the problems of the country, they will project images and cultivate styles to the neglect of the substance of politics" (ibid.:6). In short, leaders give voters what they perceive will move them, whether delusive nonsense or cold, hard realities.

12. A *Wall Street Journal*/NBC News survey conducted in January 1990 showed that by a margin of 63 to 24 percent, responding voters preferred that different parties control Congress and the White House (Washington Wire 1990). They may like the idea, but a Chapter 5 poll shows that voters weren't sure it was in force in the fall of 1988.

13. The survey data are supplemented by focus group discussions, where one major aim was to assess not only interest but also the capacity of voters to contribute to an upgrading of the quality of campaign practice. Anyone who listened to a sizeable number of the sixteen Markle group discussions would agree that such people have both the intellectual and the moral capacities for effective citizenship. Many also expressed the willingness to be at least somewhat more involved.

14. Sig Mickelson, appointed the first head of the News and Public Affairs division of CBS Television in 1952, writes of the hopes that the immediacy of television would introduce a new order of political campaigning, featuring better candidates, better-informed voters, greater participation, and the end of manipulative campaigns. Instead, he concludes, ratings have super-

seded the campaign process in the eyes of television executives, candidates are marketed like toothpaste, discussion of issues has been supplanted by "sound bites" representing philosophy by bumpersticker, and campaigns have degenerated into a series of nonevents (the flag factory, the tank ride) staged for television by handlers. "Television's grip on the viewing public turned out to be a virus weakening it from within" (Mickelson 1989).

15. This irony has not escaped international as well as domestic notice. Said Polish solidarity leader Lech Walesa at a luncheon with U.S. Senators in the fall of 1989: "Please take care of this country. Who is going to lead us if not you?" And "The energy of the new democracies abroad contrasts with the sometimes tattered democracy at home," says Senator Wyche Fowler (D., Ga.). "What's happening in Europe ought to be held up as a mirror to how well we are doing" (Rogers and Seib 1990).

16. Writing of the 1948 Senate election in Texas, Robert Caro articulates the value of carefully assessing a single election: "Explore a single individual deeply enough, Emerson noted, and truths about all individuals emerge. This is as true about campaigns as it is about men. Study a particular election in sufficient depth—study not merely the candidates' platforms and philosophies and promises but its payoffs, study it in all its brutality—focus deeply enough on all of these elements, and there will emerge universal truths about campaigns in a democracy, and about the nature of the power that shapes our lives" (1990:xxxi).

2. Good Democratic Practice: Responsibilities in Presidential Elections

1. On performance standards for print and broadcast news media, see the Hutchins Commission report, A Free and Responsible Press (Leigh, ed. 1947), and Robinson and Sheehan 1983:19. For a more elaborate analysis of media responsibilities than is offered in this chapter, see Siebert, Peterson, and Schramm, eds., Four Theories of the Press (1956). Their description of the "Social Responsibility Theory" is similar to what is suggested here. Numerous conferences for journalists, many now carried on C-Span, follow each national election and feature discussions of journalistic campaign coverage standards.

For an example of what are typically inconclusive but revealing discussions of the prevailing ethical standards among political consultants and candidates for the presidency, see Runkel 1989. The American Association of Political Consultants (AAPC) has a Code of Ethics that requires its members "to appeal to the good and commendable ideals in the American voters and not to indulge in irrational appeals . . . not to disseminate false or misleading information intentionally [and] not to indulge in any activity which corrupts or degrades the practice of political campaigning" (Broder 1989c).

Finally, there are many treatments of the demands of citizenship in classical writings on democratic theory, but relatively few discussions of citizenship demands in an era of television campaigns. For one quite demanding conception of civic obligation, see Benjamin Barber 1984.

2. The concepts of "good democratic practice" offered here will strike some readers as simplistic and naïve, given the brute realities that underlie citizen disinterest and the rough and tumble of hardball electoral politics in the real world. Such critics tend to regard any call for political or civic elevation as inherently futile and thus intrinsically naïve, since humans are seen as permanently and single-mindedly committed to self-interest motives and thus intensely unwilling (or even congenitally unable) to subordinate them to community interests.

Still others may resist suggestions for improvement either because of satisfaction with the political status quo, or simply because of a belief that the status quo is too powerfully supported to be displaced. Still, unhappiness with political practice in the 1988 and later elections was intense and widespread, suggesting a greater-than-usual willingness to consider the possibilities for improvement (Oreskes 1990a: 1).

The argument here is that improvement must begin with an explication of basic principles: idealistic "rules of the game" like those in the text, which, by casting the inadequacies of current practice into stark relief, help to pinpoint specific, desirable changes in the status quo. Those who find the "rules" spelled out here wanting for any reason are encouraged to formulate and publish alternatives for discussion.

3. American democratic ideals have figured importantly in international perceptions of America's moral stature and influence in the world. "America can hardly be said to be in decline," writes Oklahoma Democratic Senator David Boren, chair of the Senate Select Committee on Intelligence, "when hundreds of millions of people around the world take great risks to embrace our ideals. The words and ideas of Thomas Jefferson are on the lips of people from Managua to Prague, and the raising of the Statue of Liberty in Tiananmen Square symbolizes that the 20th century has been the American Century'" (1990).

4. The standards set forth in the chapter are hypotheses about the specific behaviors required to establish and sustain the democratic moral order described in the text (see next note). As hypotheses, they are subject to revision and change in the light of disconfirming experience. It is for this reason that they are portrayed as dynamic and subject to change in the body of the text.

5. Two things must be said about the particular concept of good democratic practice offered in the text. First, it is eclectic in origin. It draws on shared understandings, as revealed on editorial and op-ed pages, of informed observers concerning the "oughts" and "shoulds" of contemporary campaign practice. And it draws selectively from a great number of democratic theories, both normative and descriptive. For there is no single, widely accepted theory (see, e.g., Held 1987). The various uses and definitions of democratic theory within political science alone, for example, make use of economic assumptions (Downs 1957), public-opinion theories and spatial models (Page 1978), social-choice theories (Arrow 1963; Riker 1982), and responsible-party doctrines (Ranney 1962), among others.

In a critique of "foundationalist" thinkers who would impose conceptual purity on the political world, Benjamin Barber (1988:3–21) argues that the political domain takes our philosophical understandings (of democracy, justice, etc.) as its own mutable subject matter. In other words, there are no immutable definitions of democracy or anything else. Such political concepts must be rethought and redefined in the crucible of ongoing political practice. In this spirit, the text responds to the widespread unhappiness with political practice in the 1988 presidential campaign with a concept of "good democratic practice" intended to articulate the inchoate public expectations implicit in 1988's unhappiness.

Second, it is worth emphasizing that the present use of democratic concepts is unabashedly normative, rather than descriptive or explanatory. That is, the aim of the "good democratic practice" concept is to influence behavior in directions expected to increase the vitality and the democratic character of the American electoral system. In social science parlance, the intent here is to "change" the data, not to "fit" them.

This is in contrast to the orientation of so called "empirical" democratic theorists like Joseph A. Schumpeter (1947), who sought to reconfigure the idealistic theory away from the extensive participatory demands in the writings of Rousseau or J. S. Mill, in order to better fit the "reality" of citizen distance, apathy, and indifference to politics. In the following passage, Giovanni Sartori (1987:110) illustrates this approach: "How does the theory of democracy fare with respect to the findings on the poverty of public opinion and on the grand simplifications that occur in voting? My reply is that, despite all our misgivings about the practice, still the theory has a good fit for it. The electoral theory of democracy argues . . . that (a) democracy postulates an autonomous public opinion, (b) which sustains, via elections, consented governments, (c) which are in turn responsive to the opinions of the public. Nothing of the above is contradicted or falsified by the facts, by our evidence."

6. In explaining the relation between the theory of democracy and the theory of social choice, William H. Riker asserts: ". . . all democratic ideas are focused on the mechanism of voting. All the elements of the democratic method are means to render voting practically effective and politically significant, and all the elements of the democratic ideal are moral extensions and elaborations of the features of the method that make voting work. Voting, therefore, is the central act of democracy . . ." (1982:5).

7. Robert A. Dahl (1989) identifies two great historical transformations: the birth of democratic city-states in ancient Greece and Rome, where citizens participated in all governmental decisions, and the emergence in the eighteenth century of large-scale representative democracies in which democratic participation was for all practical purposes limited to voting in elections, which became more numerous and successively more inclusive in the nineteenth and twentieth centuries. Dahl speculates on whether a third democratic transformation might not be in the offing that would reverse the downsizing described in the text. The transformation would in-

volve a significant increase in citizen participation in economic and political life, primarily in economic and governmental organizations below the level of the nation-state.

8. Sartori (1987:152) credits this insight to Carl Friedrich, who termed it the principle of "anticipated reactions." See Friedrich 1941:Chapter 25.

9. The following excerpt—from an election-day editorial on democracy that the *Wall Street Journal* occasionally repeats—expresses the normative faith in this principle: "We sense increasingly that there is strength in the simple act of humble man choosing his own rulers, and precisely because he makes his choice neither the way the elites do nor the way the civics books describe. He knows from his own life the important things—whether he and his friends have jobs, whether his son may be sent to war. He has the smell of men, and needs no complex argument to know much about them. He knows, not from abstract reasoning but from what happens on the streets, what is fair and unfair.

"The common man's instincts can mislead and need to be tempered, of course, but the same is true of the elegant theories of his betters. So while the decisions that common men make today are not the whole of the system, they are a way of keeping rulers and policies down to earth, a crucial input that explains much of the strength in democracy's past and bodes well for continued strength in the future" (Whither Democracy 1988).

10. ". . . in a democracy," writes Robert A. Caro, "political power comes ultimately not from a gun's barrel or a monarch's manifesto but from a voting booth. Understanding political power in a democracy requires understanding elections" (1990:xxxi).

11. Curtis B. Gans, director of the Committee for the Study of the American Electorate, identifies six threats to democracy posed by nonvoting: (1) the threat of government by elites, of, for, and by the interested few; (2) the threat to policy formation in the general interest; (3) the threat of decreased voluntarism, as low turnout correlates with declines in other forms of socially conscious activity; (4) the threat of a "bleak future," as 18–24-year-olds presently vote at a 16.6 percent rate; (5) the threat to cohesion that accompanies ticket-splitting and party loss of vote share; and (6) the threat of demagoguery and authoritarianism (1988a:196).

12. This expectation, which underlies much editorial-page criticism of presidential candidates, can be traced to the "responsible-party" doctrine mentioned in note 5 above (e.g., Ranney 1962).

13. It also led two former members of Michael Dukakis's presidential campaign policy staff—noting that President Bush had begun to endorse many of the same measures candidate Bush had criticized his opponent for advocating—to complain that "the process by which we choose our leaders [has been reduced to] no more than a charade—a high stakes bait and switch" (Aronson and Georges 1990).

14. A mandate is a command or authorization, given by the electorate to its elected representative, the president, to act in particular ways on public issues. As used here the term further implies prior electoral approval for

planned action not on one single matter, like George Bush's 1988 campaign promise not to raise taxes, but on the most significant collection of issues facing the nation at a given time.

The reluctance of the 1988 candidates to seek this kind of a policy mandate can be traced to the political fortunes of 1984 Democratic presidential nominee Walter Mondale, and former Arizona Governor Bruce Babbitt in 1988, both of whom advocated tax increases as part of their programs. Like Ronald Reagan in 1984, George Bush achieved victory in 1988 without being specific about very many of his plans.

The view became fashionable in Washington during the 1988 campaign that a mandate for strong action to solve the most pressing economic and domestic problems could be fashioned after, rather than before, the election. *Washington Post* staffer Paul Taylor interviewed several campaign observers and participants who seemed to grant legitimacy to issueless, positionless campaigns. "I'm not sure you can prepare the country for what you would have to do, and still be elected," said one unidentified Dukakis staffer. Said the Urban Institute's Isabel Sawhill: "Maybe what the election is all about is finding an individual that the public trusts enough, both in a personal sense and in the sense of competence, to begin the process of educating them after the election about what really needs to be done." Democratic candidate Michael Dukakis's Issues Director, Christopher Edley, Jr., argued that campaigns should ask voters to choose among "a set of values not a set of draft budgets . . ." And former Reagan political director Mitchell Daniels said that the president-elect would be able to begin building a political mandate for hard budget choices after November 8 (Taylor 1988, p. 16).

Presidents have governed without mandates. But other approaches, such as building ad hoc coalitions, or using prerogative powers, do not make comparably efficient use of the resources of the presidency. That requires prior approval of the electorate and a governing consensus (party-based or otherwise) among legislators and the president's team, built in the election. Such prior approval can reduce the likelihood of policy stalemate. And it can reduce political resistance to other leadership strategies when they are employed.

15. "In societies where the government relies on popular participation through elections and through continuous scrutiny of the government's activities," writes Doris Graber, "political socialization must equip citizens with sufficient knowledge to participate effectively. If it fails to do this, elections, at best, become a sham; people go through the motions of making a choice without understanding what this choice means. At worst, elections become a mockery in which clever politicians manipulate an ignorant electorate. Likewise, surveillance of governmental activities is impossible if people lack a grasp of the nature of government and public policies" (1988:150).

16. Walter Lippmann argued persuasively that it is unreasonable to expect ordinary citizens to "run the democracy," that is, to have an informed view

on every important issue confronting the nation (Steel 1980:212). Still, it is reasonable to expect people, with the help of the press, candidates, and discussion with others, to develop a sense of what the country's major problems are, and of what an informed consensus of expert opinion thinks we ought to do about them. This small improvement alone would create pressure on candidates to deal with the policy agenda.

17. Sartori (1987:102—110) argues that since representative democracy shifts the burden of rationality from electorates to their representatives, the fact of ignorant, politically indifferent publics does no necessary violence to the theory of democracy. Only when, as in what Sartori calls referendum democracy, citizens must pass judgment on the intricate substance of policy, does Sartori think it necessary that they be well informed. The argument in the text suggests that a greater degree of citizen preparation than the low level Sartori tolerates is necessary for meaningful evaluation of the qualifications of candidates if democratic control is to be more than nominal and superficial.

18. Or at least rendered a superficial form. Any reasonable understanding of democracy would seem to require that those who fill the role of citizen be purposive agents, capable of acquiring the knowledge and exercising the self-discipline needed to make reasoned political choices. See Held 1987:180.

19. Paul J. Quirk (1989:65) writes: "There is an important role for unaffiliated participants, such as experts in various areas of policy, who can offer informed and relatively unbiased perspectives on the issues. The more penetrating and informed the campaign debate, the more honest and responsible the candidates will be and the more accurately the public will discern its interests."

20. Idealism aside, it makes only selfish, short-run sense for politicians to, in effect, consume the "seed corn" of the system (i.e., deplenish the tolerance and commitment of voters) just to get elected one more time. Evidence presented in Chapter 6 suggests that while "attack" campaigns may increase the electoral chances of their sponsors, they do so at significant cost both to voter turnout and to supportive political attitudes.

21. The following statement from Abramson, Atherton, and Orren (1988:22) illustrates communitarian values: "Democracy is not a process for allowing a majority to rule over minority interests antagonistically; it is a process of persuasion through which we seek to create and maintain a good life in common."

22. In a chapter discussing the "social responsibility theory" of the press, Theodore Peterson suggests that the economic responsibilities of news organizations are compatible with their public service responsibilities, because such organizations must establish economic self-sufficiency in order to be free from special interest pressures. (Siebert, Peterson, and Schramm, eds. 1956:73—103). Others regard economic imperatives as setting limits on the press's ability to function as civic educator and guardian of democracy (e.g., Entman 1989:3, 17).

23. On April 10, 1989, the Markle Commission convened a distinguished group of journalists to discuss these responsibilities. Although the discussion would generally support the standards discussed in the text, there was significant disagreement concerning how active the news media should be in attempting to improve the campaign process. ABC News reporter Sander Vanocur and *Baltimore Sun* reporter Jack Germond, for example, expressed the view that it is not the media's job to attempt to improve the process, and that journalists should confine themselves to "reporting what happens, period." On the other hand, *Washington Post* reporter David Broder, Washington Media Associates' Sherry Jones, and *New York Times* reporter R. W. Apple, among others, endorsed the view that the media should play an activist role in behalf of the process. Examples of what that would involve included increasing efforts to educate the electorate (Jim Squires, *Chicago Tribune*), attempting to "teach" the electorate that the election was their process, and not the private preserve of candidates (Broder), calling public attention to the fact that the candidates are evading the issues (Apple), and the like.

The disagreements extend to basic understandings of the media's role in the campaign process. For example, Eugene Patterson, a member of the Markle Commission and former chair of the Times Publishing Company, takes strong exception to the depiction of the media as an integral part of the electoral process, as is done in Figure 2-1. In his view, the figure misrepresents the media's status, which he regards as external to a formal process linking candidates and voters.

24. This runs against the grain of journalistic norms which stress news, i.e., coverage of recent happenings. Suggested here is that the media have an obligation to provide both types of coverage during a campaign season.

25. Kathleen Hall Jamieson, speaking at the Ripon College Media Conference, broadcast on C-Span on October 20, 1989, noted that in her book *Packaging the Presidency* (1984) she had said that the press prevents presidential candidates from lying. But that, she said, was before a candidate like Dukakis, who failed to respond vigorously and effectively to Bush advertising distortions, had been seen in American politics. Behavior like Dukakis's left it to the media to blow the whistle, which they did only belatedly and with great reluctance in 1988.

26. Larry J. Sabato (1981) suggests that national political reporters are reluctant to "truthsquad" political ads because of the importance the political consultants who create the ads have acquired as sources of "insider" campaign information for reporters. David Broder (1989c) quotes Democratic media consultant Dan Payne on the same point: "If you call the right consultants, you can find out what's going on in three or four races at once, in exchange for publicizing that person and increasing his reputation. It's a symbiotic relationship."

27. Ripon College Media Conference, October 20, 1989, C-Span broadcast.

28. Jamieson suggests that repetition is the key. It apparently takes a minimum of three audio exposures to override and correct an inaccurate visual impact.

3. The Research Strategy

1. For an example of an effort at systematic assessment of candidate "performance," see Benjamin I. Page's (1978:38) assessment of candidate issue stands. Page content-analyzed candidate speeches, interviews, and position papers to identify twenty-one Nixon positions and twenty-three Humphrey positions in the 1968 presidential election for comparison of candidate positions with public sentiment on the same or similar issues. The present study identified the 1988 candidates' positions on the "most important" public issues of the day (eight Bush and twelve Dukakis positions) for inclusion in the Harris surveys as tests of voter awareness of candidate issue positions. See Table 5-7 and surrounding discussion.

2. The Markle research program began with Labor Day because of its own late start, but also because Labor Day has long been considered the traditional beginning of the serious stretch of any presidential campaign. Although the 1988 campaign had been in progress for more than a year, most Americans had not begun tuning into the political contest between Michael Dukakis and George Bush until the two parties' nominating conventions. Labor Day is the point when most Americans turn back to school, back to work, back to business as usual after the summer vacation months. It is also the juncture at which television viewing of all kinds tends to increase.

The significance of Labor Day as a starting point is underscored by the fact that the 1988 candidates waited until then to begin commercial advertising in earnest. Michael Dukakis had begun running ads earlier, but stepped up their frequency. And George Bush's first ads of the campaign began running in California (Oreskes 1988b).

3. The group included James David Barber of Duke University and the Markle Commission, John McConahay of Duke as methodological consultant, Robert M. O'Neil of the University of Virginia and Markle Commission Chair, Louis Harris of Harris and Associates, Lloyd N. Morrisett and Edith Bjornson of the Markle Foundation, and Bruce Buchanan of the University of Texas at Austin, Markle Commission executive director and the study's principal investigator. Copies of the survey instrument may be obtained from Buchanan at the Department of Government, University of Texas, Austin, TX 78712.

4. The possibility of including in the second survey a small group of persons who had responded to the first, thus permitting assessment of learning by specific individuals, was considered and rejected as logistically impractical. Two separate random national samples were selected instead. Learning is inferred from the differences between those two samples on statistical grounds.

5. Mark Rovner and Brooks Clapp, both of the Roosevelt Center, shared responsibility for moderating the groups, while Bruce Buchanan, the principal investigator, monitored from observation rooms unseen by participants. Copies of the protocol can be obtained from Bruce Buchanan, Department of Government, University of Texas, Austin, TX 78712.

6. Copies of the coding protocol can be obtained from Bruce Buchanan, Department of Government, University of Texas, Austin, TX 78712.

4. The News Media in Campaign '88: What They Covered and How They Covered It

1. Recording, transcribing, and coding of print and broadcast news election stories were done for the Markle Commission by Luce Press Clipping Service. Coders were trained for the task by the principal investigator, Bruce Buchanan, who also developed the coding scheme.

2. A copy of the coding scheme can be obtained from Bruce Buchanan, Department of Government, University of Texas, Austin, TX 78712.

3. Research by Thomas E. Patterson (1989) extends this result backward in time to the start of the primary season for *Time* and *Newsweek*. Using a slightly more restrictive definition of horse-race coverage, Patterson established a figure of 32 percent. S. Robert Lichter, who monitored ABC, CBS, and NBC between August 19 and November 8, 1988, reports that 282 stories dealt with issues and 168 with the campaign horse race (1988).

4. Table 4-1 shows that the total of 7,574 coded Campaign '88 stories yielded 10,373 "allocations" because many stories fit into more than one category. The "percentage in category" figures are percentages of total allocations rather than total stories. Calculated this way, 36.1 percent of the story allocations were to the campaign horse-race category. Expressed another way, 49 percent of the 7,574 coded stories had significant campaign horse-race content, as well as other content. Coders were instructed to classify individual stories into as many categories as the story content warranted. This provides a much more accurate reflection of the nature of news coverage than arbitrarily classifying each story into one and only one category, as political content analysis has occasionally done. See Graber 1989:232n.48.

5. "If there were only one weekly we could select to keep up on life inside the Beltway," wrote Jude Wanniski and his colleagues in *The 1989 Media Guide*, "it would be this slim, totally serious, rather handsome periodical. NJ was founded some twenty years ago on a rock of objectivity and nonpartisanship at a time when American journalism was sliding into a romance with advocacy . . . [for the most part it has] kept the faith . . . Almost every other cover story attended to Campaign '88 in one way or another" (Wanniski, ed. 1989:113).

6. Said R. W. Apple in an article about media and voters' reactions to the candidates: "Voters' own negative feelings are clearly being reinforced by generally sour television coverage, in which Mr. Bush is portrayed as a man who spends 90 percent of his time on symbols and 10 percent, if that, on substance, and Mr. Dukakis is depicted as a cold fish who bumbles a lot . . . Newspapers have given the contest even poorer grades. In the Chicago Sun-Times, Robert Maynard, the columnist, said 10 days ago that both nominees are 'small bore,' partly because they feel constrained to campaign in 30-

second 'sound bites' for television—a problem, perhaps surprisingly, that many voters seem to understand as well as analysts of the news media . . . Television and newspaper commentators as well as voters complain constantly that the candidates are unwilling to say, because they are afraid they would lose support, how they would raise more revenues or cut Federal programs enough to reduce the deficit. They complain that they get no specifics on combatting the drug problem that now plagues all regions . . . All of this is likely not only to lead to another poor turnout—most local politicians are expecting not much more than half of the eligible electorate to show up at the polls—but also to produce a President without much of a mandate for anything" (Apple 1988).

7. One example of a possible effect is suggested by Rich Jaroslovsky, writing about the impact of the media's collective declaration that Bush had won on an NBC–*Wall Street Journal* survey of reactions to the second debate: "Our poll found a wider margin than some surveys taken immediately after the debate, suggesting a 'ripple effect' as more and more news reports crown the vice president the winner" (Jaroslovsky 1988).

8. Cable News Network, "Inside Politics," broadcast, October 17, 1988, 6:30 P.M. Eastern Time.

9. Broder also defends the tendency to focus on personality and character: "Elections are contests between individuals, not between philosophies . . . voters use issues to weigh the capabilities of the candidates and to refine their own feelings about the candidates' personalities and character. But the presidency is ultimately a test of character as much or more than a test of policy and management. And we are not mistaken if we focus primarily on the people who are candidates" (Broder 1987a:260).

10. As it happens, our group-interview evidence suggests that people may tune out such coverage, rather than fall unconsciously under its sway. See Chapter 6.

11. A perspective termed "communitarian" democracy, described by Abramson, Arterton, and Orren (1988:22), desires that political participation be a formative experience for citizens, aimed at awakening concern for larger public interests and at transcending narrow self-interest. Horse-race journalism not only does nothing to encourage citizens to view their voting choices less selfishly; it showcases a cynical view of the process, described in such terms by Jeff Greenfield: "[The media have a] fundamental view that politics is more image than substance; that ideas, policies, positions, and intentions are simply the wrappings in which a power struggle takes place" (quoted in Broder 1987a:259).

12. Debate transcript, *New York Times*, October 15, 1988.

13. It has been suggested that each qualification deserves priority attention in its appropriate season. Scrutiny of character logically comes first, as voters become acquainted with the presidential hopefuls as individuals. Ideally, questions of character and competence should be fully resolved prior to the anointment of the two finalists, so that both the Democratic and the Republican nominees can be regarded as acceptable on these grounds. That

permits issue positions and policy directions—which by the fall campaign should be the only remaining differences of importance between the candidates—to assume center stage after Labor Day (Buchanan 1988).

14. The first widespread awareness of the ability of television to intrude upon the political process in this way occurred during the 1980 election, when Jimmy Carter conceded the election to Ronald Reagan at 9:30 P.M. Eastern Standard Time. Two hours earlier, the television networks had announced that Reagan was the victor. The networks were accused of "making news" by prematurely forecasting returns as they competed in the race for ratings. In 1985, as the result of public pressure, the three major broadcast television networks, the Cable News Network, and Westinghouse Broadcasting Company agreed not to use their exit polling data to make election projections in a given state until the polls in that state had closed. But since eastern state vote totals sufficient to reveal the election's outcome became available in both 1984 and 1988 before polls in western states closed, it is clear that network cooperation alone is unlikely to solve the problem.

There is no conclusive proof that early network projections have a measurable effect on voter turnout. But the issue has prompted Congressional concern that voters be assured their votes count and help contribute to making the country's democratic system work. On April 5, 1989, the House of Representatives (for the third time since 1986) passed the Uniform Poll Closing Act (HR 18). It would require polling stations in the forty-eight contiguous states to close at the same time in presidential elections. The Senate Rules and Administration Committee held hearings for the first time and on May 17 approved the bill. The prospects for passage were good. See Bonafede 1989b:1242.

15. E. J. Dionne, Jr., for example, attributed the shift to increased voter familiarity with Dukakis shortcomings attributable to Bush advertising, a view repeated in numerous stories (Dionne 1988c). Another view, that of columnist William Safire, was that people were turned off by Dukakis's willingness to let Jesse Jackson dominate the Democratic National Convention (Safire 1988a:27). Still another theory—fashionable among academics and picked up in interpretive newspaper articles—was that voters express their vague dissatisfaction with the status quo with pre–Labor Day support of the opposition candidate, but revert to the "peace-and-prosperity" status quo as the election nears (Morin 1989:37).

16. The Communications Act of 1934 charges the Federal Communications Commission to "serve the public interest, convenience and necessity." In regulating the electronic media, the FCC has established rules that mandate public-service and local-interest programs. The print media are essentially uncontrolled except for Justice Department use of antitrust and monopoly laws to curtail monopolies.

17. An example of a story about nonvoters that combines news with implicit exhortation was an October 1988 Cox News Service piece by Joseph Albright and Marcia Kunstel (1988) entitled "Why Americans Do Not

Vote." The story reports the results of a poll identifying some characteristics of nonvoters, and thus contains "news." But it also features such admonishing sentences as this subtitle: "[Voting is] your right in our society, and it's easier to do than ever. Yet almost half of eligible Americans choose not to vote. How do those non-voters justify a democracy driven at half-speed?"

18. An example of one journalist's effort to prod citizens to prepare themselves to evaluate presidential candidates rigorously is an article by the *Austin American-Statesman*'s political correspondent, Dave McNeely. McNeely used an interview with the Washington-based Roosevelt Center for American Public Policy Studies President Roger Molander as a point of departure. McNeely describes the Roosevelt Center's "U.S. 88" project as an effort to train voters to push candidates into substantive discussions of important issues. He quotes the Roosevelt Center's program goal statement: "It is based on a simple idea: that an informed citizenry—prepared to ask presidential candidates tough, penetrating policy questions—will get thorough, thoughtful answers. And it has a clear objective: a future president prepared to deal substantively and politically with some of America's most difficult problems." McNeely's lead reveals both his own attitude and the message he hopes his column will convey: "A nonpartisan, good-government organization is trying to help the American public pay as much attention to nuclear proliferation and agriculture policy as it does to whether Gary Hart really spent the night with Donna Rice" (McNeely 1987:B2).

19. Broder's concerned and supportive attitude toward the health of participatory democracy in the United States is not unusual among political journalists. Many if not most journalists, editors, and publishers take seriously their status as members of the "fourth estate," supporters and protectors of democracy, and the unofficial eyes and ears of the people. These values are displayed in occasional pieces like Broder's, which help to shore up the sentiments on which effective participatory democracy depend. The supportive attitudes of journalists represent a potentially valuable public-interest resource that is rarely harnessed in any systematic way.

20. There is a limit, however, to the degree of independence from the candidates the press is willing to exert. Review of the specific issues discussed within the policy categories by the leading media shows that the most frequent stimulus for in-depth issue stories was the emergence of the issue as a topic of discussion in the campaign. Within the domestic-policy category, for example, one heavily featured category was toxic waste—an important problem, to be sure, but no higher than the middle among the new president's immediate priorities. Still, because it became an issue as a result of the "Boston Harbor" ads and other Bush attacks on Dukakis, the media gave it substantial "issue-story" attention. Another example was offshore drilling, the subject of a September exchange between the candidates that touched off a round of background stories.

21. Data for elections prior to 1980 were derived from the final month's campaign coverage in twenty newspapers from communities of different

size and political orientation from all parts of the country. The newspapers are identified in Graber 1988:231. Interestingly, Graber limited her 1980 analysis to the *New York Times* because she found in the earlier multi-paper studies that there was great similarity in coverage patterns among news sources throughout the country. This may indeed be the case. However, our 1988 data show that there was great variation among newspapers (though not television) in terms of the number of stories devoted to foreign policy. Papers fitting the "elite" category, such as the *New York Times*, *Washington Post*, and *Los Angeles Times*, averaged thirty foreign-policy stories each between Labor Day and election day. More regionally oriented publications like the *New York Daily News*, *Chicago Tribune*, and *Sacramento Bee* averaged only ten such stories each during the same period. Graber's foreign-policy percentages are thus probably lower than a sample of the eighteen outlets used in our 1988 study would be for the elections Graber studied. In 1988, elite publications generally published more stories in all three categories, but the discrepancies were much less striking for economic and domestic policy.

22. In Chapter 5 we report the results of two national surveys testing voters' comprehension of candidate issue positions. See Table 5−7.

23. The research of Shanto Iyengar and Donald R. Kinder (1987) shows that television news exerts subliminal influence on people's beliefs about problem importance. In other words, TV news is already helping to shape the public's sense of the nation's policy priorities. But this influence is not explicitly acknowledged by television news leaders, nor do they accept any formal responsibility for the nature of the influence news broadcasts exert. This attitude, of course, precludes attention to the nature and the quality of the influence, or attempts to refine it in the public interest. The real question, then, is not whether the media ought to try to influence the public's sense of the national agenda, but whether anything is gained or lost if media policymakers accept responsibility in this area, as many have more explicitly done in the other intermediary functions noted in the text.

24. Our senior coder reports that there were more stories about the media's treatment of Dan Quayle than about any other topic in this "self-criticism" subcategory. Other media performance topics receiving more than fleeting attention in the fall of 1988 included the propriety of the pre-election tendency among reporters to portray George Bush as the likely winner (e.g., Dionne 1988e:1), reprisals of the familiar question of whether reporters let their political views affect their practice of journalism, the tensions engendered by a media ownership and management that is conservative supervising a predominantly liberal and democratic reporting staff, and an interview with CBS News President David Burke, whose acknowledgment that television news ought to be providing more issue-analysis coverage despite public disinterest prompted several stories (Jensen 1988:72).

25. Broadcast editorial by media analyst Martin Schram, Cable News Network, "Inside Politics," broadcast, October 17, 1988, 6:30 P.M. Eastern Time.

26. The candidates and their media tacticians clearly do attempt to ma-

nipulate voters' emotions with misleading, "hot-button" advertising such as the infamous prison-furlough and Boston Harbor ads, and must accept responsibility for doing so. Most journalists agree that the media should search out and report misleading or inaccurate candidate advertising as a service to the public. See Chapter 2.

But the larger question of who is truly to blame for the increased negativity of the advertising in the 1988 presidential campaign can get tricky. It can be argued, for example, that candidates are forced to operate this way by television's ratings-driven news values. "The fault is not the candidates'; they are prisoners of what our electoral process has become . . . The villain is TV, but not because it is staffed with irresponsible people—it is the nature of the beast and those who work for it are as much prisoners of the system as the candidates" (Morris 1988). This columnist's reasoning eventually leads him to exculpate television. TV, as a commercial enterprise, has no choice but to pander to audiences that insist on easily digestible messages—"sound bites"—in return for watching. Candidate advertising, which plays to the same audience, must therefore do the same thing. The columnist can't bring himself to explicitly say so, but his argument clearly makes the audience—viewers and voters—the root cause of the sorry state of presidential campaigns.

A writer who did say so was the *Washington Post*'s Charles Paul Freund. "So whose fault is all this? Why are our candidates so often mediocre, our campaigns so often mindless, our voter turnout so often embarrassingly low? All these questions point to one villain . . . everybody on the selling end of campaigns takes the electorate as they find it" (Freund 1988).

The candidates, as might be expected of vote-seekers, limit their finger-pointing to the media. Bush media director Roger Ailes, for example, argues that since the "free" media will cover nothing but polls, pictures, mistakes, and attacks, a "rational" candidate had no choice but to feature such things as the price of getting on the all-important nightly news. Ailes also expressed amazement that the "network news leads in the evening with the new ads," leaving unspoken the inference that such priorities could not help but increase the use of negative advertising by candidates (McCarthy 1988:70).

In response to related complaints about the substantive emptiness of campaigns, Reagan media specialist Michael Deaver also points to television news. He notes that the innovations for which he is credited (as master crafter of the Reagan image) came from observing how television news would reduce a candidate's thoughtful and specific speech on an issue to a visual and a ten-second sound bite.

". . . rather than inventing the effective visual or the 30-second sound bite, we simply adapted an existing TV news technique that was already widely used. That's why it always amuses me to watch someone like Tom Brokaw, Peter Jennings or Dan Rather sitting in a million-dollar set, their physical appearance the envy of every undertaker in the nation, criticizing a politician for trying to control his or her image."

Deaver also mentions a candidate "gripe" raised in the final 1988 debate:

"As George Bush correctly noted in the final debate, complaints about a lack of attention to issues ring hollow to two campaigns that see their efforts to discuss those issues lost in 'news' about polls and minor personality traits."

He concludes that it is unreasonable to expect political campaigns to do anything other than what they have done since the founding of the republic: to seek the best possible coverage for their side of the story (Deaver 1988:34).

These arguments show that allocating praise and blame for what is widely viewed as the dismal status of campaign practice is not a simple task. As suggested in Chapter 2 and elsewhere, media, citizens, and candidates alike share responsibility—although of different kinds—for the status quo.

27. Saying that "never before in a presidential campaign have televised ads sponsored by a major party candidate lied so blatantly as in the campaign of 1988," political advertising expert Kathleen Hall Jamieson (1988) points to several specifics, most from the Bush campaign. "The picture shows a pool of sludge and pollutants near a sign reading, "Danger/Radiation Hazard/No Swimming." The text indicts Massachusetts Gov. Michael S. Dukakis for failing to clean up Boston Harbor. But the sign shown has, in fact, nothing to do with Dukakis or his record. Instead it warns Navy personnel not to swim in waters that had once harbored nuclear submarines under repair . . . A procession of convicts circles through a revolving gate and marches toward the nation's living rooms. The ad invites the inference—false—that 268 first-degree murderers were furloughed by Dukakis to rape and kidnap. In fact only one first-degree murderer, Willie Horton, escaped furlough in Massachusetts and committed a violent crime— although others have done so under other furlough programs, including those run by the federal government and by California under the stewardship of then-Gov. Ronald Reagan."

"The Dukakis campaign joined in with an ad claiming that Bush cast 'the tie-breaking Senate vote to cut Social Security benefits,' when, instead, Bush had voted to eliminate a cost-of-living adjustment in benefits, thus eroding purchasing power but not diminishing the actual level of the checks" (Jamieson 1988:28).

28. The significance of the amount of attention given to correcting the record has to do with the correction's power to neutralize the effect of the original distortion. "The problem with ads that are untruthful," writes one columnist, "is that stories can be written saying that they are, but those stories run only once. A television ad runs many times, and usually continues to run even after it is shown to be wrong. That cynical, win-at-all-costs mentality is detrimental to our political system" (McNeely 1988:D15). Put another way, "single news segments cannot erase dozens of exposures to a sludge-clotted Boston Harbor" (Kathleen Hall Jamieson, quoted in Boot 1989:28). If the media were to accept responsibility for counteracting inaccurate advertising, they would be forced by the limiting facts of human memory to use the same technique of repetition. That is why many believe

that the most effective check against such distortion is not the media but the opposing candidate.

29. The ABC News piece on campaign ads, which attracted much attention at post-election media conferences, featured four statements from George Bush's tank ad ridiculing Michael Dukakis's defense positions and one statement from a Dukakis ad criticizing Bush's record on Social Security. Each was followed with an "in fact" sentence, correcting the record (Broder 1989c).

30. Coders recorded the total number of times each candidate's name was mentioned in each story (number of candidate "mentions") and judged whether each mention was positive, negative, or neutral. A computer program was devised to perform the following calculations. The first step was to determine which stories were about which candidates. Which candidate a story was about was decided by which one was mentioned most often in that story; 1,303 stories were eliminated from the analysis because of "dead heats," i.e., exactly equal numbers of mentions for both candidates.

The next task was to assess, for each of the candidates in turn, the preponderant tone of each of his stories. This was done by counting the number of positive, neutral, and negative mentions. A story was labeled "no preponderant tone" if positive and negative mentions balanced exactly. It was given one of the other labels if a majority of the mentions was positive, negative, or neutral.

5. What the Electorate Learned

1. This finding was particularly noted when the survey results were released to the media in May 1990. The headline in the *New York Times* story, for example, read, "Study Finds 'Astonishing' Indifference to Elections" (Oreskes 1990d).

2. In June 1988, the National Republican Congressional Committee (NRCC) conducted a survey of the electorate to assist in developing future Republican campaign strategy. They found that 45 percent of their respondents did not know that Democrats controlled the House of Representatives. See Edsall 1989.

3. A national survey conducted later (between March 21 and May 8, 1989) by the Survey Research Laboratory of Virginia Commonwealth University asked a dozen "civics-knowledge" questions that had appeared on polls conducted from 1945 to 1957. The responses showed an increase—to 69—in the percentage that could identify the Democratic Party as the one with the most members in the United States House of Representatives. Media coverage of the 1988 election results may have raised the level of public awareness of this basic fact. Other findings of the Virginia Commonwealth survey, when compared to results from surveys in the 1940's and 1950's, show some long-term learning, but still reinforce the frequently repeated finding that Americans are not well informed about their national government. For example, 46 percent knew that the first ten amendments to the

Constitution are collectively called the Bill of Rights, compared to 33 percent in a 1954 poll. Seventy-five percent correctly named the vice president of the United States as Dan Quayle, compared to 69 percent in 1952 who correctly named Alben W. Barkley. See Kagay 1989:15.

4. Before we can interpret these and other open-ended results properly, certain facts about polling and the electorate must be understood. Because most polls now rely exclusively on closed-ended questions, it is easy to suppose that survey populations divide neatly into large blocs that agree or disagree with whatever proposition is put before them. That is the kind of result closed questions produce. But such results convey a misleading picture of the actual distribution of public opinion. And by implicitly encouraging the impression that only large percentages matter (e.g., 52 percent agree, 48 percent disagree) it also wrongly downgrades the perceived significance of small percentages.

The electorate is not a homogeneous mass, but a collection of disparate groups with sharply different priorities. Different groups of voters take note of different kinds of information for reasons of their own. These facts are clearly understood by political strategists, who carefully tailor messages to appeal to particular voting groups and vary the message to suit the audience. They well recognize that a swing of only 2 or 3 percentage points represents millions of voters and can easily reverse an election result (Graber 1988:19). As few as 57 people, who would comprise 3 percent of our 1,875-person sample, can represent up to 5,098,890 people; the equivalent 3 percent of the 169,963,000 adults in the United States eighteen years old and over (1989 *World Almanac*, p. 322).

5. Giving voters an issues test is unusual, so a few words about procedures are in order. The portion of the telephone interview dealing with issue questions was introduced in a manner intended to be nonthreatening. We sought to avoid creating any "test performance anxiety," in which people felt diminished for not getting answers right. So the interviewers prefaced the issue questions with: "Sometimes the candidates make their stands clear, and sometimes they don't. Now, as far as you are concerned, which candidate (read each item: e.g., "favors keeping the Pledge of Allegiance in schools voluntary?" and so on).

As Table 5-7 shows, respondents to both surveys were asked twenty issue questions. An effort was made to restrict the pool of issue positions to those which had been publicized enough to have a reasonable chance of becoming known to ordinary citizens. We also sought to include issue positions representing each of the major policy domains: domestic, economic, and foreign-policy/national-security, and to balance the mix of Bush and Dukakis positions. There weren't enough issues meeting all these criteria to include the same number of issue position questions for each candidate and each policy category. That explains the slightly unbalanced mix in Table 5-7.

6. The percent linking the right candidate to each issue obviously includes some proportion of successful guessers. The customary adjustment procedure for guessing is to deduct the percentage incorrect from the per-

centage correct. For example, this would reduce the percentages getting Bush's capital-punishment position "right" to 39 and 66, respectively. The reader can easily calculate these adjustments. But they are not reported in Table 5-7 because the calculations yield several less-than-zero percentages (e.g., the percent accurately identifying Dukakis's position on conventional forces would move from − 27 in Survey 1 to − 19 in Survey 2). The effect of the adjustments would be to significantly lower the percentages estimated to be familiar with each issue position. That would not materially affect the analysis of the results in the text, where pervasive voter ignorance of issue positions is amply acknowledged.

As an alternative to the subtraction procedure, the percentage unsure for each issue position is reported. This clutters the table somewhat, but supplies another body of information relevant to estimating the extent of the "guessing" problem. The relatively high number willing to admit uncertainty about which candidate had endorsed particular issue positions (an average of 27.5 percent per item on the first survey and 22.4 percent on the second) implies that guessing was not excessive. It also suggests that the telephone interviewers succeeded in minimizing anxieties about revealing ignorance.

7. Thomas E. Patterson and R. D. McClure (1976) found that network news failed to adequately inform voters about the choices between the candidates and their issue positions. But Iyengar and Kinder (1987) demonstrate a pervasive educational impact for television, asserting that "television news is news that matters" (p. 2). Table 5-13 offers additional evidence that attention to media and knowledge of candidate positions are positively associated.

8. The two best-recognized Group B issue positions in Survey 2—Bush's cold war position and Dukakis's proposal of a fund to promote teaching excellence—probably owe their healthy 46 and 41 percent familiarity scores more to coincidentally accurate guesses about which party's candidate would be most likely to endorse either position than to familiarity with what the 1988 candidates actually said.

Conversely, Group C's low percentages are almost certainly the result of incorrect guesses based on inaccurate political-party assumptions. For example, an uninformed voter asked which candidate had promised to create 30 million new jobs would likely guess the Democratic candidate, but would be wrong, as some 52 percent were. Incorrect assumptions might also influence guessing which party's nominee would be likely to style himself as the education president, or which would be likely to propose a day-care tax credit, both Bush rather than Dukakis positions.

9. Analysts or pundits who are willing to take the American people to task are quite rare. The few political columnists who occasionally chastise the voters for their irresponsible ways include James Reston (1988b) and Jim Fain (1989). See also Allison and Smith 1988.

10. The other clear evidence of an educational impact was the media's implicit responsibility for the 5 percent increase in those regarding the budget deficit as the most important problem. See Table 5-6.

11. The Bush campaign's tactical superiority to the Dukakis campaign has been widely noted. Bush deliberately trumpeted issues that aroused voter interest by provoking anti-Dukakis emotion. Many analysts have deplored this aspect of the 1988 campaign. Critics have suggested that candidates should be held to higher standards, and that the press ought to reduce purely "horse-race" campaign coverage. But the public's own collective responsibility for deciding what is and isn't worth "learning" has gotten much less attention. This responsibility should be born in mind when allocating praise and blame for how well the recent presidential campaign served democracy.

12. Note that the great majority of the means in both tables fall in the positive range, i.e., between 6 and 10. This is evidence that Americans generally respected the qualifications of both candidates, and saw themselves as choosing between candidates who were both at least marginally acceptable on all twelve dimensions.

The range—the gap between the lowest (5.3) and the highest (7.5) means—is rather small, only 2.2 points. Most of the mean changes across surveys and differences between candidate means are fractional—less than 1 point. But with samples as large as these, such changes and differences are all statistically significant. And since every single change in both tables was consistent with the outcome of the election (that is, all the downward changes were in Dukakis assessments, and all the increases favored Bush), the implication is that these changes and differences were politically significant as well.

13. There may well be some "method variance" in these results; that is, asking people item after item about a given candidate leads many to fall into a rut, rattling off a standard response.

14. But other factors, like peace and prosperity, and fear that the inexperienced Dukakis might turn out to be another Jimmy Carter, were arguably as or more important. See note 15 and also Chapter 6's discussion of interpersonal influences on candidate preference.

15. Those who manage political campaigns for a living are convinced that Bush campaign tactics were a decisive force in the Bush victory. ". . . it is the bipartisan consensus of the [political] consultants," writes the *Washington Post*'s Paul Taylor, "that Bush's campaign was a technical masterpiece—an example of brilliant exploitation of the new political technology" (Taylor 1989:7). Our evidence certainly argues that the Bush campaign had a measurable impact on what eligible voters knew and felt about the candidates and the issues. We uncovered no comparably pervasive source of influence at work during the 1988 campaign.

But did the influence reported here affect the outcome of the election? The surprising answer is—marginally, at best. Several political scientists were able to predict the outcome of the election within a few tenths of a percentage point well in advance of the fall campaign (Morin 1989:37). They did so with models that used variables like voters' personal financial well-being, estimates of percentage change in real disposable income, and party identification as predictors. Such things were beyond the reach of campaign strategists and unaffected by the campaign itself, and, it must be added, unaffected by media coverage of the campaign.

Cataclysmic events or riveting candidate personalities can override circumstantial factors like peace and prosperity and affect election outcomes. But neither did so in 1988. Does this mean that the changes the Markle surveys were able to measure have no significance? Emphatically not. For the presidential campaign itself, and the media's coverage of it, undoubtedly did affect other indicators of democratic health that may actually be more important than who wins a particular election: voter turnout, voter confidence in and enthusiasm for the electoral process, and perhaps even the public's disposition to support the winner once in office.

The media covered the campaign extensively, which helped to intensify the campaign's demotivating impact on voters. University of Michigan political scientist Gregory Markus makes the case: "We had only a 50% turnout, and 60 percent of those who voted said they wished they could have voted for somebody else . . . Was it due to the nature of the campaign? Sure it was. You hear that campaigns are dirty business. It was qualitatively different this year. This one was really nasty, more so than other campaigns. I don't think those kinds of campaigns serve the country very well. That's something that candidates should think about" (quoted in Morin 1989:37).

16. Which groups tend to follow the media's campaign coverage most closely? Survey 2 results (not reported in tables) show that the greater the educational attainment, the higher the percentage following closely. Older people generally tended to follow more closely than younger people. Larger percentages of self-styled conservatives and Republicans (72 percent) followed more closely than moderates and Democrats (68 percent), with liberals and Independents behind at 62 percent.

Which groups performed best on the candidate issues test? Survey 2 results show that groups with more formal education had larger percentages in the high-knowledge category. There were no significant differences in the high-knowledge percentages of different age groups or ideological groupings. But 18 percent of Republicans and 16 percent of Independents scored in the top category on the issue-position knowledge test, while only 10 percent of Democrats did so.

17. The summer 1988 press treatment of Republican vice-presidential candidate Dan Quayle's controversial service in the National Guard during the Vietnam War stirred a groundswell of displeasure with the media that had not fully subsided by the time of the election. But the most durable source of displeasure with the media was general bias. A small but insistent part of the audience—mostly self-identified conservatives and moderates, with a sprinkling of liberals—felt coverage was slanted to favor some views and interests over others. These citizens are not alone in suspecting systematic bias. Bias is a recurring theme in the critical literature on the media, with conservatives alleging liberal bias (e.g., Rusher 1988; Lichter and Lichter 1986) and liberals alleging the opposite (e.g., Hertsgaard 1988; Herman and Chomsky 1988). There is a case for objectivity, however; it is made in Broder 1987a and elsewhere in this book (Chapter 4).

The next five criticisms, support for four of which declined from the first to the second survey, all reflect disapproval of perceived distortions in coverage of the news, and give some examples of specific "biases" that troubled small clusters of respondents. Whether spending too much time digging into the candidates' past, or blowing things out of proportion, or focusing on the negative, the alleged coverage fault lies with an inaccurate or otherwise flawed representation of what critics regard as real and important.

Two complaints not mentioned by respondents to the first survey emerged later in the campaign and raised questions that also received attention from the media during the campaign. The idea that there may have been an overemphasis on coverage of polls was mentioned by 5 percent of second-survey respondents, and also became a matter of discussion on the editorial pages of the *New York Times* (A. M. Rosenthal 1988:27). And Dukakis partisans outside our sample felt that questions like that about his wife's hypothetical rape posed to Michael Dukakis by CNN's Bernard Shaw during the second presidential debate were unfair (Toner 1988c).

6. Citizens in Groups

1. In his book *Behind the Front Page, Washington Post* correspondent David Broder suggests the value of combining polling data with depth interviews: "Sometimes we combine [depth] interviewing with scientific polling, in a way that, I think, gets the most out of both techniques. We have statistics that guard against . . . error, while preserving the insights that come from interviewing. In . . . interviews you hear the connections people make spontaneously between issues and personalities, and you sense which feelings are deep and persistent, which are superficial and subject to change. When those insights are put together with the polling data, you know much more than you could learn from either technique alone" (Broder 1987a:253).

2. Other efforts to take the measure of "ordinary people" include Lane 1962, Graber 1988, H. J. Gans 1988, and Bellah et al. 1985, although not all of these studies explicitly raised the question of improvability. In some respects the people we listened to were not as "ordinary" as those in earlier studies. As demographic data in Table 6-2 show, the 161 participants in our focus groups were better educated, somewhat less conservative, and otherwise differed from average representatives of the mass electorate. This was an unavoidable consequence of the need to include only those who were faithful consumers of media campaign coverage. Still, they are sufficiently similar that it would be seriously misleading to regard their strengths and weaknesses as utterly unlike those of their more "average" counterparts.

3. Focus-group research is qualitative research. Unlike quantitative research, which concerns itself with counting things to arrive at statistically projectable data, qualitative research addresses the nature or structure of attitudes and motivations rather than their frequency and distribution. The goal of qualitative research is to explore in depth the feelings and beliefs people hold, and to learn how these feelings may shape overt behavior. For an elaboration of the characteristics of qualitative, group depth-interview

methodology, see Alfred E. Goldman and Susan Schwartz McDonald *The Group Depth Interview* (1987). See also Richard A. Krueger *Focus Groups* (1988).

Our moderators followed a discussion protocol designed by the principal investigator; its contents are disclosed in the body of the chapter. But in keeping with the methodology of qualitative research, moderators were free to repeat and/or reword questions to work toward a psychologically valid representation of how people thought and felt about candidates, issues, and media.

4. One reason (in addition to the general wish to maximize diversity and heterogeneity) for conducting groups in each major region was that polls taken the summer before the start of the group research showed that people in different regions attached different priorities to particular policy problems. This was potentially important because personal priorities affect the perception and interpretation of information such as that disseminated by the media or campaign advertising. Research shows, for example, that citizens misperceive stands taken by leaders on policy issues in ways that reinforce and support their own views (Page and Brody 1972).

5. Two of our groups, both in Houston, Texas, were reassembled with nearly identical membership a second time, which permitted assessment of cross-time learning by the same individuals. As it turned out, very little change occurred in the knowledge or the attitudes of those in either returning group.

6. The focus-group discussions were conducted by the Roosevelt Center for American Public Policy Studies, Mark Rovner and Brooks Clapp, moderators. Fourteen of the sixteen sessions were observed from behind a one-way mirror by the principal investigator. Eight of the sessions were videotaped, all sixteen audio-recorded. Participants in focus groups were paid $40.00 for taking part in a two-hour discussion. They were recruited by telephone by professional market-research organizations in each region. These firms also provided meeting rooms and recording facilities.

7. Participants in the focus groups were recruited to meet three screening criteria. First, they had to be regular readers of the major local newspaper and regular watchers of at least one network television news program. This requirement, which reduced the samples' representativeness of the electorate on such characteristics as education (see Table 6-2), was necessary to permit investigation of media influences. Second, each group had to be composed of an approximately equal mixture of pro-Bush, pro-Dukakis, and undecided members, at the time of recruitment. Finally, a reasonably heterogeneous mix on such demographic characteristics as age, sex, race, and education was sought.

8. Since I personally witnessed fourteen of the sixteen sessions (and reviewed audio and video tapes of the other two), it is primarily my own perceptions and judgments that underlie the generalizations offered in this chapter. I do make occasional use of group votes taken during sessions, plus more systematic content analysis of group discussions to show the extent and sometimes depth of feelings about particular matters.

9. Robin M. Hogarth (1987) supplies a near-exhaustive "catalogue" of human judgmental fallibilities, many of which can be traced to the difficulties of integrating cognitive, affective, and normative dispositions. Other research has shown that people tend to focus on that which is unambiguous (Fiske 1980), extreme or intense (such as flashy political advertising or colorful, "human-interest" media coverage; see Tversky 1977), or especially salient to personally important values or symbols (Kinder and Fiske 1978). Another body of research guided by attribution theory (Kelley 1973) has uncovered various systematic human tendencies toward error in the comprehension and interpretation of information.

The point of all this is to suggest that as the media cover the gamut of services potentially desired by voters, from "What happened?/What are the facts?" to "Why does it matter?/How important is it?" to "How should I feel about it?" the preponderant emphases of their coverage might well be encouraging various systematic misperceptions, distortions, or overvaluations of the sort discovered in previous research. Group interactions offer one of the best opportunities to discover and document these tendencies.

10. That, parenthetically, is why virtually all concepts of responsible citizenship require the individual citizen to engage in some degree of preparatory "learning" about issues and candidates before deciding whom to support. Also implicit is some measure of discipline or self-control in weighing evidence and values against internal impulses or prejudices. This is a well-founded expectation, as it appears that the less people know, the more susceptible they are to potentially misleading influences like political advertising (Joslyn 1985).

Some recent research on neural pathways in mammalian brains conducted by psychologist Joseph LeDoux of the Center for Neural Science at New York University suggests that emotion actually occurs before thought, and may have impact independently of thought: "Emotional reactions and emotional memories can be formed without any conscious, cognitive participation at all because anatomically the emotion system can act independently," said LeDoux (cited by Goleman 1989).

This contradicts the prevailing wisdom in psychology that emotional reactions follow from thoughts about a situation. Emotions can be triggered before the brain has had time to register fully just what it is that is being responded to. Dr. LeDoux has evidence that this emotional reaction is stored as memory in the amygdala, the brain setting for processing emotional reactions. Once stored (something that apparently happens instantaneously), emotional memories are extremely resistant to being extinguished or edited.

"Once your emotion system learns something, it seems you never let it go ... What therapy does is teach you to control it. It teaches your cortex how to inhibit your amygdala. The propensity to act is suppressed, while your basic emotions about it may remain in a subdued form," said LeDoux.

The implications for the processing of political information are fascinating. Not only is the evidence of emotional impact on political reasoning abundant (see previous note), but it might also be the case that since politics gets little cognitive attention (i.e., sustained thought) from most people, primary emotional reactions to political stimuli take particularly deep root and are even less likely to be successfully edited or controlled later.

In these terms, one important aim of citizenship training can be seen as analogous to that of therapy: to teach the cortex how to inhibit the amygdala (Goleman 1989).

11. Responses to the learning question also illustrate a number of other interesting human tendencies. One is people's strong wish to make clear where they stand and whom they support at the earliest opportunity, even when the question doesn't require or even necessarily invite it. Another is that people urgently want to explain themselves, to give reasons for how they feel. A third is how feelings, in the form of preferences, may guide and shade what is noticed and how reasoning itself is performed. We see that political reasoning in these circumstances is often little more than feelings dressed up to appear rational. See the discussion of "closed" reasoners later in the text.

12. The letter-number appendages to names in the text refer to the location of the group, and to one of the four sessions held in each location. Thus S4 refers to the fourth Sacramento group, NY2 to the second New York group, and so on. This information pinpoints the date of the comment (see Table 6-1) as well as the location of the speaker.

13. Table 5-6 shows that samples of the mass electorate put domestic affairs at the top of the next president's priorities (73 percent), followed by economics (46 percent), foreign affairs (30 percent), and miscellaneous (8 percent). The comparable focus-group percentages were 57, 26, 13, and 5, respectively.

14. See Chapter 5. Herbert J. Gans (1988) notes that social scientists are fond of bemoaning people's ignorance of basic facts about government and its problems, as we did in expressing surprise in Chapter 5 that so few people knew who Lloyd Bentsen and Dan Quayle were. "The belief that Americans must know a series of historical and other facts in order to be proper citizens is not new. As a result, every so often historians and cultural critics earn momentary national fame by complaining about the citizenry's ignorance of facts from which, among other things, these writers earn their livelihoods."

15. See Table 4-1. A prominent student of "ordinary Americans" argues that the norm of avoidance leads people like those in our focus groups to ignore the kind of news reports that contain information relevant to an understanding of the agenda likely to be faced by the president they are about to choose. He writes: "Compared to people in many other countries, many Americans, middle and others, do not seem to need daily information about the government and the other large organizations that appear in the national news. They are able, in effect, to live a good deal of their lives without a regular informational or other tie to them" (H. J. Gans 1988:59). ". . . middle America's concentration on life in the family and informal groups detaches and distances people from most formal organizations which are not immediately and directly relevant to their lives and

their most important purposes. Even though people may know that Big Business, Big Government, and very large formal organizations exert a long-term influence on their lives, their concern and their knowledge about them remain limited as long as that influence remains indirect" (ibid.: 56).

16. This pervasive tendency to ignore the political arena may reflect trust and promote stability, as some democratic theorists have argued (e.g., Berelson, Lazarsfeld, and McPhee 1954; Berelson 1952), but it is a formidable barrier to engaging the electorate in any major restoration of civic participation, or to upgrading the quality of whatever participation there is.

17. Writes H. J. Gans (1988:61–62), "The distance middle America feels from the country and the doubts it has about government and its leaders contrast sharply with the close and supportive feelings it appears to have for 'the nation.' In a November 1985 *New York Times* poll in which 49 percent of the people said that they trusted the federal government to do what is right only some of the time or almost never, 87 percent also said they were very proud to be Americans. Bellah and his colleagues in *Habits of the Heart* reported similarly that 'we . . . found a widespread and strong identification with the United States as a national community. Yet, though the nation was viewed as good, "government" and "politics" often had negative connotations.'

"People can feel close to and identify with the nation because it is neither Big Government nor 'the country,' both of which are associated with domestic politics. For them, the nation is a symbol . . . people appear to treat it as an abstract and expressive symbol to be identified with rather than used as a basis for debating (say) foreign policy.

"Consequently, the nation may be the kind of symbol people can fit to their own needs and wishes, and many seem to believe that doing so entails no special obligations. The 1983 *New York Times* Patriotism Study showed that only a third of the sample felt that any action was required to love one's country. In answer to another question, 60 percent of the actions people considered patriotic were actually compulsory: serving in the armed forces and obeying the law. Two-thirds of those who were asked what made them proud about the country referred to various kinds of freedom, and another 12 percent to the standard of living or the opportunity for upward mobility . . . hostile acts against the nation such as the taking of hostages and terrorist attacks appear to evoke personal feelings of insult and humiliation . . . At other times the nation turns into a revered symbol—for example around national holidays and the birthdays of national figures . . . they are . . . services of the civic religion."

18. Media influence was apparently not a subject to which most participants had devoted much thought, however. For despite the best efforts of two experienced moderators, discussions of the media often seemed somewhat forced. There was little evidence of strong feeling one way or another; much less, for example, than for campaign advertising (see below).

19. The media attitudes expressed in the Markle groups were broadly consistent with those uncovered a year later in a late 1989 poll conducted for the Times Mirror Company by the Gallup organization. The poll found that

although the credibility of news organizations had declined since a similar poll four years earlier, people still reported viewing the press favorably: 82 percent for network news, 80 percent for local news, and 77 percent for newspapers (Rosenstiel 1989).

20. See Chapter 4, note 29 for a reference to the most widely noticed ABC news piece pointing out candidate misstatements.

21. Ellen Goodman, columnist for the *Boston Globe*, echoed this fear in a column complaining about excessive media attention to the horse race: "It reminded me of what a seasoned political reporter said to me just a few days ago. She went out into the heartland to find out what people were talking about this election year. She found out that they were talking about campaign strategy" (Goodman 1988).

22. Using only photographs, University of California at Irvine political scientist Shawn Rosenberg asked seven hundred subjects during the last year to rate real and mock politicians on characteristics like competence, trustworthiness, leadership ability, and political demeanor. He found that the best-looking, best-dressed candidates got much higher marks. He also found that he could push positive ratings up or down by as much as 20 points by showing pictures in which hair styles, clothing, and makeup had been altered (Davidson 1989).

23. Some analysts (e.g., Patterson and McClure 1976) believe there is more issue content in political advertising, on average, than in the news itself. One study suggests that people get little issue content from television news campaign coverage (Patterson 1980), leaving the field open to the influence of advertising.

24. Schumpeter revised the traditional doctrines of democracy to reflect the realities of the mass public's political ignorance and apathy. For Schumpeter, it is the competition by potential decision makers for the peoples' vote, not extensive citizen participation, that is the vital feature of democracy. In this view, citizens participate only by voting for leaders and by discussion.

The theories of Berelson and his colleagues, Dahl and Sartori, all descend directly from Schumpeter's attack on earlier, more idealistic democratic theories. Schumpeter's portrayal of earlier theory as unrealistic and his characterization of the "democratic method" and the role of participation in that method have become almost universally accepted in recent writings on democratic theory.

More recent theorists have viewed modest rates of citizen participation as an asset to functioning democracies. Bernard R. Berelson, Paul F. Lazarsfeld, and William N. McPhee (1954), for example, argue that limited citizen participation and apathy have a positive function for the whole system by cushioning the shock of disagreement, adjustment, and change. Classical theories, says Berelson, concentrated too much on and asked too much of the individual citizen. High levels of participation and interest are required from a minority of citizens. The apathy of the majority plays a valuable role in maintaining the stability of the system as a whole.

In Dahl's (1956) scheme, "Elections are central to the democratic method because they provide the mechanism through which the control of leaders by non-leaders can take place" (Pateman 1970:8). "Democratic theory is concerned with the processes by which ordinary citizens exert a relatively high degree of control over leaders" (Dahl 1956:3). The fact that individual citizens can switch their support from one set of leaders to another ensures that leaders are relatively responsive to nonleaders. Dahl extends Berelson by suggesting the possible dangers in increasing the participation of the common people. Lower socioeconomic groups are the least politically active, and the spawning ground for larger percentages of authoritarian personalities. Increased participation of this group might destabilize a democratic system.

Sartori is one of the few democratic theorists to specifically ask: "How can we account for the inactivity of the average citizen?" (Pateman 1970:11). He says we must simply accept it, because we cannot coerce citizens to participate or penalize the active minority. Apathy, in sum, is nobody's fault.

25. This may indeed be the case. Sociologist Herbert J. Gans makes a relevant argument: "Statistics and other data indicating people's widespread shortage or superficiality of knowledge about current events are sometimes used to demonstrate their lack of intelligence, their apathy, or their lack of 'future' orientation, said to make them incapable of considering issues to be resolved in the future. Some people undoubtedly are ignorant, or apathetic, or unable to think ahead, but many say they are bewildered by the complexity of the political world. As a result, large numbers (77 percent in 1985) agree with another frequently used poll statement, that 'politics and government seem so complicated that a person like me cannot really know or understand what is going on.'

"Complexity may overwhelm some, but it is most likely just an excuse for others, since there is no shortage of information that can make public policy comprehensible to persons of ordinary intelligence. Lacking incentive to learn, a sizable number of people make a fairly deliberate choice not to know too much and thus not to reduce the distance between themselves and the larger social order. Their families and informal groups are more important, and until they have a reasonable degree of control over their own lives, they are not very interested in society at large.

"Consequently, social scientists, civic leaders, political activists and others like them who properly warn that seemingly faraway national—or local—organizations actually have a major impact on people's lives have always had difficulty getting their message heard . . . If interviewed, people understand fully that potential threats can directly affect them someday . . . Nonetheless, they have structured their own ways of perceiving and living, to keep these matters distant until they become an immediate danger" (H. J. Gans 1988:57–58).

The foregoing assessment by Gans is as good a description as any of the problem facing those who would seriously upgrade the quality of citizen participation in the candidate evaluation process.

Still, the implications for American-style democracy are regrettable. Some may be apparent in the recent success of campaign tactics that avoid much discussion of the national problem agenda and instead stress evocative symbolic appeals.

26. Jefferson writes: "Men by their constitutions are naturally divided into two parties: 1. Those who fear and distrust the people, and wish to draw all powers from them into the hands of the higher classes. 2. Those who identify themselves with the people, have confidence in them, cherish and consider them as the most honest, and safe, although not the most wise depository of the public interests" (Letter to Henry Lee, Monticello, August 10, 1824, in Koch and Peden, eds. 1972:715).

27. Writes Lippmann biographer Ronald Steel: "In the *Phantom Public* as he called this sequal to *Public Opinion*, Lippmann . . . now declared it a 'false ideal' to imagine that the voters were even 'inherently competent' to direct public affairs . . . In a review of the book, H. L. Mencken described Lippmann as one who 'started out life with high hopes for democracy and an almost mystical belief in the congenital wisdom of the masses,' and had come around to the conclusion that the masses were 'ignorant and unteachable.' Mencken exaggerated, as always, but was not totally off the mark." Lippman, as Steel notes elsewhere, had been disillusioned by the lost peace and the success of propaganda during the First World War (Steel 1980:212–215).

28. The consensus in 1988, for example, was that international economic competetiveness, how to deal with changes in the Soviet Union and Eastern Europe, the budget and trade deficits, and domestic health, housing, and welfare crises were on the next president's shortlist. Some groups were more issue-oriented than others. But very few of our participants seemed to have heard much discussion of the state of the nation or of major upcoming presidential priorities.

29. More recent evidence, a *Times-Mirror* Gallup poll, suggests that citizens at large may have more explicit expectations in this area than our focus group participants. Six in ten Americans appreciate the media's role as a watchdog over unethical or illegal behavior, reflecting an increase since a similar poll in 1984 in the number expressing such views (Rosenstiel 1989).

7. 1992 and Beyond: The Markle Commission Recommendations

1. The *Report* was the subject of numerous editorials and newspaper stories, e.g., Oreskes 1990a; Schwartz 1990; Feinsilber 1990; Blaming the Voters First 1990.

2. Berelson et al. 1954:307–310 found that "certain requirements commonly assumed for the successful operation of democracy are not met by the behavior of the 'average' citizen . . . Many vote without real involvement in the election . . . The citizen is not highly informed on the details of the campaign . . . " These findings, summarized in Dalton 1988:15, are consistent with the classic *American Voter* study results (Campbell et al.

1960), which found a lack of ideological awareness among the electorate, no evidence of ideological structure, and weak relationships between individual positions on issues. Angus Campbell and his colleagues concluded that the electorate "is almost completely unable to judge the rationality of government actions; knowing little of the particular policies and what has led to them, the mass electorate is not able either to appraise its goals or the appropriateness of the means chosen to secure these goals" (1960:543). Russell J. Dalton notes that this study was followed by a series of surveys showing that many citizens could not name their elected representatives, were unfamiliar with the institutions of government, and did not understand the mechanics of the political process. A more recent study (Bennett 1989:434) concludes that "Americans are less politically informed today than in the 1960's primarily because they are less interested in politics and less dependent on newspapers for public affairs information . . . they do not 'hear' or 'see' because they are not interested . . . "

3. There is disagreement, however, on the origin of the problem. In its editorial reaction to the May 6, 1990, release of the Markle Commission Report, the *Wall Street Journal* took exception to what it termed "blaming the voters first," arguing that the system is rigged by a "Beltway ruling class" that has effectively sidelined the average voter. The editorial cites the book *Politics by Other Means* (Ginsber and Shefter 1990) in support of its contention that elections have become virtually insignificant. "Rather than engage the voters directly [as in elections], competing interests have taken political combat inside the Beltway, using weapons such as congressional investigations, media revelations and judicial proceedings . . . The American people have responded to being sidelined from the real political struggles in predictable fashion: they stay home on election day" (Blaming the Voters First 1990).

The editorial overlooks important facts. First, no combination of interests is powerful enough to thwart the involvement or the impact of the American electorate once it has collectively determined to exert its will. The "tax revolt" of the early 1980's was a demonstration of that fact, as was the popular uprising that thwarted a Congressional pay raise in 1989. The sovereign power does indeed rest with the "sleeping giant" that is the mass electorate. But many vested interests benefit from keeping the giant asleep, and it slumbers much of the time.

Second, research shows that the reasons for nonvoting are varied and complicated. A small segment of eligible voters may abstain for the kind of informed and principled reasons alleged in the editorial. But many more stay home because of registration barriers (Piven and Cloward 1989), frequent changes of residence (Wolfinger 1990), the declining strength of partisanship, and simple ignorance and indifference (Abramson and Aldrich 1982). For example, a November 1989 poll conducted for the People for the American Way by Peter Hart found that young people ages fifteen to twenty-four asked to describe a "good citizen" were unable to name any citizenship responsibilities beyond "being a good person" (*Democracy's Next Generation* 1989:72). Only a small fraction volunteered political participation as the defining character of a good citizen, and a commanding majority (70 percent) said that their parents had the greatest impact on their thinking about citizenship.

If parents, schools, and other influential forces in the lives of young Americans conveyed the sort of civic expectations described in this chapter, it is more than a little likely that citizens' feelings of political efficacy would increase along with their informed participation in elections at every level. It would then be interesting to see what became of the kind of "insider's games" the *Journal* deplores.

4. The italicized recommendations for citizens, like those appearing later in the chapter for candidates and media, exactly reproduce the recommendations released by the Markle Commission on the Media and the Electorate on May 6, 1990. The order of appearance of the recommendations has been altered, however, for better integration with this chapter's structure. The commentary surrounding the recommendations, while supportive of and consistent with them, is my own.

5. A nation willing to finance a nonpartisan organization (the National Endowment for Democracy, privately chartered but funded largely through congressional appropriations) devoted to preparing those in foreign lands to function as democratic citizens (Karl 1989:2214) should seemingly be willing to devote similar intellectual and economic resources to finding ways to revitalize the commitment and preparedness of its own voters.

6. This language, borrowed from "Advancing Civic Learning" in *Higher Learning in the National Interest,* a 1981 report by Ernest L. Boyer and Fred M. Hechinger issued by the Carnegie Foundation for the Advancement of Teaching, shows again that concern for the citizenship problem is not new.

7. See also such writings as Pratte 1988 and Ichilov, ed. 1990.

8. "George Bush campaigns at a flag factory and everybody says, 'What does that have to do with the problems of the country?'" said one aide to the House Democratic leadership. One year later, he said ruefully, "We've spent four months trying to perfect an anti-flag burning statute." See Toner 1989.

9. The campaigns preceding the 1990 congressional, state, and local elections saw a sharp increase in the critical attention paid in the media to campaign consultants and handlers. Many news organizations increased their surveillance of both televised candidate advertising and the consultants who produced it. Wrote one reporter of the California campaigns: "Several of the state's major newspapers, including the San Francisco Chronicle, the Los Angeles Times and the Sacramento Bee, as well as several television stations are now treating the political commercials the way reporters have long handled the candidates' major speeches. Each time a new advertisement comes out, the newspapers run the text, accompanied by an analysis that often challenges, clarifies, contradicts or offers context for claims made in the commercial" (Oreskes 1990c). Similar coverage appeared in newspaper treatment of attack advertising in local Texas political races (Elliot 1990). David Yepsen, the chief political reporter for the *Des*

Moines Register, wrote of campaign consultants: "They play by their own rules—put another 'victory' on the old résumé to peddle around Washington and chuckle about how they conned those hicks in the sticks" (Toner 1990). The consultants, writes another reporter, "are finding themselves on the receiving end of a kind of negative campaign" (ibid.) Roger Ailes, for one, remains unmoved by the criticism. He dismissed consultant-bashing as no more than a phase created by journalists who "are running out of things to cover other than substance," adding "I can take whatever they dish" (ibid.).

10. At a symposium sponsored by the Commission on Presidential Debates, the argument for requiring candidate participation was made by *Washington Post* reporter David Broder: "Whose campaign is it? We have accepted, I think, far too passively the notion that it is up to the candidates and their advisers to determine what takes place and what's talked about, and how it's talked about in a presidential campaign . . . [Campaigns] belong to the public and . . . the public has great leverage because voters pay for it through the voluntary income tax checkoff system. Legislation could be written to require debate participation as a condition for receiving the federal subsidies available to qualified candidates in the primaries and to the two major-party nominees in the general election" (quoted by Germond and Witcover 1990).

11. This bipartisan, nonprofit organization is jointly directed by the Democratic and Republican party chairmen. The Markle Commission chose not to center its recommendation around the existing Commission on Presidential Debates format. But it is true that the political parties have traditionally assumed responsibility for civic education (Sabato 1988:20), and debate sponsorship is consistent with that mandate. It is salutary too that the parties, now widely perceived as in serious decline, should seek to make involvement with this important educational event a part their efforts at self-revitalization.

But the strongest argument for centering debate management in party hands rests with the pre-nomination leverage each party can exert on would-be nominees to agree to presidential debates well in advance of the nominating conventions. Better-known candidates with little incentive to debate lesser known opponents could still refuse to do so, as, for example, Richard Nixon refused to debate George McGovern in 1972. But they would find it much more difficult if they had joined other party hopefuls in a well-publicized pledge, during the primary season, to engage in debates if nominated. Debates are complex events to arrange and deploy. The rationality with which they can be staged and managed would be greatly increased if candidates were committed and debates scheduled a full year in advance. The parties are in the best position to bring this about.

12. It might also be desirable, as a way of increasing public opportunities to directly compare the positions and arguments of the candidates, to encourage the staging of surrogate debates between well-known supporters of the major-party presidential nominees. This would serve to increase the attention given to issues and problems by both media and voters. It would

also de-emphasize personality and style, as there would be little reason to dwell on the personal characteristics or situational performances of surrogates, as often happens with the candidates themselves. Multiple surrogate debates would also make it possible to experiment with a variety of formats.

13. Worth noting here are two similar proposals that received attention during the spring of 1990 on op-ed pages and at conferences that discussed the media's political coverage responsibilities (Oreskes 1990b). One, by Timothy J. Russert (NBC News Washington Bureau Chief) called upon the networks to commit to broadcasting four prime-time debates to be moderated by their news anchors (Russert 1990). The other, suggested by *Washington Post* reporter Paul Taylor, would give each candidate for president five minutes of free time a night, on alternating nights, on each of the nation's 1,378 over-the-air television stations and 10,337 radio stations for the final five weeks of the fall campaign, beginning in 1992 (Taylor 1990:23).

Also widely discussed during that spring of stocktaking were proposals set forth by David Broder, who had taken upon himself the role of self-described "crank," bent on using his widely read column to assist efforts to improve what he had come to regard as a corrupted process. He suggested five steps print and broadcast reporters and editorialists could take that would lead to improvement: (1) deny candidates "custody" of the agenda-setting process; (2) hold consultants accountable for past negative campaigns; (3) make candidates answer personally for every television ad and piece of direct mail put out in their names; (4) treat ads as if they were speeches, and cover them accordingly; and (5) encourage editorialists and columnists (not reporters) to denounce those who "sabotage the election process by their paid-media demagoguery" (Broder 1990b).

14. See Table 4-6 for a breakdown of the media stories coding category.

15. Political biography that is genuinely relevant to the task of assessing a candidate's suitability for the presidency can be difficult to produce, however. The challenge to journalists charged with developing biographical insight lies in knowing where to look and what to look for in a candidate's background. Suggestions in this regard, drawn from the work of James David Barber (1980; 1985) and others, can be found in Chapter 2.

REFERENCES

Abramson, Jeffrey B., F. Christopher Arterton, and Gary R. Orren. 1988. *The Electronic Commonwealth: The Impact of New Media Technologies on Democratic Politics*. New York: Basic Books.

Abramson, Paul R. 1983. *Political Attitudes in America*. San Francisco: W. H. Freeman.

Abramson, Paul R., and John H. Aldrich. 1982. The Decline of Electoral Participation in America. *American Political Science Review* 76:502–521.

Albright, Joseph, and Marcia Kunstel. 1988. Why Americans Do Not Vote. *Austin American-Statesman*, October 2, p. D1.

Allison, Graham, and Katie Smith. 1988. A Democracy with Ever Fewer Voters. *New York Times*, March 11, p. 27.

Almond, Gabriel, and Sydney Verba. 1963. *The Civic Culture: Political Attitudes and Democracy in Five Nations*. Princeton, N.J.: Princeton University Press.

Ambrose, Stephen E. 1987. *Nixon: The Education of a Politician, 1913–1962*. New York: Simon and Schuster.

Apple, R. W., Jr. 1988. From Jersey to Missouri, Voters Are Fed Up. *New York Times*, October 11, p. 1.

———. 1989. Will The Networks Succeed in Getting the Candidates to Talk Substance in 1992? *New York Times*, May 10.

Aronson, Michael, and Christopher J. Georges. 1990. Dukakis Triumphs . . . *New York Times*, June 7, p. A15.

Arrow, Kenneth J. 1963. *Social Choice and Individual Values*. 2d ed. New York: Wiley.

Asher, Herbert B. 1984. *Presidential Elections and American Politics*. 3d ed. Homewood, Ill.: Dorsey Press.

Associated Press. 1988. Poll Respondents Endorse Reagan But Find Fault with Social Policies. *Austin American-Statesman*, December 27.

Atkin, C. K., and G. Heald. 1976. Effects of Political Advertising. *Public Opinion Quarterly* 37:209–224.

Barber, Benjamin. 1984. *Strong Democracy: Participatory Politics for a New Age*. Berkeley, Calif.: University of California Press.
———. 1988. *The Conquest of Politics: Liberal Philosophy in Democratic Times*. Princeton, N.J.: Princeton University Press.
Barber, James David. 1980. *The Pulse of Politics*. New York: Norton.
———. 1985. *The Presidential Character: Predicting Performance in the White House*. 3d ed. Englewood Cliffs, N.J.: Prentice-Hall.
Barone, Michael. 1990. *Our Country: The Shaping of America from Roosevelt to Reagan*. New York: Free Press.
Becker, L., I. Sobowale, R. Cobbey, and C. Eyal. 1978. Debates' Effects on Voters' Understanding of Candidates and Issues. In *The Presidential Debates*, edited by G. Bishop, R. Meadow, and M. Jackson-Beek, pp. 126–137. New York: Praeger.
Bellah, Robert N., Richard Madsen, William M. Sullivan, Ann Swidler, and Steven M. Tipton. 1985. *Habits of the Heart: Individualism and Commitment in American Life*. Berkeley: University of California Press.
Bennett, Stephen Earl. 1989. Trends in Americans' Political Information, 1967–1987. *American Politics Quarterly* 17:422–435.
Berelson, Bernard R. 1952. Democratic Theory and Public Opinion. *Public Opinion Quarterly* 16:313–330.
Berelson, Bernard R., Paul F. Lazarsfeld, and William N. McPhee. 1954. *Voting*. Chicago: University of Chicago Press.
Berke, Richard L. 1988a. Lightest Turnout in 40 Years Is Seen. *New York Times*, October 22.
———. 1988b. 50.16% Voter Turnout Is 64-Year Low. *New York Times*, December 18.
Blaming the Voters First. 1990. *Wall Street Journal*, May 18, p. A10.
Blumenthal, Sidney. 1988. Coming in from the Cold: Should We Be Worrying about Ourselves instead of the Soviets? *Washington Post National Weekly Edition*, June 27–July 3.
Bonafede, Dom. 1989a. Taking on the Press. *National Journal*, April 8.
———. 1989b. The Networks' Call. *National Journal*, May 20.
Boot, William. 1989. Campaign '88: TV Overdoses on the Inside Dope. *Columbia Journalism Review*, January/February, pp. 23–29.
Boren, David. 1990. New Decade, New World, New Strategy. *New York Times*, January 2, p. 25.
Boyd, Robert S. 1988. "Focus Groups" of Democrats Helped Shape Bush Campaign. *St. Paul Pioneer Press Dispatch*, November 9, p. 11A.
Boyer, Ernest L., and Fred M. Hechinger. 1981. *Higher Learning in the National Interest*. New York: Carnegie Foundation for the Advancement of Teaching.
Boyer, Peter J. 1988. *Who Killed CBS? The Undoing of America's Number One News Network*. New York: Random House.
Broder, David. 1987a. *Behind The Front Page: A Candid Look at How the News Is Made*. New York: Simon and Schuster.
———. 1987b. Iowans Reflect Democracy at Its Finest. *Austin American-Statesman*, August 12.

———. 1988. Washington Fears Facing Economic Reality. *Austin American-Statesman*, September 26.

———. 1989a. No-Hands Government. *Washington Post National Weekly Edition*, January 9–15.

———. 1989b. Sense and Sensitivity. *Washington Post National Weekly Edition*, January 16–22, p. 4.

———. 1989c. Who Should Play Cop for Campaign Ads? *Washington Post National Weekly Edition*, February 13–19, p. 8.

———. 1989d. Breeding Public Cynicism. *Washington Post National Weekly Edition*, March 20–26.

———. 1989e. Another Politically Mean Season. *Washington Post National Weekly Edition*, November 13–19, p. 12.

———. 1990a. Our Strangling Democracy. *Washington Post National Weekly Edition*, January 8–14, p. 4.

———. 1990b. How To Stop a Political Mudbath in Five Easy Steps. *Washington Post National Weekly Edition*, January 22–28, p. 23.

Buchanan, Bruce. 1987a. Open All Candidates before Election. *New York Times*, October 2.

———. 1987b. *The Citizen's Presidency: Standards of Choice and Judgement*. Washington, D.C.: Congressional Quarterly Press.

———. 1988. Sizing Up Candidates. *PS: Political Science and Politics* 21:250–256.

Buckley, William F., Jr. 1988. Bush Scored Big against Media. *Houston Chronicle*, October 17.

Burnham, Walter Dean. 1981. The System of 1896: An Analysis. In *The Evolution of American Electoral Systems*, edited by Paul Kleppner et al. Westport, Conn.: Greenwood Press.

———. 1989. The Reagan Heritage. In *The Election of 1988: Reports and Interpretations*, edited by Gerald M. Pomper, pp. 1–32. Chatham, N.J.: Chatham House.

Butterfield, Fox. 1990. Dukakis Tells of Major Errors in Race. *New York Times*, April 22, p. 20.

Campbell, Angus, Phillip E. Converse, Warren E. Miller, and Donald E. Stokes. 1960. *The American Voter*. New York: Wiley.

Carmody, Deirdre. 1988. Many Students Fail Quiz on Basic Economics. *New York Times*, December 29.

Caro, Robert A. 1990. *Means of Ascent: The Years of Lyndon Johnson*. New York: Knopf.

Carter, Hodding III. 1988. On the Dreary, Dirty Campaign Trail. *Wall Street Journal*, August 25.

A Chance to Expand Democracy. 1990. *New York Times*, January 31, p. A18.

A Closer Look: The Tank Ad. 1988. *USA Today*, October 20, p. 4A.

Commission on Freedom of the Press. 1947. *A Free and Responsible Press: A General Report on Mass Communication*. Chicago: University of Chicago Press.

Cose, Ellis. 1989. *The Press: Inside America's Most Powerful Newspaper Empires—from the Newsrooms to the Boardrooms*. New York: Morrow.

Curry, George E. 1988. League Attacks Debate Rules, Quits as Sponsor. *Chicago Tribune*, October 4.

Dahl, Robert A. 1956. *A Preface to Democratic Theory*. Chicago: University of Chicago Press.

——. 1989. *Democracy and Its Critics*. New Haven: Yale University Press.

Dalton, Russell J. 1988. *Citizen Politics in Western Democracies*. Chatham, N.J.: Chatham House.

Davidson, Jean. 1989. Clothes Do Make the Politician. *Austin American-Statesman*, October 30, p. C1.

Davis, L. 1964. The Cost of Realism: Contemporary Restatements of Democracy. *Western Political Quarterly* 17:37–46. Cited by Pateman 1970:21.

Deaver, Michael. 1988. Sound-Bite Campaigning: TV Made Us Do It. *Washington Post National Weekly Edition*, November 7–13.

Democracy's Next Generation. 1989. Washington, D.C.: People for the American Way.

Dionne, E. J., Jr. 1987. Survey of Electorate Finds Weak Political Parties and Conflicts over Change. *New York Times*, October 1.

——. 1988a. Drugs as 1988 Issue: Filling a Vacuum. *New York Times*, May 24.

——. 1988b. Bush Struggling to Shed Questions on Quayle Service. *New York Times*, August 21.

——. 1988c. The Art of Creating Reality out of Campaign Symbolism. *New York Times*, September 5, p. 1.

——. 1988d. Poll Shows Bush Sets Agenda for Principal Election Issues. *New York Times*, September 14.

——. 1988e. Just Talking of Landslide Has Rival Camps Uneasy. *New York Times*, October 23.

——. 1988f. Voters Fault Selection of Presidents. *New York Times*, November 22.

——. 1989. Seeking Reasons besides Dukakis, Democrats Mull Defeat. *New York Times*, February 19, p.11.

Downs, Anthony. 1957. *An Economic Theory of Democracy*. New York: Harper.

Drew, Elizabeth. 1989. *Election Journal: Political Events of 1897–1988*. New York: William Morrow and Company.

Drogin, Bob. 1988. Dukakis Begins Cramming for Sunday Debate. *Los Angeles Times*, September 21, p. 12.

Edsall, Thomas B. 1989. It's Never Too Soon to Start Planning the Next Campaign. *Washington Post National Weekly Edition*, March 6–12, p. 16.

Elliot, David. 1990. Republicans Plan Quick TV Hits. *Austin American-Statesman*, May 23, p. A1.

Entman, Robert M. 1989. *Democracy without Citizens: Media and the Decay of American Politics*. New York: Oxford University Press.

Estrich, Susan. 1989. Willie Horton, Racism, and Our Campaign. *Washington Post National Weekly Edition*, May 1–7, pp. 9–10.

Fain, Jim. 1989. Slime Politics—Campaign Mud-Slinging Will End When the Public Stops Buying It. *Austin American-Statesman*, June 28, p. A8.

Feinsilber, Mike. 1990. Voters Showed Indifference in '88, Panel Says. *Fort Worth Star-Telegram*, May 6, p. 4.

Fishel, Jeff. 1985. *Presidents and Promises: From Campaign Pledge to Presidential Performance.* Washington, D.C.: Congressional Quarterly Press.

Fiske, Susan T. 1980. Attention and Weight in Person Perception: The Impact of Negative and Extreme Behavior. *Journal of Personality and Social Psychology* 38:889–908.

Freund, Charles Paul. 1988. But Then, Truth Has Never Been Important. *Washington Post National Weekly Edition*, November 7–13, p. 29.

Friedrich, Carl. 1941. *Constitutional Government and Democracy.* 2d ed. Boston: Ginn.

Gans, Curtis B. 1988a. Nonvoting: The Nature of the Problem, Its Importance to American Democracy and Some Approaches to Its Solution. In *Media Technology and the Vote: A Sourcebook*, edited by Joel L. Swerdlow, p. 196. Boulder, Colo.: Westview Press.

Gans, Curtis B. 1988b. Is TV Turning Off the American Voter? *New York Times*, July 3.

Gans, Herbert J. 1988. *Middle American Individualism: The Future of Liberal Democracy.* New York: Free Press.

Garramone, G. M. 1984. Voter Responses to Negative Political Ads. *Journalism Quarterly* 61 (Summer): 771–775.

Germond, Jack W., and Jules Witcover. 1989. *Whose Broad Stripes and Bright Stars? The Trivial Pursuit of the Presidency, 1988.* New York: Warner.

———. 1990. Are Presidential Debates Inevitable? *National Journal*, May 19, p. 1244.

Ginsberg, Benjamin, and Martin Shefter. 1990. *Politics by Other Means: The Declining Importance of Elections in America.* New York: Basic Books.

Glass, David P. 1985. Evaluating Presidential Candidates: Who Focuses on Their Personal Attributes? *Public Opinion Quarterly* 49:517–534.

Goldman, Alfred E., and Susan Schwartz McDonald. 1987. *The Group Depth Interview: Principles and Practice.* Englewood Cliffs, N.J.: Prentice-Hall.

Goldman, Peter, and Tom Mathews. 1989. *The Quest for the Presidency 1988.* New York: Touchstone Books.

Goleman, Daniel. 1989. Brain's Design Emerges as a Key to Emotions. *New York Times*, August 15, p. 15.

Goodman, Ellen. 1988. "Politics as Theater Dominates Voters' View." *Austin American-Statesman*, October 1, p. A16.

Graber, Doris. 1988. *Processing the News: How People Tame the Information Tide.* 2d ed. New York: Longman.

————. 1989. *Mass Media and American Politics*. 3d ed. Washington, D.C.: Congressional Quarterly Press.

Grove, Lloyd. 1988. Campaign Ads Play Fast and Loose with the Truth. *Washington Post*, October 22.

Harwood, Richard. 1988–1989. Nobody Reads Anymore. *Washington Post National Weekly Edition*, December 26–January 1.

Held, David. 1987. *Models of Democracy*. Stanford, Calif.: Stanford University Press.

Herman, Edward S., and Noam Chomsky. 1988. *Manufacturing Consent: The Political Economy of the Mass Media*. New York: Pantheon Books.

Hertsgaard, Mark. 1988. *On Bended Knee: The Press and the Reagan Presidency*. New York: Farrar Straus Giroux.

Hoffman, David. 1989. George Bush Takes Up the Baton. *Washington Post National Weekly Edition*, January 16–22.

Hogarth, Robin M. 1987. *Judgement and Choice: The Psychology of Decision*. 2d ed. New York: Wiley.

Holloway, Diane. 1989. Pawn Game Makes ABC Rethink Moves on Presidential Coverage. *Austin American-Statesman*, March 13, p. C24.

Huckfeldt, Robert, and John Sprague. 1988. Discussant Effects on Vote Choice: The Political Interdependence of Discussion Partners. Paper presented at the Annual Meeting of the American Political Science Association, Washington, September 1–4.

Ichilov, Orit, ed. 1990. *Political Socialization, Citizenship Education, and Democracy*. New York: Columbia Teachers College Press.

Ignatius, David, and Michael Getler. 1988. So Many Sweeping Changes around the World, So Little Said by the Candidates. *Washington Post National Weekly Edition*, November 7–13, p. 10.

Iyengar, Shanto, and Donald R. Kinder. 1987. *News That Matters: Television and American Opinion*. Chicago: University of Chicago Press.

Jamieson, Kathleen Hall. 1984. *Packaging the Presidency: A History and Criticism of Presidential Campaign Advertising*. New York: Oxford University Press.

————. 1988. Is the Truth Now Irrelevant in Presidential Campaigns? *Washington Post National Weekly Edition*, November 7–13, p. 28.

Jamieson, Kathleen Hall, and David S. Birdsell. 1988. *Presidential Debates: The Challenge of Creating an Informed Electorate*. New York: Oxford University Press.

Jaroslovsky, Rich. 1988. "Poll Gives Bush 55% to 38% Lead over Dukakis: But Journal/NBC Survey Shows Wide Discontent with Whole Campaign. *Wall Street Journal*, October 18, p. A3.

Jensen, Elizabeth. 1988. News Prez: Media Feed Public's Disinterest in Campaign. *New York Daily News*, October 19.

Joslyn, Richard. 1985. *Mass Media and Elections*. Reading, Mass.: Addison-Wesley.

Kagay, Michael R. 1989. Public's Knowledge of Civics Rises Only a Bit. *New York Times*, May 28.

Kalb, Marvin. 1988. TV, Election Spoiler. *New York Times*, November 28.

Karl, Jonathan D. 1989. Cultivating Democracy on Authoritarian Terrain. *National Journal*, September 9.

Kelley, Harold H. 1973. The Process of Causal Attribution. *American Psychologist* 28 : 107–128.

Key, V. O. 1966. *The Responsible Electorate: Rationality in Presidential Voting, 1936–1960*. New York: Vintage.

Kilborn, Peter T. 1988a. As Nominees Shun Tax Issue, U.S. Panel Quietly Ponders It. *New York Times*, October 13.

———. 1988b. Bush Vows Talks on His First Day to Cut the Deficit. *New York Times*, November 23, p. 1.

Kinder, Donald R., and Susan T. Fiske. 1986. Presidents in the Public Mind. In *Political Psychology: Contemporary Problems and Issues*, edited by Margaret G. Herman, pp. 193–218. San Francisco: Jossey-Bass.

Kinder, Donald R., and D. O. Sears. 1985. Public Opinion and Political Behavior. Vol. 2 of *Handbook of Social Psychology*, 3d ed., edited by G. Lindzey and E. Aronson. New York: Random House.

Koch, Adrienne, and William Peden, eds. 1972. *The Life and Selected Writings of Thomas Jefferson*. New York: Modern Library.

Kotler, Philip, and Eduardo L. Roberto. 1989. *Social Marketing: Strategies for Changing Public Behavior*. New York: Free Press.

Krippendorff, Klaus. 1980. *Content Analysis: An Introduction to Its Methodology*. Beverly Hills, Calif.: Sage.

Krueger, Richard A. 1988. *Focus Groups: A Practical Guide for Applied Research*. Newbury Park, Calif.: Sage Publications, Inc.

Lamb, Brian. 1988. Campaign Substance Was There for the Viewing. *Wall Street Journal*, December 29.

Lane, Robert. 1962. *Political Ideology: Why the American Common Man Believes What He Does*. New York: Free Press.

Leigh, Robert D., ed. 1947. *A Free and Responsible Press: Report of the Commission on Freedom of the Press*. Chicago: University of Chicago Press.

Lewis, Anthony. 1988. A Corrupted Process. *New York Times*, October 13, p. 27.

Lewis, Flora. 1990. Year of Elections. *New York Times*, January 9, p. 23.

Lichter, S. Robert. 1988. How the Press Covered the Primaries. *Public Opinion*, July/August, pp. 45–49.

Lichter, S. Robert, Stanley Rothman, and Linda S. Lichter. 1986. *The Media Elite*. Bethesda, Md.: Adler and Adler.

Lippmann, Walter. 1965. *Public Opinion*. New York: Free Press. Originally published in 1922.

Lipset, Seymour Martin. 1959. *Political Man: The Social Bases of Politics*. Garden City, N.Y.: Doubleday.

———. 1963. *The First New Nation*. New York: Norton.

Los Angeles Times Poll. September 9–11, 1988. LAT 160: September 1988 Political Survey.

———. October 8–9, 1988. LAT 165: Lloyd Bentsen/Dan Quayle VP Debate.

McCarthy, Larry. 1988. The Selling of the President: An Interview with Roger Ailes. *Gannett Center Journal* 2 (Fall): 65–72.

McNeely, Dave. 1987. "U.S. 88" Training Voters to Measure Candidates against Issues. *Austin American-Statesman*, June 25.

———. 1988. Candidates Duck the Truth in Negative Campaign Advertising. *Austin American-Statesman*, October 27.

McQueen, Michel. 1988. The Gender Gap: Economic Issues Split Sexes in Their Choice of Bush or Dukakis. *Wall Street Journal*, September 23, p. 1.

McWilliams, Wilson Cary. 1989. The Meaning of the Election. In *The Elections of 1988: Reports and Interpretations*, edited by Gerald M. Pomper. Chatham, N.J.: Chatham House.

Margolis, Michael. 1979. *Viable Democracy*. New York: Penguin Books.

Markey, Edward J., and Bob Graham. 1989. Putting Their Mouths Where the Money Is. *New York Times*, July 19.

Markham, James M. 1987. Europeans Amused by U.S. Scrutiny of Candidates. *New York Times*, November 12.

Mickelson, Sig. 1989. *From Whistle Stop to Sound Bite: Four Decades of Politics and Television*. New York: Praeger.

Miller, Arthur H., Martin P. Wattenberg, and Oksana Malanchuk. 1986. Schematic Assessments of Presidential Candidates. *American Political Science Review* 80: 521–540.

Miller, Mark Crispin. 1988. TV's Anti-Liberal Bias. *New York Times*, November 16.

The Moral Relativism Issue. 1988. *Wall Street Journal*, October 3, p. A16.

Morin, Richard. 1988a. Bringing Focus Groups into Focus. *Washington Post National Weekly Edition*, October 10–16, p. 38.

———. 1988b. Relieved Rather than Elated: A Campaign That Failed to Engage the Voters Drags toward the Finish Line. *Washington Post National Weekly Edition*, November 7–13, p. 42.

———. 1989. The True Political Puppeteers: Pocketbooks and Partisan Ways. *Washington Post National Weekly Edition*, February 20–26.

Morris, Donald R. 1988. We Must Start Now to Restore the Political Process. *Houston Post*, November 1, p. E2.

Morrison, Donald. 1988. *The Winning of the White House 1988: By the Editors of Time Magazine*. New York: Time, Inc.

Nelson, Jack. 1988. Top Democrats See Dukakis in Deep Trouble. *Los Angeles Times*, September 21.

Neuman, Russell. 1986. *The Paradox of Mass Politics: Knowledge and Opinion in the American Electorate*. Cambridge, Mass.: Harvard University Press.

Nunn, Sam. 1988. Our Allies Have to Do More. *New York Times*, July 10.

Oakes, John B. 1988. Bush's Calumnies: A Dangerous Game. *New York Times*, November 5, p. 17.

Oreskes, Michael. 1988a. Bush Overtakes Dukakis in a Poll. *New York Times*, August 23, p. 1.

———. 1988b. On What Is Usually Opening Day, 1988 Campaign Enters the Homestretch. *New York Times*, September 6, p. 10.

———. 1988c. Dukakis in TV Ads, Strikes Back in Kind. *New York Times*, October 22, p. 8.

———. 1988d. TV's Role in '88: The Medium Is the Election. *New York Times*, October 30.

———. 1989. What Poison Politics Has Done to America. *New York Times*, October 29, section 4, p. 1.

———. 1990a. America's Politics Loses Way As Its Vision Changes World. *New York Times*, March 18, p. 1, 16.

———. 1990b. If Politics Is Broke, Can Talk Fix It? *New York Times*, April 6, p. A9.

———. 1990c. Campaign Advertising Gets Press Scrutiny in California. *New York Times*, April 29, p. 14.

———. 1990d. Study Finds "Astonishing" Indifference to Elections. *New York Times*, May 6, p. 16.

Ornstein, Norman J., and Mark Schmitt. 1989. The 1988 Election. *Foreign Affairs* 68(1): 39–52.

Osborne, David. 1988. *Laboratories of Democracy*. Cambridge, Mass.: Harvard Business School Press.

Page, Benjamin I. 1978. *Choices and Echoes in Presidential Elections*. Chicago: University of Chicago Press.

Page, Benjamin I., and Richard A. Brody. 1972. Policy Voting and the Electoral Process: The Vietnam War Issues. *American Political Science Review* 66:979–995.

Pateman, Carole. 1970. *Participation and Democratic Theory*. Cambridge: Cambridge University Press.

Patterson, Thomas E. 1980. *The Mass Media Election: How Americans Choose Their President*. New York: Praeger.

———. 1989. The Press and Its Missed Assignment. In *The Elections of 1988*, edited by Michael Nelson. Washington, D.C.: Congressional Quarterly Press.

Patterson, Thomas E., and R. D. McClure. 1976. *The Unseeing Eye: The Myth of Television Power in National Elections*. New York: Putnam.

Piven, Frances Fox, and Richard A. Cloward. 1989. *Why Americans Don't Vote*. New York: Pantheon.

The Pledge vs. the Good Old U.S.A. 1988. *New York Times*, August 31, p. 22.

Powell, G. Bingham, Jr. 1986. American Voter Turnout in Comparative Perspective. *American Political Science Review* 80:17–44.

Pratte, Richard. 1988. *The Civic Imperative: Examining the Need for Civic Education*. New York: Columbia Teachers College Press.

Quirk, Paul J. 1989. The Election. In *The Elections of 1988*, edited by Michael Nelson. Washington, D.C.: Congressional Quarterly Press.

Randolph, Eleanor. 1988. "Quayle Hunt" Turns News Media into Target for Angry Public. *Washington Post*, August 25, p. A10.

Ranney, Austin. 1962. *The Doctrine of Responsible Party Government: Its Origins and Present State*. Urbana: University of Illinois Press.

Reid, T. R. 1989. No, No, a Thousand Times No: Adman Ailes Doth Protest His Negative Image. *Washington Post National Weekly Edition*, August 7–13.

Report of the Markle Commission on the Media and the Electorate. 1990. New York: John and Mary R. Markle Foundation.

Reston, James. 1988a. If Only Bush Would . . . *New York Times*, May 9.

———. 1988b. Voodoo Voters. *New York Times*, September 13, p. 27.

Riker, William H. 1982. *Liberalism against Populism: A Confrontation between the Theory of Democracy and the Theory of Social Choice.* Prospect Heights, Ill.: Waveland Press, Inc.

Riker, William H., and Peter C. Ordeshook. 1968. A Theory of the Calculus of Voting. *American Political Science Review* 63:25–43.

Roberts, Steven V. 1988. Missile Shield's Future. *New York Times*, September 10.

Robinson, John P., and Mark R. Levy. 1986. *The Main Source: Learning from Television News.* Beverly Hills, Calif.: Sage.

Robinson, Michael J. 1988. Isn't There a Better Way to Run an American Election? Some Views on Improving the Process. *New York Times*, November 13, section 4, p. 1.

Robinson, Michael J., and Andrew Kohut. 1988. Believability and the Press. *Public Opinion Quarterly* 52:174–189.

Robinson, Michael J., and Margaret A. Sheehan. 1983. *Over the Wire and on TV: CBS and UPI in Campaign '80.* New York: Russell Sage Foundation.

Rogers, David. 1988. Debate, Dan Quayle's Big Test, Will Give Nation Close Look at the Controversial Baby Boomer . . . *Wall Street Journal*, October 4, p. A32.

Rogers, David, and Gerald F. Seib. 1990. Congress Reconvenes to a Host of International and Domestic Issues Vying for Limited Resources. *Wall Street Journal*, January 23, p. A20.

Roseboom, Eugene H. 1959. *A History of Presidential Elections.* New York: Macmillan Company.

Rosenbaum, David E. 1989. From Guns to Butter. *New York Times*, December 14, p. 1.

Rosenstiel, Thomas B. 1987. Public Faults Media Focus on Candidates' Character. *Austin American-Statesman*, November 19.

———. 1989. Confidence in Press's Objectivity Drops, Surveys Say. *Austin American-Statesman*, November 19, p. A11.

Rosenthal, Andrew. 1988a. After Third TV Debate Networks' Policy Shifts. *New York Times*, October 15.

———. 1988b. Foes Accuse Bush Campaign of Inflaming Racial Tension. *New York Times*, October 24, p. 1.

Runkel, David R. 1989. *Campaign for President: The Managers Look at '88.* Dover, Mass.: Auburn House.

Rusher, William. 1988. *The Coming Battle for the Media.* New York: William Morrow Company.

Russert, Timothy J. 1990. For '92, the Networks Have to Do Better. *New York Times*, March 4, section 4, p. 23.

Sabato, Larry J. 1981. *The Rise of Political Consultants*. New York: Basic Books.

———. 1988. *The Party's Just Begun: Shaping Political Parties for America's Future*. Glenview, Ill.: Scott, Foresman.

Safire, William. 1988a. The Northern Strategy. *New York Times*, October 13.

———. 1988b. Fire in The Belly. *New York Times*, October 17, p. 23.

Sartori, Giovanni. 1987. *The Theory of Democracy Revisited*. Chatham, N.J.: Chatham House.

Scheer, Robert. 1988. Political Pro Is Pulling All the Strings. *Los Angeles Times*, October 21.

Schleuder, Joan, Maxwell McCombs, and Wayne Wanta. 1989. Inside the Agenda Setting Process: How Political Advertising and TV News Prime Viewers to Think about Issues and Candidates. Paper presented to the Theory and Methodology Division of the Association for Education in Journalism and Mass Communication, Washington, D.C.

Schneider, William. 1989. 1988 Lessons Reversed in 1989 Vote. *National Journal*, November 18.

Schumpeter, Joseph A. 1947. *Capitalism, Socialism and Democracy*. 2d ed. New York: Harper and Brothers.

Schwadel, Francine. 1989. Consumer Trust: An Elusive Quarry. *Wall Street Journal*, September 20, p. B1.

Schwartz, Maralee. 1988. Political Grapevine: A Conventional Solution to A Conventional Problem. *Washington Post National Weekly Edition*, December 19–25.

———. 1990. Study: U.S. Voters Apathetic, Uninformed. *Washington Post*, May 6, p. A18.

Seib, Gerald F., and Robert E. Taylor. 1988. Bush and Dukakis Duck $50 Billion S&Ls Problem That One of Them Will Have to Face as President. *Wall Street Journal*, October 25.

Seymour-Ure, Colin. 1974. *The Political Impact of Mass Media*. Beverly Hills, Calif.: Sage.

Shapiro, Michael A., and Robert H. Rieger. 1989. Comparing Positive and Negative Political Advertising. Paper presented at the Annual Meeting of the International Communications Association, Political Communications Division, San Francisco.

Siebert, Fred S., Theodore Peterson, and Wilber Schramm, eds. 1956. *Four Theories of the Press*. Urbana: University of Illinois Press.

Skelton, George. 1987. Voters Say Ability Ranks above Issues or Character. *Austin American Statesman*, October 1.

Smith, Tom W. 1987. The Art of Asking Questions, 1936–1985. *Public Opinion Quarterly* 51:595–608.

Squire, Peverill, Raymond Wolfinger, and David P. Glass. 1987. Residential Mobility and Turnout. *American Political Science Review* 81:45–66.

Stanley, Harold W., and Richard G. Niemi. 1989. *Vital Statistics on American Politics*. 2d ed. Washington, D.C.: CQ Press.

Steel, Ronald. 1980. *Walter Lippmann and the American Century*. Boston: Little, Brown.

Sudman, Seymour. 1987. The People and the Press. *Public Opinion Quarterly* 51:400–403.

Sussman, Barry. 1988. *What Americans Really Think and Why Our Politicians Pay No Attention*. New York: Pantheon.

Swerdlow, Joel L., ed. 1989. *Media Technology and the Vote: A Source Book*. Boulder, Colo.: Westview Press.

Taylor, Paul. 1988. The Bush-Dukakis Pact: Mum's the Word on the Deficit. *Washington Post National Weekly Edition*, May 30–June 5.

———. 1989. Pigsty Politics: The 1988 Presidential Race Set a New Standard for Negative Ads. *Washington Post National Weekly Edition*, February 13–19, p. 7.

———. 1990. The Five-Minute Fix. *Washington Post National Weekly Edition*, April 23–29, p. 23.

Taylor, Paul, and David S. Broder. 1988. How The Presidential Campaign Got Stuck on the Low Road. *Washington Post National Weekly Edition*, November 7–13, p. 14.

Thorson, Esther. 1989. Television Commercials as Mass Media Messages. In *Messages In Communication Science: Contemporary Approaches to the Study of Effects*, edited by James J. Bradac, pp. 195–230. Beverly Hills, Calif.: Sage.

Toner, Robin. 1988a. Dukakis Seeks to Assure Allies on Support for NATO. *New York Times*, June 15.

———. 1988b. Dukakis and Bush Trade Fire in Heavy Barrages. *New York Times*, August 31, p. 1.

———. 1988c. Dukakis Returns to Stump As Aides Paint Rosy Picture. *New York Times*, October 15, p. 9.

———. 1989. The Monument to '88 Lives in Politics of '89. *New York Times*, October 6, p. 9.

———. 1990. Political Advisers: Hired Guns under Fire. *New York Times*, May 24, p. A10.

Transcript of Bush's Inaugural Address: Nation Stands Ready to Move On. 1989. *New York Times*, January 21, p. 10.

Trueheart, Charles. 1988. The Three Faces of Dukakis. *Washington Post National Weekly Edition*, February 22–28.

Tversky, Amos. 1977. Features of Similarity. *Psychological Review* 84: 327–352.

Wanniski, Jude, ed. 1989. *The 1989 Media Guide: A Critical Review of the Print Media*. Morristown, N.J.: Polyconomics, Inc.

Washington Wire. 1990. *The Wall Street Journal*, January 19, p. 1.

Whither Democracy? 1988. *Wall Street Journal*, November 8, p. A14.

Why There Are No Issues. 1988. *New York Times*, May 3.

Wicker, Tom. 1988. The Hispanic Factor. *New York Times*, September 9.

Wills, Gary. 1988. Introduction: A Moral Derailing. In *The Winning of the White House, 1988*, edited by Donald Morrison. New York: Time, Inc.

Wilson, James Q. 1986. *American Government: Institutions and Policies.* 3d ed. Lexington, Mass.: D. C. Heath.

Wolfinger, Raymond E. 1990. How to Raise Voter Turnout. *New York Times*, June 6, p. A15.

Wolfinger, Raymond E., and Steven J. Rosenstone. 1980. *Who Votes?* New Haven: Yale University Press.

Zurawik, David. 1988. No Debate—TV Colors Our Thinking. *Dallas Times-Herald*, September 27.

INDEX